COMPUTATIONAL EXPERIMENTS
IN GRAMMATICAL CLASSIFICATION

JANUA LINGUARUM

STUDIA MEMORIAE
NICOLAI VAN WIJK DEDICATA

edenda curat

C. H. VAN SCHOONEVELD
INDIANA UNIVERSITY

SERIES MINOR
61

1969
MOUTON
THE HAGUE · PARIS

COMPUTATIONAL EXPERIMENTS IN GRAMMATICAL CLASSIFICATION

by

H. T. CARVELL *and* JAN SVARTVIK

1969

MOUTON

THE HAGUE · PARIS

LIBRARY OF CONGRESS CATALOG CARD NUMBER: 68-23805

Printed in The Netherlands by Mouton & Co., Printers, The Hague.

PREFACE

This book is an account of the application of certain computational techniques to a specific linguistic problem. In order to enable the reader to judge the value of the techniques for similar investigations, the analysis is given in considerable detail.

The problem is the relation of verbs to prepositional phrases in English. In such strings there appears to be a scale of closeness and openness whose poles may be illustrated by the following examples: *She sent for his coat* and *She came with his coat*. These two sentences have the same constituent structure ($N_1 V p N_2$), but different transformational properties, such as the passive *His coat was sent for* but not *His coat was come with*. Chomsky provides the ambiguous active sentence *He decided on the boat*, which may or may not take passive transformation depending on whether it has the sense of *He chose the boat* or of *He decided while on the boat* (see Chomsky 1965, pp. 105f.).

There are many problems of this type in descriptive linguistics, and the linguist may not even be sure that he possesses an adequate and reasonable set of linguistic categories for their solution; and if not, his problem is substantially more difficult than that of correctly assigning examples to given categories. (The simpler problem is given special consideration in an appendix). The authors believe that no particular linguistic philosophy is likely to offer an obvious solution of these problems, and that what is required for this purpose is a suitable method of analysing data.

There are at present a number of computer techniques being developed which may be called automatic classification techniques. They have arisen in response to problems in various disciplines, but usually have only a tenuous connexion with their parent problem, since they are based on an abstraction from it. Consequently they have been applied in many unrelated fields, and in particular it is argued in this book that the methods are valid in grammatical study. The analysis described is principally that of the authors' use of one particular classification program, and the subsequent detailed "follow-up" procedures. The book considers the extent to which these procedures offer a solution, how valuable the solution is, and, more importantly, the potential value of such procedures in the light of this experiment. In order to put the classification techniques in perspective, some space is devoted to a consideration of some of the variations in approach that are possible, although the book does not attempt to give an exhaustive description.

The contributions to this joint product can, in the main, be divided into mathematical/computational and linguistic, and the responsibility for these is Carvell's and Svartvik's respectively. The work on the monograph was done under the auspices of the Survey of English Usage, University College London, while we were on the Survey staff; it was largely made possible by a British Government grant, DSIR (later OSTI) reference ID/02/2/04. We should like to acknowledge the part played in the work by Survey colleagues and especially by the Director, Professor Randolph Quirk. Our debt extends also to W. L. B. Nixon, Diane Morgan and other members of the University of London Institute of Computer Science and to scholars in association with taxonomic work outside the University of London, notably P. H. A. Sneath, Medical Research Council, University of Leicester, J. C. Gower, Rothamsted Experimental Station, Harpenden, and R. Needham, Cambridge University. We would, further, like to acknowledge comments on a preliminary version of this monograph from D. L. Bolinger, Judith Carvell, N. Fairclough, A. Henrici, R. Hodson, B. Mohan, Karen Needham, M. Sackin, J. Sinclair, and N. Thun.

Rugby and Göteborg　　　　　　　　　　　　　H. T. Carvell
December 1967　　　　　　　　　　　　　　　　Jan Svartvik

CONTENTS

1

INTRODUCTION

A consideration of the problems raised by classification obviously assumes not only that there are problems but that classification is desirable. If in fact the latter assumption is challenged we would reply that we believe, or hope, that in every field of experience, phenomena are clustered into types, so that it becomes natural and convenient to consider phenomena in relation to those types and to relate fresh experience to them. We do of course use classification all the time in our daily life. Consider for example such groupings as *infant, baby, adolescent, teenager, adult,* etc. which for ordinary purposes are much more convenient and suggestive, though not more precise, than simply giving the age of each individual referred to.

This book discusses the use of numerical taxonomy in linguistics and, in particular, its application to a specific problem of classification in English syntax. We hope that the argumentation and general principles used here will apply also to many other fields of linguistic classification. This is a report on a pilot experiment, conducted in 1963-65, and the methods and tentative conclusions are not to be thought of as final.

Before beginning a consideration of classificatory problems on a general scale, it may be helpful to look at our illustrative problem, which was raised by a specific, reasonably well-defined aspect of English grammar: viz. the relation of verbs to prepositional phrases. We have, for example, the $N_1 \ V \ p \ N_2$ structures

(1) She sent for his coat.
(2) She came with his coat.

Clearly, the two sequences have different grammatical properties. Unlike (2), (1) will admit, for instance, passive transformation:

(3) → His coat was sent for.

(4) → *His coat was come with.

The behaviour of (1) is in this respect like that of an $N_1 \ V \ N_2$ structure where N_2 is object, as in

(5) She ironed his coat.

(6) → His coat was ironed.

We shall refer to sequences which contain one or more prepositions as "prepositional strings". For the present experiment we have restricted ourselves to finite active clauses of the structure $N_1 \ V \ p$ N_2, a formula used for clauses with only one preposition (p) and postprepositional nominal element (N_2) besides subject (N_1) and finite verb (V).

These strings are commonly divided by grammarians into two groups: "verbs with prepositional object" (1) and "verbs, with prepositional adjunct" (2). The dichotomy is often based on the feeling that in the first group the verb and the preposition form a close unit, in the second group they do not. However, although it is indispensable to the analyst, such linguistic feel should not be made the only basis for ordering the material. It is a desideratum that a general classification should be as widely understood and accepted as possible by other practitioners in the field. But this is feasible only if the classifier's intuition is correlated with objective criteria, which lay his classification open to outside inspection, a procedure which is generally agreed on as a prerequisite in all scientific work. Hence the grammarian's attempt to objectify his *Sprachgefühl* by defining his classes in terms of testable criteria.

Attempts have indeed been made to use formal linguistic criteria for classifying these strings, for instance by Jespersen, who points out that the close connexion is shown by "the possibility of the passive construction ... and in the end-position of the particle (prep.) in interrogative sentences and relative clauses". Also, "we find the same preposed word as the object at the same time of a single verb and a verbal phrase", as in "these laws my readers are bound to *believe in* and to *obey*". As regards strings exemplified by

He was sent for and taken care of, Jespersen observes that "the particle has greater cohesion with the verb than with what (in the active) is the object either of the particle alone (preposition) or of the whole phrase" (1907-49, Part III, Sections 13.9 and 15.6).

Also Kruisinga uses the last criterion and points out the "inseparable" character of strings like *look upon*. Furthermore, "the verb can be used without the preposition or adverb, although the passive of such verbs is rarely possible without a preposition", as in *She sat the horse with ease* (1931-32, Part III:2, Section 1964 ff.).

Sweet offers another criterion: "When an intransitive verb requires a noun-word to complete its meaning, the noun-word is joined to it by a preposition, forming a prepositional complement, as in *he came to London; he looked at the house; I thought of that; he thinks of going abroad.*" "When the combination of an intransitive verb with a preposition is logically equivalent to a transitive verb, we call the combination a group-verb." (1891, Part I, p. 91). Lees uses the term "verb-preposition transitives" (1963, p. 9).

Poutsma requires three features for prepositional objects, "none of which should be lacking": "a) The preposition-group is felt as a more less indispensable adjunct of the verb or adjective with which it stands; b) The preposition is of a vague meaning, conveying no distinct notion of place, time, cause, purpose, agency, instrumentality, etc.; c) The preposition is intimately connected with the verb so as to form a kind of unit with it, not seldom one which in the same or some cognate language may be expressed by a verb without a preposition" (1904-26, Part I, p. 257).

The last criterion and others are discussed by Olsson: "the traditional distinctions between 'predicative adjuncts' and 'objects' and between 'objects' and 'adverbial adjuncts' (especially 'adverbials of place') cannot be upheld" (1961, pp. 70f.). His approach is through commutation and 'x-level' (extra-lingual) analysis.

Chomsky gives the ambiguous active sentence *John decided on the boat*, which may or may not have passive transformation depending on whether it has the sense of *He chose the boat* or of *He decided while on the boat*. In order to account for this, he makes a distinction between "Verb-Complement" and "VP-Complement", respectively, where only the former is "subject to pseudopassiviz-ation by the passive transformation" (1965, pp. 105 f.).

These extracts may suffice to illustrate the lack of agreement among grammarians on the mode of classification of prepositional strings in English. Before returning to our own approach to this problem we shall consider some general aspects of classification.

2

PROBLEMS OF CLASSIFICATION

Tentatively, we would think that something similar to the following procedural steps are likely to take place whenever a classification of this kind is attempted.

(a) We have the intuition that there exists a distinctive important group, in this case one with close connexion between the elements V and p.

(b) This intuition is very crude but also very strong.

(c) Our intuition basically leads us to focus our attention on this group, and hence our intellectual response is to decide that it is sensible to divide prepositional strings into two classes: strings with close connexion between V and p elements, and the rest, i.e. strings with little connexion between these elements.

(d) In an attempt to define this first class the passive criterion is found to be adequate in most cases, and is evidently important. Yet this criterion alone gives us results which are "counter-intuitive", since it would exclude strings which we intuitively want to include, for example

(7)   Ice consists of water.

which has no passive transform

(8)   → *Water is consisted of (by ice).

or

(9)   He looks like a weasel.

(10)   → *A weasel is looked like (by him).

Our first criterion seems therefore inadequate to objectify our intuition, and hence we may feel the need for more criteria.

(e) Additional criteria will also be found helpful to take care of marginal cases. Furthermore, even within the class that accepts the original criterion, it will appear that some strings accept it more readily than others, which suggests that they are not all of one and the same type.

Apart from some query cases, setting up dichotomous classes presents no great difficulty, so long as they are defined by single criteria, for example

Members of Class I satisfy some Criterion P.

Members of Class II do not satisfy Criterion P.

The linguist may maintain that, for his purpose, a dichotomy is all he wants. This seems of course a fully justifiable attitude provided that the purpose of the classification is a restricted one. For instance, a linguist studying voice in the verb would seem to be justified in drawing a line between strings which allow passive transformation and those which do not (see, for example, Svartvik 1966, pp. 20f.). But the argument here applies to general, all-purpose classifications, describing overall structure of the particular strings.

Even in a general classification the linguist may insist on a dichotomy, although there is usually no evidence for assuming that such a classification is a good one. He may succeed in setting up dichotomous classes, at worst by forcing recalcitrant examples into the classes, or, at best, by listing as "marginal" those examples which are not classifiable as members of classes set up on the basis of the selected criteria. This approach is particularly unsatisfactory if there is a large number of marginal cases, which are left unclassified as "a mixed bag". As an example of this we might mention prepositional phrases with place-indicating function, such as

(11) He is in the garden.

(12) They had slept in the bed.

The function of these phrases is adverbial, which is apparent from the use of question forms with *where*:

(13) Where is he?

(14) Where had they slept?

Yet the phrase in (11) is structurally indispensable, and (12) admits passive voice transformation (see Zandvoort 1963, p. 204):

(15) *He is.
(16) The bed had been slept in.

2.2 ARGUMENTS IN FAVOUR OF MULTIPLE CRITERIA

To avoid the dilemma arising from a classification based on a very few criteria which are considered to be important (what taxonomists call "diagnostic key features" (see Sections 3.3-4, pp. 31 ff. and 3.6, pp. 37 f.), we shall advocate one based on the correlation of many criteria. The different classes will then be set up according to "overall similarity", i.e. the number of features which their members share.

Before we go on to describe the principles of our approach, it may be appropriate to ask ourselves what we want from a general linguistic classification (see further Section 3.4, pp. 33 ff.). Let us postulate three requirements:

(a) It should be comprehensive, i.e. account for all the data, including unclear, ambiguous, and marginal cases.

(b) It should be based on formal linguistic criteria and hence be objective and empirically verifiable. Objectivity is of course a relative concept, but it should be incumbent on the analyst to try and reduce as far as possible the subjective element in his classi-fication.

(c) There should be a judicious balance between high predictive power and simplicity, so that for a classification of prescribed complexity, the predictive power is as great as possible. (A classi-fication has high predictive power if the knowledge that a string is in a given class enables us to make several predictions about the string with certainty or near-certainty. See Section 3.4 d, pp. 34 f.).

A classification satisfying these three requirements fully would in some sense be an optimum classification, and, to the extent that such a classification is implicit in the language itself, we may summarize by saying that we require a natural classification.

We believe that we can arrive at a good classification with high predictive power only by using multiple criteria. Consider, for example, the following points:

(a) The analysis of strings in the data by any particular criterion is often uncertain or unclear, for example,

(17) Her fears confined her dreams within herself.

(b) Particular strings may have certain constraints imposed on them by exponence. The two strings

(18) Emma asked for a reply.
(19) Emma asked for her coat, ... (OTU 8, b 96)[1]

are likely to cause different informant reactions due to N_2 exponence, which influences the possibility of, say, the passive transformation criterion:

(20) A reply was asked for.
(21) *Her coat was asked for.

At the same time as we want to recognise this fact, we also want to point out resemblance otherwise.

(c) Transformation potential is restricted by contextualisation. The following strings, for example,

(22) The girl was turned to.

and

(23) The Prime Minister was turned to for help by people suffering from the depression in the north-eastern industrial areas.

produced immensely different responses from informants.

(d) Informants may vary in their responses, which may be due to misunderstanding, uncertainty, or dialectal and/or idiolectal variations.

(e) The choice of criteria is likely to be subject to involuntary bias on the linguist's part. This may be due either to a field of

[1]   For the meaning of *a* and *b* see Bibliography. For OTU, see Section 3.3, p.32.

inquiry which is too narrow, or to a selection of criteria which is unduly influenced by what he has uppermost in his mind at the particular time. The use of a large number of criteria will not entirely remove this effect, but it will minimize it.

Unless the purpose of the classification is a special one, it would thus seem essential, linguistically, to take a comprehensive view. There are also compelling technical reasons for using multiple criteria.

2.3 DIFFICULTIES IN USING TWO CRITERIA

Let us suppose we are using two criteria, and that we are trying to divide the data into two classes. In order to isolate some of the difficulties, we consider three cases which might occur:

Case I: When we prefer our classes to be defined by yes-answers.[2]

Case II: When a single criterion is felt to be inadequate.

Case III: When there are a number of query answers.[3]

(We use the following notation: X and Y are classes, L and M are criteria. "$+L$" = "satisfying L"; "$-L$" = "not satisfying L"; and "$?L$" = "query L".)

Case I

Because this seems so natural, it is easy to forget the no-answers. Suppose we wish to use the two criteria as follows:

---

[2]   The motive for this is the requirement for high predictive power. In itself, it is not very illuminating to know that a given string does not take a given transformation.

[3]   It is essential to emphasize that query answers should be considered as "genuine" and linguistically important, and not as due to some insufficiency on the informant's part. Queries may be conditioned by a range of factors, including structural ambiguity inherent in the language. See further Sections 4.4 (pp. 51 ff.), 8.233-4 (pp. 127 ff.), and fn. 10, p. 123.

if a string is $+L$ it is placed in Class X, and
if it is $+M$ it is placed in Class Y.

This can work only if we never have $+L$ and $+M$, and can be comprehensive only if we never have $-L$ and $-M$. In this case we say that L and M are *opposed*:[4]

	$+L$	$-L$
$+M$		√
$-M$	√	

If we have established that L and M are opposed, it will obviously be simpler to use only one of them, although the second criterion could be used to confirm the first. The requirement of Case I would however have been satisfied. Less useful is the similar situation when L and M are *equivalent*:

	$+L$	$-L$
$+M$	√	
$-M$		√

These situations with criteria in complete equivalence or opposition are not very likely in practice, where we normally have *over-lapping* criteria:

	$+L$	$-L$
$+M$	√	√
$-M$	√	√

Thus, in a sample of 128 prepositional strings of the structure N_1 Vp N_2 we got the following distribution (P = possibility of passive transformation, e.g. *The coat was sent for;* A = possibility of question transformation with adverbs such as *where, when, how, why*, e.g. *When did she usually smoke?* as the transform of *She usually smoked in the morning.*):

---

[4] A blank cell implies that there are no occurrences with this particular correlation, and "√" implies that there are.

	$+P$	$-P$
$+A$	1	55
$-A$	32	40

It may be convenient to consider the single instance of $+P/+A$ as extra-systemic and marginal, but this will not do for 40 instances of $-P/-A$ (approximately 30% of the sample). In this situation two ways are open: either setting up a third class defined as $-P/-A$ or using more criteria. Defining a class negatively would seem, as we said, to defeat our avowed intention to obtain the highest possible predictive power (see the definition of linguistic predictivity in Section 3.4 d, pp. 34f.). The second alternative is preferable because it takes care not only of the $+P/+A$ and $-P/-A$ categories but is also likely to refine the other two classes.

Case II

Let us suppose that in general $+L$ holds for the strings we wish to place in X, and $-L$ for those we wish to place in Y. L may be felt inadequate because $-L$ holds for some strings we wish to place in X; this situation may be called *unwanted failure*. Conversely, $+L$ may hold for some strings we wish to place in Y; this situation may be called *unwanted acceptance*. Finally, if both these situations co-occur, the resulting situation may be called *overlap*.[5]

Remembering that M may approximate towards either equival-

[5] A relevant case of "unwanted failure" is exemplified by (9) and (10) in Section 2.1, and a relevant case of "unwanted acceptance" is exemplified by (12) and (16) in Section 2.1. If with a given criterion L there are cases of unwanted failure only, $+L$ may be a sufficient but not necessary condition for membership of X; similarly, if there are cases of unwanted acceptance only, $+L$ may be a necessary but not sufficient condition for membership of X; if there are cases of both unwanted failure and unwanted acceptance, $+L$ can neither be a necessary nor a sufficient condition for membership of X.

ence or opposition to *L*, we exhibit what seem to be the natural attempts at resolving the difficulty.[6]

	M and L partially equivalent		M and L partially opposed	
	Table	Condition that a string is in X	Table	Condition that a string is in X
Unwanted failure	$+M$: X(+L) X(−L); $-M$: X(+L) Y(−L)	$+M$ or $+L$	$+M$: X(+L) Y(−L); $-M$: X(+L) X(−L)	$+L$ or $-M$
Unwanted acceptance	$+M$: X(+L) Y(−L); $-M$: Y(+L) Y(−L)	$+M$ and $+L$	$+M$: Y(+L) Y(−L); $-M$: X(+L) Y(−L)	$+L$ and $-M$
Overlap	$+M$: X(+L) ?(−L); $-M$: ?(+L) Y(−L)	?	$+M$: ?(+L) Y(−L); $-M$: X(+L) ?(−L)	?

We should now have to check whether the system was consistent with intuition, or could be made so by suitable choices in the indeterminate cases; or whether it was consistent except for these, but required further refinement in them. In practice we could probably find a criterion *M* which, in combination with *L*, was better than *L* alone, but which was still not perfect. We would usually be driven to increase the complexity by looking for further criteria. A simple extension of these ideas might suffice, for example, "a string is in X if $+M$ or $+L$ or $+N$", but we feel that usually a more complex analysis would be necessary.

---

[6] "Partially equivalent" is used to mean "much nearer equivalence than opposition". "Partially opposed" is used to mean "much nearer opposition than equivalence". We use *or* for what is commonly written "and/or".

Case III

This is simple if we can find a criterion M that never conflicts with L (where the table defines our use of "conflict"):

	$+L$	$?L$	$-L$
$+M$	$\surd$	$\surd$	
$?M$	$\surd$	$\surd$	$\surd$
$-M$		$\surd$	$\surd$

This gives a reasonable generalisation of equivalent criteria (Case I), and gives just one reasonable classification:

	$+L$	$?L$	$-L$
$+M$	X	X	
$?M$	X	?	Y
$-M$		Y	Y

We shall again have no difficulty if we can find instead a criterion M which (in a similarly generalised sense) opposes L. (Except once again in the probably rare case of $?L$ and $?M$.) In practice, however, we normally find L and M overlap to a greater or lesser extent:

	$+L$	$?L$	$-L$
$+M$	$\surd$	$\surd$	$\surd$
$?M$	$\surd$	$\surd$	$\surd$
$-M$	$\surd$	$\surd$	$\surd$

For simplicity, let us suppose we find a criterion M which reinforces L.[7] We then have two principal choices:

(a) to make one of L and M *subordinate* to the other.
(b) to make L and M *co-ordinate*, or of equal status.

We now define these terms.

---

[7] There would be no essential difference in the argument if $-M$ reinforced $+L$.

If we adopt (a), and make, say, M subordinate to L, we may classify as follows:

Put a string in X if $+L$ and in Y if $-L$; and if $?L$, put the string in X if $+M$ and in Y if $-M$.

	$+L$	$?L$	$-L$
$+M$	X	X	Y
$?M$	X	?	Y
$-M$	X	Y	Y

If we adopt (b), we have a number of choices; for example, we may generalise the "$+M$ *and* $+L$" of Case II in two ways:

	$+L$	$?L$	$-L$
$+M$	X	X	Y
$?M$	X	?	Y
$-M$	Y	Y	Y

	$+L$	$?L$	$-L$
$+M$	X	?	Y
$?M$	?	?	Y
$-M$	Y	Y	Y

and we may similarly generalise "$+M$ *or* $+L$":

	$+L$	$?L$	$-L$
$+M$	X	X	X
$?M$	X	?	Y
$-M$	X	Y	Y

	$+L$	$?L$	$-L$
$+M$	X	X	X
$?M$	X	?	?
$-M$	X	?	Y

Again, we may think of L and M as equivalent, especially if they come near to being so, in our generalised sense, and classify thus:

	$+L$	$?L$	$-L$
$+M$	X	X	?
$?M$	X	?	Y
$-M$	?	Y	Y

It is evident that we cannot specify in advance how the dichotomy is to be achieved; this can only be done by considering the particular criteria. In addition, we have no guarantee that any of these methods will be entirely satisfactory.

2.4 INADEQUACY OF TWO CRITERIA

In conclusion we remember that all three cases — I, II, and III — may co-occur. We suggest in the light of this and earlier sections that:

(a) it is not always reasonable to insist on a dichotomy;

(b) division into more than two classes is likely to be difficult, especially when there are query-answers;

(c) more information will, in general, be needed, which can be gained by increasing the number of criteria;

(d) it will not be possible to lay down in advance simple rules of the type we have just considered. Each situation will have to be judged on its merits;

(e) a more satisfactory method for doing this must be found, but it would be expedient to look first at a particular case.

2.5 USING THREE CRITERIA

Increasing the number of criteria to three for classifying the sample of 128 strings, we chose criterion Q = possibility of question transformation with pronoun (*who/what*), as in *What did she send for?*, in addition to P and A.[8] 7 out of 8 possible patterns occurred:

Pattern	Criteria			Occurrence
	P	Q	A	
I	+	+	+	1
II	+	+	−	31
III	+	−	+	0
IV	+	−	−	1
V	−	+	+	26
VI	−	+	−	28
VII	−	−	+	29
VIII	−	−	−	12

[8] For a more detailed presentation of the criteria see Section 4.3 (pp. 41ff.). The same sample was used here as for two criteria in Section 2.3.

The table suggests for example that:

(a) $+P$, but not $-P$, has high predictive value.

(b) $+Q$ has less predictive value since it occurs frequently with both $+P$ (32 occ.) and $-P$ (54 occ.) and also with both $+A$ (27 occ.) and $-A$ (59 occ.).

(c) $+A$ implies $-P$ but little about Q, hence it has less predictive value than $+P$.

2.6 USING FOUR CRITERIA

Adding a fourth criterion, D (possibility of deleting p N_2 without structural change, as in *I won't ask for details* → *I won't ask*), we got the following distribution with 12 out of 16 possible patterns:

Pattern	Criteria				Occurrence
	P	Q	A	D	
I	+	+	+	+	1
II	+	+	+	−	0
III	+	+	−	+	17
IV	+	+	−	−	14
V	+	−	+	+	0
VI	+	−	+	−	0
VII	+	−	−	+	0
VIII	+	−	−	−	1
IX	−	+	+	+	21
X	−	+	+	−	5
XI	−	+	−	+	19
XII	−	+	−	−	9
XIII	−	−	+	+	20
XIV	−	−	+	−	9
XV	−	−	−	+	7
XVI	−	−	−	−	5

Queries have not been included in the tables; if they are added, we get the following additional patterns:

XVII	+	+	?	—	5
XVIII	+	—	?	—	2
XIX	?	+	+	—	3
XX	—	+	+	?	1
XXI	—	+	?	—	3
XXII	—	+	—	?	1
XXIII	—	?	+	+	2
XXIV	—	—	+	?	1
XXV	—	—	?	+	2

Although some clustering suggests the existence of a hierarchy, this is by no means borne out by the whole material. In fact, there is considerable cross-cutting: of 86 occurrences of $+Q$, for instance, we have 32 occurrences of $+P$, 58 occurrences of $+D$, and 27 occurrences of $+A$. It is also interesting to notice that $+Q$ occurs with no other feature $(+Q-P-A-D)$ 9 times and with all other features $(+Q+P+A+D)$ once. More striking still, we have $+Q+P-A-D$ 14 times and $+Q-P+A+D$ 21 times. Yet $-Q$ *is* predictive: $-Q+P$ occurs only once out of 42 occurrences of $-Q$. This suggests that there is no single key feature for each class, but that the classes are defined by certain correlations of features.

2.7 INADEQUACY OF FOUR CRITERIA

Extending the number of criteria from one to four, we have progressively increased the number of classes in our data (with positive and negative but not query responses considered):

1 criterion	(P)	2 classes
2 criteria	(P, Q)	4 classes
3 criteria	(P, Q, A)	7 classes
4 criteria	(P, Q, A, D)	12 classes

It seems at this point legitimate to ask: why stop at 4, why not use 40, or 400? It is obvious that there is complex structuring involved, and if our objective is to gain as much insight as possible into the problem, the odds are that the more criteria we apply the more facts will be revealed.[9]

---

[9]   The use of multiple criteria has been persuasively advocated by, for example, P. H. A. Sneath. See Sneath 1957a, 1957b, and Sokal & Sneath 1963.

3

THE NATURE AND OBJECT OF CLASSIFICATION

Since we have now reached the stage of considering a classification based on a large number of criteria, it seems appropriate to examine the nature of classification itself. We shall henceforth use the term in the following extended sense: "a classification of a set of objects is a system of reference for the objects together with rules for referring them to it".

3.1 THE MENTAL CLASSIFICATION PROCESS

We begin by considering briefly a particular class of classifications, viz. those we acquire without consciously formulating or learning them (and which in some cases we have no knowledge of). Our minds receive a vast amount of "data" which, at least in the case of sense data, we cannot describe directly. (Notice the difficulty of a painter wishing to reproduce faithfully what either of his eyes sees.) Yet we have a highly organised system of thought, in which our conscious minds recognise a very much smaller number of variables, giving our mental processes a deceptive air of simplicity. There are at least two problems which could be considered:

(a) How does this system arise? We envisage the means by which the system arises as a very complex process in which information assessed according to the classification system as it stands in turn modifies the classification. We do not know how this happens, and shall not discuss the matter further. We shall only consider mental processes as applications of the system, ignoring the fact that they are a conscious link in its continuous formation.

(b) What is the nature of the system? To answer this is to describe the system as a static object, and this is all that will be attempted here. For simplicity we consider the system as a division into classes where a class is thought of very vaguely as a collection of objects which our minds would treat in some respects in the same way. We leave open the question of the relationships between these classes.

3.2 CLUSTERING AND DIAGNOSIS

Two questions then arise, which may be called the problems of clustering and diagnosis respectively:

(a) What are these classes?

(b) What is the relationship between the objects and the classes which causes an inspected object to be assigned to a particular class?

To these we propose tentative answers as follows. The classified objects have a large number of properties which our minds recognise,[1] for example, in the case of physical objects: physical properties, contexts in which they are observed, uses, the results of their being used, and so on. We have in our minds certain classes whose members are, in terms of their properties, similar to one another, and less similar to objects we should place in other classes: the classes are formed on the basis of the overall similarity of their members. It is also likely that, for any class, there are certain properties typical of it, in the sense that they are possessed by most members and that all members possess most but not necessarily all of them.

These properties, or rather a subset of them, are used for (possibly tentative) diagnosis, i.e. the assignment of new objects to the class. These may be called "key features". They will have high predictive power, correlating highly with other properties: to know that an object possesses most or all of them will make us almost

---

[1] In practice, the features used for diagnosis on a given occasion can only be those available, and others more highly associated may therefore not be available for use. We are not conscious of the difference between the two processes involved in clustering and diagnosis, because we normally apply both as a continuous process.

certain it possesses many others, and we shall rarely have to modify our impression drastically.[2]

We thus possess a general system enabling us to describe and respond to various types of objects economically and efficiently — in fact, enabling us to think.

Certain points emerge from this and the previous section, explicitly or implicitly:

(a) The factors which determine the classes differ from those which determine how new members are assigned to them, which may be expressed shortly as "the problem of clustering differs from that of diagnosis".

(b) The features which are felt to be important will be those which are used for diagnosis, i.e. those which are highly correlated with many others; and conversely, features not highly correlated with many others will be felt unimportant.

(c) Since the means our minds use are obscure, we cannot rely on introspection when devising a system of classification. However, there is not necessarily any simple connexion between the end products of a process, and the process itself; in particular between the obvious or defining characteristics of classes formed in a particular way, and the process which formed them. Consequently our classification procedure, which derives ultimately from Sneath (see fn. 9, p. 28), relates in a simple way to its objectives. In fact, the *process* we use conforms to the hypothesis of Section 3.2, which was *not* a description of a process.

3.3 TERMINOLOGY

Before stating the aims it is convenient to define our use of the following terms:

---

[2] Whenever a classification problem arises, even if unrecognised as such, our natural reaction, conscious or (more generally) unconscious, is to look for "key" or "important" features, without being aware of the possible complexities.

OTU or OPERATIONAL TAXONOMIC UNIT: any one of the objects to be classified which is actually used in setting up the classification. (For a discussion of OTUs see Sokal & Sneath 1963, pp. 120 ff.)

INDIVIDUAL: any one of the objects to be classified, whether or not it is used in setting up the classification.

POPULATION: the collection of all individuals.

CRITERION: any test applied to the OTUs.

FEATURE: the response of an OTU to a criterion. Hence we may speak about "positive" and "negative" features.

CLASSIFICATION METHOD: the means by which the data, i.e. the OTUs and their features, are processed objectively (in our case by computer) to give a classification of the OTUs. See also the definition of classification, p. 29.

RELEVANT (as applied to criteria): having a significant relationship to the classification.[3]

OTU CLASSIFICATION, POPULATION CLASSIFICATION, DIAGNOSTIC KEY: the output of the method will be a classification of the OTUs, which we call the OTU classification. A means should then be found for extending this to the whole population. Such a means we call a diagnostic key[4] and the classification resulting from it the population classification. Where there is no risk of ambiguity, "classification" will be used for both "population classification" and "OTU classification".

GROUP, or CLUSTER: any set of OTUs, particularly those of the OTU classification.

CLASS: any set of individuals defined by the diagnostic key.

CLASSIFICATION PROCEDURE, or simply "procedure": the principles of conducting the experiment, including the method, the choosing of the OTUs and the criteria, the phase of setting up a diagnostic key, and the final interpretation.

CRITERION-COMPLEX: any set of criteria considered simultaneously. These are usually, though not always, logically inter-dependent;

[3]   This has been referred to in Section 3.2, and is discussed further in Section 3.6 (pp. 37 f.).
[4]   For a discussion of diagnostic keys see, for example, Sokal & Sneath, 1963, pp. 275 ff. and Möller 1962.

see, for example, TR 4, CON 4 and CON 9 (Section 4.3, pp. 43 ff.; see also Section 7.12, pp. 72 ff.). Criteria to which there are more than two responses may, if it seems preferable, be treated in this way as complexes of binary criteria.

3.4 THE AIMS OF CLASSIFICATION

The aims given below (which include the provisional linguistic requirements stated in Section 2.2, p. 17) are set forth primarily to clarify our ideas about what we are trying to do. They are in some cases counsels of perfection, to be kept in mind although they may be difficult or impossible to realise fully. They are not meant to be independent, and while it is conceivable that some may be mutually opposed, we feel that in general they reinforce one another. They should serve as a standard for judging the procedure — both in the abstract and in the light of the results it produces — and also as a standard against which to examine the results themselves. Finally, they may be helpful in the formulation of new methods of attack. We do not imply that a classification procedure can be mechanically deduced from the aims. The procedure we have adopted has several parts, and their relationship to these aims is complex. Where the procedure has been consciously deduced from explicitly formulated aims, it has probably been by considering them singly. Progress is most likely when one problem is dealt with at a time.

In the following specification of the aims of classification, the comments serve as more or less precise definitions or clarifications of our use of the headings. We believe that the resultant classification should be

(a) SIMPLE. The classification should be reasonably simple to understand and to use. This is perhaps a basic requirement.

(b) COMPREHENSIVE. As stated in Section 2.2 (p. 17), it should account for all the data, including the unclear, ambiguous, and marginal cases.

(c) GENERAL. It should relate to the overall nature of the set of linguistic objects classified, rather than to one particular aspect, and should in consequence be useful for general purposes.

It is not anticipated that this will lead to equivocal results, although it may lead to cross-classification.[5] We hope that if it is sensible to consider the data from a number of aspects, this will be revealed or at least suggested by the analysis. To give a plausible example: it may be convenient to consider constraints as in part grammatical (systemic), and in part lexical (exponential).

(d) PREDICTIVE. Partial or complete knowledge of the relationship of a given individual to the classification (which is normally knowledge of a class containing that individual) should enable us to predict with certainty or near-certainty many other facts about it. Two senses of "predictive" may be distinguished, one applicable to the OTU classification and the other to the population classification. We are therefore considering two related requirements.

The first is that the OTU classification should be *internally predictive*.[6] We expect the data to have some structure, so that there should be significant correlations between the features, possibly of particular interest when more than two are considered. The classification should be based on these correlations, and hence should reveal which combinations of features "go together"; in particular, if classes are formed, such groups of features should be associated with the classes. The classification could always be

---

[5] The term "cross-classification" is discussed in Section 7.24 (pp. 92ff.). We do not believe that non-general (i.e. special) classifications cannot be useful. The point is that we believe that classification of the type considered here is of basic importance, and one aspect of this type is generality. We may call this type "natural classification"; see Sokal & Sneath 1963, pp. 11-20. See also Section 2.2 (pp. 17ff.).

[6] To say that a classification is internally predictive means that it is predictive vis-à-vis the OTUs and the set of selected features; to say that a classification is externally predictive means that it is predictive vis-à-vis all individuals (not only the OTUs) and all features (not merely those selected). This means that if we wish internally predictive to imply externally predictive, we must hope that the OTUs are a fair and representative sample of the population of all individuals, and that the features selected are a fair and representative sample of all possible features. It is obvious that it is the latter requirement which presents most difficulty.

extended (if extension was necessary) so that a complete statement of the relationship of an OTU to the classification should give implicitly all its features. This statement should in general be much simpler than an enumeration of the features, and so the classification should serve as a device for economical description. More generally, a partial statement should enable a substantial number of features to be inferred with reasonable confidence.[7]

The second requirement, which is less precise, is that the population classification should be *linguistically predictive*. It relates, for example, to the classification enabling us to predict simply as many as possible of the transformations that an individual will accept. We hope that with greater general knowledge, the linguistic predictive power of a given classification will increase, and also that it will become easier to find linguistically predictive classifications. A classification can be linguistically predictive only if it is externally predictive (as defined in fn. 6).

(e) OBJECTIVE. It should be possible for other investigators to use different data and to obtain essentially the same results, or to repeat the experiment (using different informants) and get virtually identical results. (Ideally, if the criteria are chosen independently according to the same principles and applied to the same data, the results should be very similar. This is of course a very strong requirement.) The results should be as little dependent as possible on the bias of the individual linguist. It should be noticed that this bias can be of two types: for both the criteria he thinks of and those he judges sufficiently important to use are determined by his

---

[7] Further desiderata include: (a) a knowledge of how many features are necessary to establish accurately a given amount of information; (b) a knowledge of how many more features need to be considered in order to make (with the same "reasonable degree" of confidence) a further given number of inferences; (c) a measure of the efficiency of a given OTU classification. This might for example be achieved by defining a numerical measure of the volume of the description of all OTUs (i.e. a statement of their features) in terms of a given classification, and, in addition, a numerical measure of the complexity of that classification, so that it would be possible to compare numerically the labour involved in stating the features of the OTUs in terms of the classification with the labour involved in doing so without the classification.

skill, experience and prejudice.[8] The method itself should be completely precise rather than partially intuitive.[9]

(f) CONSISTENT WITH INTUITION. The classification should, broadly speaking, match our intuition, while being more objective, detailed, and in many respects more sensitive to the differences obtaining in different corpora. This does not in itself imply the use of any particular method.[10]

(g) EXTENDABLE. The classification should relate simply and sensibly to similar classifications for other corpora, and to classifications of other sets of linguistic objects.

(h) STIMULATING. We expect that the classification should be related to and should partially reveal some underlying structure, and hence should deepen our insight into the language.

3.5 THE NATURE OF FEATURES

In Section 2.7 (pp. 27 f.) we have shown that there are good reasons for favouring multiple criteria. It would seem that the more criteria we use, the more likely we are to arrive at a natural classification: relevant criteria will reinforce one another, whereas irrelevant criteria will prove immaterial to the final classification.

Two questions naturally arise, "What is a feature?" and "Are all features of the same status a priori, *quite apart from their relevance*?" It would be pleasant to have convincing answers to these questions and to have, for example, a clear concept "atomic

---

[8] There is always a danger that a classification may give more information about its designer than about the data it purports to classify.

[9] If this requirement is satisfied, the method can in principle be implemented on a digital computer, subject to practical limitation of computer storage and time. In practice the use of a computer is essential for all but trivially small applications. We do not of course preclude the modification of the method or of the procedure in the light of experience so that it shall give increasingly satisfactory results, as judged by these aims: in particular, so that the results are consistent with intuition. We anticipate a simultaneous improvement in our understanding of what we are studying and of our method of studying it.

[10] A bad classification method might invariably give results which matched the experimenter's intuition, for example one using heavily weighted criteria.

feature" to represent a "basic" linguistic property, together with a means of relating all features to atomic features.[11] This, however, seems very difficult especially as we do not possess a complete grammar of the language, but are, on the contrary, looking for a tool to improve our knowledge of the grammar and our general understanding of the language.

A glance at the features used in the experiment will show that their definitions depend on previous linguistic knowledge, and, indeed, on previous linguistic classification. For reasons of economy, it was inevitable that they should be non-atomic, however "atomic" might be defined. However, whether or not atomic features can be defined, some features can be broken down into simpler ones.[12] It might be argued that such compound features should be weighted in proportion to the number of relatively basic features they represent, but in the absence of a clear notion of atomic features, this seems unrealistic and artificial. We trust that an additional advantage of using a large number of criteria will be to offset, in some measure, these unavoidable imperfections.

3.6 WEIGHTING OF CRITERIA

We define a numerical coefficient of similarity between the OTUs and evaluate it for all pairs. How this is done will be explained in Section 7.11 (pp. 66 ff.), but here we may state the general principle that while we may treat different types of criteria slightly differently, we do not weight criteria or features: there is no a priori division

---

[11] An "atomic feature" would be a feature which could not be resolved into subfeatures. Furthermore, it would be possible to express all features in terms of atomic features. It is questionable (a) whether there is in fact such a thing as "atomic feature" in language and, if there is, (b) whether it is possible to identify atomic features without having a full knowledge of the structure of language.

[12] For example, a feature "animate" (in opposition to "inanimate") may be broken down into "personal" and "common", and in turn "common" may be reduced to "common 1" and "common 2"; see Section 4.3 (pp. 48f.). This example illustrates some of the difficulties in the use of "subfeatures", since the reduction process creates an imbalance in the relationship existing between individual features. See Section 7.12 (pp. 72ff.).

into those that are important and those that are not. We consider this a principle of vital importance in numerical taxonomy. There is no need to discuss this further here, but we refer instead to the forceful argument of, for example, Sokal & Sneath (1963, pp. 118 ff.). Their basic thesis is that the features we feel are important are exactly those which are, in our sense, relevant, i.e. those that correlate highly with other features; and that in so doing they will, if we have chosen a large and representative set of criteria, contribute towards the formation of classes and other aspects of this particular classification method in proportion to their relevance. Furthermore, if we wish to select features for diagnosis — i.e. find key features — we shall inevitably choose from the most relevant features. The linguist writing on a specific problem will already have devised — intuitively — the rudiments of a classification, and if he feels repugnance to the notion of basing a classification on a large number of unweighted features, this is presumably because he is thinking in terms of sets of important or significant features — in other words, of key features. His repugnance may be overcome by the reflection that a human classifier must have classified with key features. This will apply whether he has deliberately set out to classify or not. The approach here is an attempt to press the process back a stage, and we hope to finish an experiment with the features weighted, or rather ordered, on convincing evidence.

Features which co-occur freely with all other combinations are completely irrelevant, but if there are a large number of criteria and OTUs, it need not be feared that such irrelevant features will have a distorting effect on the final analysis. Similarly, unreliable criteria — that is, those which are very frequently answered differently by different informants — will not be as pernicious as it might be feared, provided there are a sufficient number of OTUs. The reason for this is that, in general, we shall have two fairly similar OTUs differing with respect to a particular response, and each similar to a group of others. According to the clustering method employed, the appropriate class may or may not be formed as early, but it should still be formed (see Section 7.321, pp. 98 ff.).

4

A TAXONOMIC EXPERIMENT: LINGUISTIC TASKS

The procedure of classification adopted in studying the degrees of verb-preposition cohesion (see Chapter 1) consisted of the following steps:

I Basic Linguistic Tasks.
    (a) Delimiting the problem.
    (b) Choosing the corpus.
    (c) Selecting the criteria.
    (d) Eliciting informant reactions.

II Computational Tasks.
    (e) Selecting a classification method.
    (f) Preparing the data.
    (g) Program execution.

III Analytical and Critical Tasks.
    (h) Obtaining a diagnostic key.
    (i) Assessing the results statistically where possible.
    (j) Interpreting the results linguistically.

Basic linguistic tasks will be dealt with in this chapter, computational tasks in Chapters 5-7, and analytical tasks in Chapters 8-10.

4.1 DELIMITING THE PROBLEM

There are many different kinds of structures which include prepositional strings, for example,

(24) $N_1 \, V \, p \, N_2$	"I work in a bookshop."	(a19)
(25) $N_1 \, V \, N_2 \, p \, N_3$	I gave a book to him.	
(26) $N_1 \, V \, p \, N_2 \, p \, N_3$	They looked behind them at the now tenebrous graveyard ... (a29)	

(27) $N_1 \, V \, N_2 \, p \, N_3 \, p \, N_4$ "I ... have tea in town on Mondays, ..."   (b91)

(28) $N_1 \, V \, p \, N_2 \, p \, N_3 \, p \, N_4$ "he'd change over from one set of false teeth to another in the middle of a lecture."   (b104)

(29) $N_1 \, V \, p \, N_2 \, p \, N_3 \, p \, N_4$ Her eyes travelled over the mounds, $p \, N_5 \, p \, N_6$ to the spot, along the column, to its crown, to its arched upper window.

For this first experiment in numerical taxonomy it was desirable to delimit the problem to a set of structures which were fairly homogeneous within the domain of the specific problem. (There are good reasons to believe that the use of prepositional strings is greatly context-conditioned. The possibility of mobility of $p \, N$ in the clause, for example, varies according to the type and number of other clause elements present.)

We chose active finite verb clauses with only one prepositional phrase and no other nominal element (object or predicative), expressed by the formula $N_1 \, V \, pN_2$. This type consists of, minimally, four elements, any one of which may of course be zero by ellipsis in co-ordinate parallel structures. $N_1 =$ subject, $V =$ finite verbal group, $p =$ preposition, and $N_2 =$ postprepositional element. N_1 and N_2 refer to the entire highest layer operating at those places in the clause structure, for instance,

(30) he was thinking, specifically, of **the heavy bag of potatoes which he was carrying;**   (b91)

p can be either simple (*on, with, to* ...) or complex (*out of, from under* ...), as well as *pNp* sequences operating as structural units (*in front of, in case of* ...). The elements may occur in different order, for example, discontinuous (31) or reversed (32):

(31) $\left| V \right| \overline{N_1} \left| V \right| \, p \, N_2$ "Must we talk about him?"   (b102)

(32) $p \, N_2 \, N_1 \, V$ With intermittent yelps of hysteria, Dinah's dog tore along (full pelt, ...) (a18)

Presence of non-prepositional clause adjuncts, such as adverbs or subordinate clauses, was recorded but did not influence the choice of material.

4.2 CHOOSING THE CORPUS

The corpus consisted of two texts in the files of the Survey of English Usage (a and b, see Bibliography) taken from novels, each text totalling some 5000 running words. The data were abstracted from all strings with the properties described above which occurred in the two texts. The corpus yielded 146 such strings.

4.3 SELECTING THE CRITERIA

There are, naturally, several factors which limit the number of criteria. They include the linguist's ingenuity, the linguistic categories available in the particular problem, the informants' time, and (though this is not relevant in the case of large machines) the computer's storage. Taking these factors into consideration, the choice of criteria is necessarily bound to be a compromise guided by commonsense. (The selection of criteria is one of many aspects of classification which should particularly profit by reappraisal in the light of gained experience.)

Criteria have to be thought of, and in isolating an idea for serious consideration we *must* have in our minds some notion of "reasonably conceivable relevance".

On the basis of preliminary experiments we had good grounds for believing that certain criteria could make no significant contribution to the classification, since their responses appeared to correlate freely with all combinations of other features. Even if it were possible, it would be manifestly absurd to exercise no judgment whatever in the selection. (It may be objected that by admitting this we have destroyed all claim to objectivity, but in fact we have merely lost the right to claim 100% objectivity.)

Some criteria may be frequently inapplicable, for example those depending on a part of the string not necessarily present, or such criteria as TR4: 1-4 (see below). If we assume that a criterion is used by the method once for every pair of OTUs to which it applies — this is strictly true for our method — then the number of uses increases rapidly with the number of times it applies. If the number of times a criterion is applicable is n, the number of uses (indicating the degree of usefulness) is $n(n-1)/2$; thus, for $n =$ 1, 2, 3, 4, 10, 100, 146, the number of uses is 0, 1, 3, 6, 45, 4950, 10585 respectively. Thus if a criterion is used only once, then it provides no basis for comparison, and its number of "uses" is therefore zero. There may however be points in favour of retaining a criterion even though it is not often used. It may be found that it is very relevant in some small group of OTUs in which it frequently or invariably applies. Again, we may want to know what happens to the OTUs to which it applies. Since we shall have a method for investigating such questions in the stage of setting up the population classification, we shall discover the answer as a matter of course if we retain the criterion, whereas our task will be considerably complicated if we have a separate body of data containing the responses to interesting but infrequently applicable criteria. It may be noticed that the number of criteria we need, and whether a criterion is so frequently inapplicable as to be useless, depends on the number of OTUs.

The criteria are of two main types. We may call them CONSTITUENT (CON) and TRANSFORMATIONAL (TR) CRITERIA. The first type refers to overt features which are actually present in the particular string under analysis. The second refers to potential features, which informants attribute to the strings. (Other possible names for the two kinds of features are overt/observed and covert features.)[1]

TR 1 $P =$ possibility of passive transformation, with agent optional.

    (33)   "He'll deal with it, ..." /he = the dog, it = the rat/
                                           (a 24)

    (34) → It will be dealt with (by him).

---

[1]   For a more detailed categorization of criteria, see Quirk 1965, p. 205. Our use of "transformational" is wider than his, corresponding to "potential constituent" as well as "transformational features".

There are various constraints to P, as well as to other transformational features. It may be convenient to distinguish between systemic and exponential constraints. The former can be illustrated by

> (35)   She smokes like a chimney.   (a 21)
> (36) → *A chimney is smoked like (by her).

which under no circumstances allows P. The latter can be shown by

> (37)   They looked at themselves.
> (38) → *Themselves were looked at.

as compared with

> (39)   They looked at the old car.
> (40)   The old car was looked at.

In the present experiment, exponential constraint was disregarded for transformational criteria.

TR 2 C = possibility of coordination of $V\,p$ with transitive (nonprepositional) verb.

> (41)   `He looked at /and admired/ the effigy.
> cf. (42)   *he sprang backwards with /and emitted/ a yelp, ...
>   (a25)

This criterion requires considerable ingenuity on the informant's part, since he himself has to try and find a suitable verb, whereas, for other criteria, his task is restricted to giving simple yes-, no-, or query-answers to questions put to him by the linguist.

TR 3 Q = possibility of question-transform with *wh*-pronoun (*who/what*).

> (43)   Treece turned to Viola.   (b104)
> (44) → Who did Treece turn to?

Since we had two informant sources for these responses with marked disagreements, TR 3 was divided into Qa and Qb. (See the end of Section 8.233 and Section 8.234, pp. 137 ff.).

TR 4 A = possibility of question-transform with *wh*-adverb.

When Criterion *A* was satisfied, the type of *wh*-adverb was further specified in the following four columns.

1. *Ap* = *where*?

    (45)   He kneeled down in front of her ...   (b96)
    (46) → Where did he kneel down?

2. *App* = *where* + end-placed *p*?

    (47)   Presently they retired to the Kardomah Café ...   (b91)
    (48) → Where did they retire to?

as well as *Ap*

    (49) → Where did they retire?
    (50)   He pulled into the kerb ...   (b90)
    (51) → Where did he pull into?

but not *Ap*

    (52) → *Where did he pull?

3. *At* = *when*?

    (53)   Dr. Adrian Carfax happened at that moment to be passing by, ...   (b100)
    (54) → When did Dr. Adrian Carfax happen to be passing by?

4. *Am* = *how*?

    (55)   Watching him, Madeleine continued in a vague and level manner: ...   (a20)
    (56) → How did Madeleine continue?

(Other possible question adverbs, *why*, *how long*, etc., were also tested but they did not apply to our corpus and were consequently left out from the processing.)

Variation in the reactions from the two sources for (TR 3) and uncertainty among informants suggest that there are at least two types of the *Q* and *A* question-forms. (We shall use the prosodic transcription conventions of Crystal and Quirk, 1964.) The normal types have unmarked tonicity (i.e. place in the tone unit of the syllable carrying the nuclear tone) and falling tone:

(57) /what does he :sùffer ·from #
(58) /who did the rat :lòok ·at #

as the normal question forms of

(59) "... he suffers from schizophrenia, ..."   (b104)
(60) "The rat looked at me."

and

(61) /where has he :gòne #

as the normal question form of

(62) "he's gone to the football match."   (a26)

The "abnormal" types have rising tone and shifted tonicity on the *wh*-element in recapitulatory (or reclamatory) questions, which require previously fully realised affirmatives:

(63) /whát does he ·suffer ·from #
(64) /whó did the ·rat ·look ·at #
(65) /whére has he ·gone #

In such recapitulatory questions *wh*-pronouns may be used alongside the normal *wh*-adverb, and hence the criterion is less discriminating:

(66) /whát had he ·gone ·to #

In applying these criteria, it was our aim to consider only the normal type as satisfying the criteria.

TR 5 D = possibility of deletion of $p\ N_2$, without structural change.

(67) "I won't ask for details."   (a29)
(68) → I won't ask.

but

(69) Emma was referring to the fact that ...   (b92)
(70) → *Emma was referring.

This is a difficult criterion to work with, and informants are often doubtful about the "sameness" of the full and partially deleted strings. We may have a situation similar to that of TR 3, so that there is one fully deletable type which does not entail structural change, and another elliptic type.

TR 6 $M =$ possibility of mobility of p N_2 to front position in the clause.

> (71)   he sprang backwards with a yelp, nipped in the lip.
>
> (a25)
>
> (72) → with a yelp he sprang backwards, nipped in the lip.

but

> (73)   "Mr. Bryce deals with the bibliophiles ..."   (a20)
> (74) → *with the bibliophiles Mr. Bryce deals.

Emphatic front position is almost always possible with emphatic intonation and stress, but in applying the criterion here we attempted to accept only non-emphatic functions. (The rarity of M in N_1 V p N_2 strings reduces its usefulness as a criterion in this particular study. It is likely to be more useful in classifying multiple-p N strings).

TR 7

> 1.   → $N_1 an =$ animate gender possible for N_1.
> 2.   → $N_1 in =$ inanimate gender possible for N_1.

Both $N_1 an$ and $N_1 in$:

> (75)   Madeleine/the tree ... stood at a little distance, ...
>
> (a27)

Only $N_1 an$:

> (76)   Emma looked out of the window, ...   (b93)

Only $N_1 in$:

> (77)   "(I wanted to ask you) what happened about Mr. Eborebelosa."   (b92)

TR 8

1.   → N_2an = animate gender possible for N_2.
2.   → N_2in = inanimate gender possible for N_2.

Both N_2an and N_2in:

(78)   She hurried to the gate/woman, ...   (a24)

Only N_2an:

(79)   "... I've been wanting to talk to you."   (b92)

Only N_2in:

(80)   From some distance she waved and nodded, ...   (a29)

CON 1-4 refer to N_1 and CON 5-8 to N_2. Since both sets use the same criteria applied to different elements in the strings, only the first set is illustrated here.

CON 1 form class.

1.   *Npron* = pronoun (*he, they, someone,* etc.)
2.   *Nname* = name (*Emma, Machiavelli, London, The Hague,* etc.)
3.   *Nnoun* = noun. It includes here, for convenience, nominalizations:

(81) "The bookshop does cater for **what's called the culti-vated reading public** — ..."   (a19)

CON 2 modification.

1.   *Npre* = premodification.

(82)   a few bright discs   (a26)

2.   *Npost* = postmodification.

(83)   professors nibbling cheese straws   (b107)

CON 3 *Ndef/Nindef* = finitude. As definite were included *N*s with determiners (*the*, *his*, etc.), and such pronouns as require a previous referent; thus *he* is definite in "he is coming" while *it* is indefinite in "it is raining".

CON 4 gender was specified in the following six columns:

1. *an* = animate
2. *pers* = personal (animate)
3. co^1 = common type 1 (animate)
4. co^2 = common type 2 (animate)
5. *conc* = concrete (inanimate)
6. *abst* = abstract (inanimate)

The distinctions were based on the following substitution-classes:

PERSONAL	COMMON 1	INANIMATE
$\begin{bmatrix} I \\ you \\ he \\ she \\ he/she \\ they \end{bmatrix} + who$	$\begin{bmatrix} he/it \\ she/it \\ he/she/it \\ it/they \end{bmatrix} + \begin{bmatrix} who \\ which \end{bmatrix}$	$\begin{bmatrix} it \\ they \end{bmatrix} + which$
boy, people, doctor, ...	horse, child, Fleet Street, ...	box, ability, grammars, ...

"Common 2" was set up as an intermediate category between "common 1" and "inanimate" for N_1 collocating with verbs like *try, see,* and *like* (e.g. *rat, snake,* etc.). Together these categories seem to make up a gender scale with personal and inanimate concrete as polar opposites:

$$\uparrow \left.\begin{matrix} \text{personal} \\ \text{common 1} \\ \text{common 2} \end{matrix}\right] \text{animate}$$

$$\downarrow \left.\begin{matrix} \text{abstract} \\ \text{concrete} \end{matrix}\right] \text{inanimate}$$

(The reason for placing abstract rather than concrete nearer to animates is that they seem to behave like animates more often than concretes:

(84)   Dusk was creeping up.

(85)   ... after the dog went the frantic voice of Dinah, ... (a24)

Such instances of unexpected nominal behaviour within *Nin* with regard to this scheme are however explained as metaphors, and do not affect the present analysis).

CON 9 adjuncts in clause.

1. Ad = presence of other adjuncts.
2.   adjunct = adverb (*Adv*).

(86) **Outside** the dusk was creeping up between the market stalls, ...   (b93)

3.   adjunct = verb construction, finite or non-finite (*Vcon*).

(87) **Observing what they took to be a bull in the next field,** they turned for home.   (a22)

4.   adjunct placed between V and p N_2 elements ($V + Ad + p + N_2$).

(88) Carfax sat down and began to puff **militarily** at his pipe; ...
                                                                (b103)

CON 10 specification of p exponents. In order to save machine time only those prepositions occurring more than once were included. (Since the original corpus included both finite and non-finite clauses, this does not strictly apply to the present limited corpus including only finite clauses).

There are thus 67 criteria, 15 of which are transformational and 52 constituent. This total does not, however, reflect the number of independent criteria applicable to the classification, since some coding was such that, say, only one out of three criteria (each one of which was in a separate column) could apply. This was particularly the case with the 24 in CON 10 stating p exponence, inasmuch as, by definition, there was only one p in each string. Another situation is illustrated by the criteria *A*, *Ap*, *App*, *At* and *Am*. Because of the large number of occasions when a criterion was inapplicable, and hence did not count in matching pairs, the number of criteria which counted in any given comparison of a pair of OTUs was usually between 20 and 25, approximately equally divided between constituent and transformational criteria.

Although one might expect TR criteria to have the greater classificatory power, in many cases CON criteria turned out to be closely correlated with TR criteria. CON criteria have, moreover, certain advantages over TR criteria:

(a) They are more reliable, since they refer to actual realizations. The element of uncertainty (cf. what has been said above on constraints imposed by exponence and context) is thereby considerably reduced.

(b) They require no informants, and hence are not subject to idiolectal variation.

(c) They provide valuable information about actual linguistic events. The fact that CON criteria are naturally less discriminating may be balanced by their large number, which is of course one of the basic principles of numerical taxonomy. The strength of CON features is often far from obvious. It is clear that N_2 may be either *an* or *in, pron* or *noun* as in

(89)   I don't believe in that man.
(90)   I don't believe in anyone.
(91)   I don't believe in public philosophies.
(92)   I don't believe in them.

and this would come out of TR criteria. On the other hand, in

(93)   He usually smokes in the morning.

N_2 cannot be *an:*

(94)   *He usually smokes in somebody.

nor, indeed, can it be *pron* in strings of this class:

(95)   *He usually smokes in it.

(which is ungrammatical, unless, of course, it is interpreted in a non-temporal sense, such as "in his smoking jacket").

These restrictions would come out equally well, and more reliably, with CON features.

4.4 ELICITING INFORMANT REACTIONS

Two female postgraduate students gave their native informant reactions to the strings tested by the relevant criteria. Furthermore, supplementary responses were given jointly by two academic staff members, male and female, for questions with *who/what* (Criterion TR 3).

The informants were asked to answer the TR questions given by the analyst with "yes", or "no", or "query". "Query" was commonly used when an informant was uncertain about her own usage or when she thought a certain transform, which she would not use herself, might be used by other native speakers.

Prior to eliciting informant reactions, the strings had been analysed manually with some of the TR criteria and were ordered in provisional groups. Within these groups, however, the strings occurred in the same order as in the texts. It is possible that the previous ordering may have, in some small measure, influenced the responses, since it seems easier for an informant to accept transformations in a long series of highly related strings less critically than he would if the strings were presented to him in random order.

We would like to emphasize the hazards of using informant reactions in dealing with syntactic problems. The decisions are not so much of the type "yes" or "no" as "more or less likely". We treated queries as fully information-bearing answers, so that we had a three-point scale ("yes" — "query" — "no"), and whenever the computer programs allowed it, this three-point scale was used when transferring the features to entries in the data input. Even so, the possibilities of erratic results, due to misunderstanding, idiosyncracies, individual bias, etc., are so great that the output must be interpreted with caution.

The dangers of getting erratic results in this kind of informant reaction test might be reduced by the use of more elaborate techniques than have been attempted in the present experiment. In response to a given TR, for example, there is all the difference in the world between

(a)

yes	query	no
	1	

with one single informant, and

(b)

yes	query	no
17	3	0

or

(c)

yes	query	no
3	17	0

or

(d)

yes	query	no
2	6	12

where 20 informants might be used and where (b) would be entered as "yes", (c) as "query" and (d) as "no".

The use of many informants, however, raises other problems: there is not only the difficulty of finding enough willing and suitably "naive" subjects with sufficient time at their disposal, but also that of test-condition control, which increases with the number of informants. It would therefore be interesting to try to find other more satisfactory means of scaling the responses than by using statistical averages. (For the use of informant reactions in investigating linguistic acceptability, see Quirk & Svartvik, 1966.)

As indicated by frequent hesitation and qualifications to the "bare" responses used in the present experiment, it was obvious that "yes", "query", or "no" answers were all too often felt by the informant to be inadequate representations of his reactions. One might therefore achieve greater refinement, for instance, by increasing the number of possible answers or by measuring the time elapsing between hearing a question and producing the answer to it.

5

AN OUTLINE OF THE TECHNICAL PROCESSES

Hitherto in this study we have discussed general problems of classification and described the basic linguistic tasks in the classification procedure of an experiment in numerical taxonomy. It is our intention now to discuss the nature of the classification method[1] we use (Chapters 6 and 7), and, in considerable detail, its application to our specific problem, especially to the finding of diagnostic keys (Chapter 8). Chapter 8 is in part an endeavour to provide material for an evaluation, in our context, of these methods of numerical taxonomy rather than to gain linguistic insight into the particular aspect of English grammar that we have chosen for illustration. In the following two chapters, we give a final version of the OTU classification and assess the bearing of the results on our problem, and, in Chapter 11, the suitability of the method for this kind of linguistic research.

We may consider the analysis proper to be that part of the work, which was conducted without any reference to linguistic considerations; it includes both work of the electronic computer and of the human experimenter. It is described in Chapters 6, 7, 8 and 9, and since these sections necessarily contain the more technical parts of this study, it will probably be helpful to make a preliminary survey of them. We shall first state the main tasks of the analysis, then list the subsections containing the basic ideas, and finally give a synopsis of these four chapters.

---

[1] The CLASSIFICATION METHOD is used to mean the way in which the data' that is, the OTUs and their features, are processed objectively (in our case by a computer) to give a classification of the OTUs. The CLASSIFICATION PROCEDURE is taken to mean the principles of conducting the experiment; this includes the method, the choosing of the OTUs and the criteria, the phase of setting up a diagnostic key, and the final interpretation. For the use of other terms, such as "classification" and "OTU", see Section 3.3 (pp. 31 ff.).

COMPUTATIONAL TASKS

Stage 1 (Section 7.11). — We obtain a similarity matrix by calculating a measure of resemblance between every pair of OTUs.

Stage 2 (Section 7.3). — On the basis of these numbers, we obtain an OTU classification by clumping the OTUs into groups whose members will, broadly speaking, resemble those of the same group and differ from those of other groups.

ANALYTICAL TASKS

Stage 3 (Chapter 8) — We obtain a diagnostic key by selecting from the groups those features which seem to be particularly associated with them, which may be used for identification (i.e. key features). In addition, we may select somewhat less important features as being predictable from the groups. In our context, however, this is not so important, because we hope to make future use of the groups we obtain and to find that various other features that we did not use in forming the classification are predictable from these groups. We are in a sense trying to classify important features and to find the structure of the class so formed, but we cannot hope, in this experiment, to go beyond the first stages of this.

Chapters 6 and 7 explain how the programs processed their material, and so do not introduce the data except for purposes of exemplification. Chapter 8, on the other hand, (in conjunction with Appendix 1) both develops and applies techniques for interpreting the computer output.

Not all the subsections are of equal importance to every reader. The minimum necessary for a linguist who wished to have a general idea of the processes, but did not wish to subject them to critical examination, would be, in addition to the synopsis below:

Chapter 6: Sections 7.1, 7.11 (as far as the basic definition of SIMILARITY COEFFICIENT), 7.2 (including its subsections), 7.31, 7.32, 7.321, 7.333, 7.334; 8.1, 8.22, 8.23 (including its subsections), 8.41 (first two paragraphs), 8.42, 8.43; Chapter 9.

Section 7.12 (coding and the nature of criteria) will be of interest only to those actually engaged in similar work; Section 7.13 is also of rather specialized interest.

SYNOPSIS OF CHAPTERS 6-9

Chapter 6: *Procedural choices.* — We state some of the general choices made in adopting our classification procedure, and consider the nature of our particular classificatory problem. We conclude by estimating the optimum number of criteria.

Chapter 7: *The similarity matrix.* — We discuss the definition, interpretation and processing of the similarity matrix.

Section 7.1: *Computing the similarity matrix.* — The similarity matrix is defined as a set of members, the similarity coefficients. These are conceived as measures of resemblance between the OTUs.

Section 7.11: *Calculating the similarity coefficient.* — We define the similarity coefficients for the programs we used. The similarity coefficient of two OTUs is in general an estimate of the proportion of features common to both.

Section 7.12: *Coding and the nature of criteria.* — We discuss the difficulties of coding that are almost certain to arise in this work (principally because the criteria are not independent).

Section 7.13: *Interpreting the similarity coefficient.* — This section considers the justification for considering the similarity coefficient as a measure of resemblance.

Section 7.2: *Interpreting the similarity matrix.* — We consider certain simple types of structure whose existence can be inferred by mere visual inspection of the similarity matrix, provided the OTUs have, by some means, been arranged in a suitable order.

Section 7.3: *Obtaining a classification from the similarity matrix.* — We discuss some of the technical methods of obtaining a classification (normally a cluster analysis) from the similarity matrix.

The section sets the method we used against a background of alternatives, but it does not aim to be comprehensive; in particular, it does not discuss the sophisticated methods initiated by R. Needham (1961) or R. Le Schack (1964). A number of methods are discussed in Bonner 1964.

Section 7.31: *General problems.* — We discuss the need for programmed methods, and make some general comments on the possibilities.

Section 7.32: *Cluster analysis and linkage systems.* — We define the clustering method (single linkage) which was used, and also some related approaches. This discussion is in terms of linkages, but the principles apply more generally.

Section 7.33: *Practical considerations.* — We consider certain practical problems, and also apply the single linkage method to a small selection of the criteria and OTUs used in the experiment.

Appendix 1 and Chapter 8, respectively, define and execute methods of simplifying the output and finding a diagnostic key. The total analysis is rather more detailed than the material justifies.

Section 8.1: *The need for a key.* — This section suggests that the computer output, while simpler than the data, is still too complex to be comprehended without classification, and indeed that in our situation we are only interested in a diagnostic key.

Section 8.2: *A key based directly on the output.* — A key is given which attempts to describe the output as it stands before any further processing. Two numerical methods are employed for selecting key criteria. One was designed to eliminate effects which might be due principally to chance, and the other, given in Appendix 1, uses a function designed to measure the value of any specified criterion in predicting any given partitioning of the OTUs.

Section 8.3: *A key based on inter-group analysis.*

Section 8.4: *A key constructed by a concept-formation process.* —

We investigate, by different methods, the relationship between the OTU classification groups, and form new groups by uniting these.

Chapter 9: *Classification of OTUs.* — This section gives the final version of the OTU classification, and quotes every OTU.

There are two extreme ways of looking at the type of work discussed here: it is inhuman and ridiculous; or, conversely, it is mathematical, objective, and infallible. The truth lies in between: the approach is partially subjective, i.e. it relies essentially at some points on human judgments that we do not know how to refute or sustain objectively; and it is partially objective, in that we submit the data to an objective process which, we may reasonably expect, will eliminate some of the human errors of judgment. We consider that it is a valuable research tool, not to be despised because it is neither completely subjective nor completely objective. "There is no more common error than to assume that, because prolonged and accurate mathematical calculations have been made, the application of the result to some fact of nature is absolutely certain." (Whitehead, quoted in Moroney 1956, p. 271). It "would be a naive error to assume that the quickest path to objectivity lies in being objective at every stage of one's inquiry". (Hudson 1965, p. 19).

PROCEDURAL CHOICES

In evaluating the experiment it may be helpful to know some of the choices that were made, and a little about the nature of some of the alternatives. At most points we were able to make the best choices we could conceive of, but some choices were governed by the availability of programs. Here there will be a little repetition of points made earlier. It is simplest to ignore for the moment the processes used in setting up the diagnostic key. We begin with the general choices (the choices of method will be discussed in detail in Sections 7.1 and 7.3). The basic choice was:

(1) To seek a general purpose classification.

Choices concerning the criteria were:

(2) To use (a priori) unweighted criteria (see Section 3.6, pp. 37f.).
(3) To use many criteria.
(4) To make a free choice of conceivably relevant criteria.

Choices concerning the classification method were:

(5) To search for a polythetic classification (see below).
(6) To avoid systems which necessarily produce very specialised types of output, for example clines (see Section 7.21, pp. 88 ff.). In fact, the method we actually used had as its objective the production of a nested hierarchy. Such a form may not be realistic — our total analysis should help to decide this. We stress, however, that the method divides naturally into two parts, the production of a similarity matrix and a cluster analysis, and it is only the latter that relates to the nested hierarchy. The similarity matrix is entirely general, and lends itself to other interpretations (see Sections 7.2, 7.32, 8.3, and 8.4).[1]

[1] There are two especially interesting, and completely distinct, types of program (due to J. C. Gower; and J. B. Kruskal, R. N. Shepard and J. Doran)

We may say that (1) requires the others, with the possible exception of (2); though weighted criteria would probably be principally suitable for special purpose classifications. We do *not* believe special purpose classifications are valueless, but rather that general purpose classifications are especially valuable. In view of the importance of the latter, we give for comparison some examples of special purpose classifications:

a. Shuffling a feature matrix to achieve a satisfactory appearance and conformity to more or less ill-defined intuitions.

b. A classification based on one criterion of immediate interest. This becomes part of a subjective experiment: the observer finds what sort of objects the classes contain. The subjective element is perhaps present in our case also, but to a lesser degree and in a different way.

c. An attempt to objectify an intuition. For example, "degree of cohesion" might be estimated intuitively and weights calculated a posteriori for the features so that the "value" of an OTU was roughly the original estimate (see Appendix 3, pp. 247 ff.). Notice that this method must give a cline (see Section 7.21, pp. 88 ff.) as output, and is really an analysis of features together with the finding of a diagnostic key (see Section 3.3, p. 32) and also a test as to whether an intuition can be objectified.

(a) and (b) are examples of what Sneath has called MONOTHETIC and POLYTHETIC classifications respectively. "The ruling idea of monothetic groups is that they are formed by rigid and successive logical divisions so that the possession of a unique set of features is both sufficient and necessary for membership in the group thus defined. They are called monothetic because the defining set of

---

which can produce clines. The methods they employ can place the OTUs as points in a space of 1, 2, 3, or more dimensions, and are intended primarily as visual aids. In our case, these analyses would be based on a space of 145 dimensions (i.e. one dimension less than the number of OTUs); another possible approach to this space would be to "see" where the natural constellations are and how they relate to each other. Such an approach has been attempted. Needham (1961) has devised an approach which leads to cross-classification (see further Section 7.24, pp. 92 ff.). We used a program written by J. Doran in Appendix 5 (see also fn. 13, pp. 151 f.).

features is unique." Polythetic groups have been defined thus by Beckner:

"A class is ordinarily defined by reference to a set of properties which are both necessary and sufficient (by stipulation) for membership in the class. It is possible, however, to define a group K in terms of a set G of properties $f_1, f_2, ..., f_n$ in a different manner. Suppose we have an aggregation of individuals (we shall not as yet call them a class) such that:

(1) Each one possesses a large (but unspecified) number of the properties in G.

(2) Each f in G is possessed by large numbers of these individuals and

(3) No f in G is possessed by every individual in the aggregate.

By the terms of (3), no f is necessary for membership in this aggregate; and nothing has been said to either warrant or rule out the possibility that some f in G is sufficient for membership in the aggregate." (Sokal & Sneath 1963, p. 14.)

In the context of biological classification, it has been suggested that general purpose classifications are most realistically considered as special purpose classifications with a very broad range of application. Our approach is consistent with this, but not with the related but more radical suggestion, made in the same context, that classification experiments will not lead to new hypotheses, but will merely regurgitate the antecedent hypotheses or knowledge that determined the choice of criteria. If this is considered as a logical proposition rather than an empiric one, there are various objections: for example, that rankings and associations of criteria may be revealed which were not already known to the experimenter; that the type of structure of a population (e.g. hierarchical) may not be obvious in advance even if certain key features are; and that the groups proposed by the classification method may correlate with completely unforeseen features.[2] The suggestion implies, in fact,

---

[2] At a meeting of the Classification Society, Miss J. M. Lambert described a particularly interesting example: in the classification of ecological sites in a particular region, the principle division was found to be strongly associated with the land drainage situation in the early 19th century.

that we are already in possession of most of the knowledge we need, or that we cannot even imagine any criteria which might help. From this point of view, experiments in grammatical classification may be in an unusually strong position. It is possible to select criteria without having any *hypothesis* leading us to do so; we certainly do not know the order of importance, or relevance, of our criteria; and any pre-existing knowledge we have is likely to be largely intuitive.

For our present work, at least, taxonomic methods are probably best considered as heuristic,[3] that is, consisting of procedures which we may reasonably hope to be valuable, but which may fail to give the best results. Indeed, they are not guaranteed to give good results; rather, they should be valued by the frequency and extent of their usefulness. This is for at least four reasons:

(1) The necessarily subjective element in the procedure which occurs in both finding and selecting the criteria, and in eliciting informant reactions (see also Section 7.13, pp. 83 ff.).

(2) The use of small samples. The data were 146 strings consisting of finite active verb clauses with only one prepositional phrase and no other nominal element (object or predicative), expressed by the formula $N_1 \, V \, p \, N_2$. The corpus consisted of two stretches of 5000 words each, both drawn from novels (see Section 4.2, p. 41).

(3) The tentative nature of the classification methods which have been proposed by workers in the field. It may be possible to define what is in some sense a perfect method, in which case it will probably be prohibitively long to apply (see Appendix 1, pp. 221 ff.).

(4) The subjective element in the formation of our diagnostic keys. There is, however, no doubt that they could be constructed objectively by computer.

We begin by attempting to put our particular problem in perspective. There are many different types of populations we might wish to classify, and while many procedures may always be valid,

---

[3] The term "heuristic" is used here more loosely than is customary in computational contexts. It is normal to describe a process as heuristic if it uses non-analytic methods because, so far as is known, no completely analytic method could in practice be used. This strict definition applies to (3), but it is also relevant to (1).

some populations present characteristic difficulties. Examples of relevant and basically independent factors are:

(1) Whether the population is best considered as finite or infinite; and if finite, whether or not it is too large to be handled conveniently and described in detail. The population may even be one in which there is continuous variation, as, for example, in the classification of soils, or of ecological sites.

(2) Whether all properties of the population can in principle be stated in advance or not, and in particular whether its members are specifiable or not.

(3) Whether the population is fixed; and, if not, whether future changes may affect its overall character.

The case we are using as example in this study may be considered infinite and fixed. With regard to (2), we do not know what are and what are not grammatical strings, nor what are and what are not strings likely to occur; OTUs were specified by the corpus and by the analyst's judgment. We may notice that the chosen criteria are also taken from a population which is, and will normally be, infinite and unspecifiable. This is considered later in Section 7.13, pp. 83 ff. The smaller and the more specifiable the population of criteria, the more confidence we shall have in the resulting classification but, perhaps, the less interest. These observations lead to two conclusions:

(1) In our case we have to make a sample of the individuals (i.e. of the population being classified) and also of the possible criteria (which would be true also if the number of individuals or criteria was large).

(2) Whenever the population is not small, and perhaps also when it is not specifiable, we must have a method of diagnosis, or extension to the whole population. (For a small, specifiable population, we can use the OTU classification as it stands, although even then we may well not wish to do so).

One of the basic necessities for this approach is the use of a large number of criteria (see Sokal & Sneath 1963). We give some considerations which might, between them, help to determine the number of criteria desirable:

(1) We need to be able to define a reasonable measure of resemblance between OTUs (see Sections 3.5-6, pp. 36 ff., and 7.13, pp. 83 ff.).

(2) We are interested in the proportion of features shared by any two OTUs; it is reasonable to suppose that, beyond a certain point, this proportion will not be significantly altered by the addition of further criteria (Sokal & Sneath 1963, pp. 114-8).

(3) It will generally be true that beyond a certain point, depending on the nature of the data, it will become very difficult to find criteria that might conceivably be relevant.

(4) The degree of delicacy required in the present work is at least that which would be likely to distinguish the 146 OTUs.

(5) It is also at least the number needed to distinguish with confidence a satisfactory number of distinct groups, provided that the data show such a number to be realistic.

(6) There is also a subsidiary limitation, brought about by the nature of the classification method used, and not by the nature of the problem (see Section 7.321, pp. 98 ff.).

We give the following very approximate estimates for the required number of criteria, under the six headings above:

(1) This number depends on the nature of the data, and any estimate can only be a guess. We suggest at least 60.

(2) Again, at least 60.

(3) In our case, we used 44 criteria, if p exponence is considered as a single criterion (see Section 4.3, pp. 49 f.). However, this number by no means represents an upper limit. In a subsequent taxonomic experiment involving passive verb clauses, 108 criteria were used (see Svartvik 1966). In principle, the number of possible, relevant constituent or "overt" criteria is necessarily limited, whereas the number of possible transformation or "covert" criteria (see Section 4.3, p. 42) is much greater.

(4) If all the criteria were of the "yes/no" type, if they were all independent, if each answer was equally likely, and if the OTUs were an entirely random sample, 15 criteria would be the number needed to make it more likely than not that all the descriptions would be different. In our case the OTUs were sometimes very

similar, partly because of the structured nature of the data, and partly because the OTUs were from a limited number of texts; and there was one pair with the same coding (OTUs 10 and 17).

(5) To distinguish for example 10 groups, only four binary criteria are required. However, to distinguish sensible groups, bearing in mind that some combinations of features will be rare, substantially more than four will be required; and these will be *key criteria*. Since initially we do not know which the key criteria are, we shall need more than the minimum number of key criteria. We can only guess how many are needed: we suggest at least 10 key criteria and 40 initial criteria.

(6) We estimate below (see Section 7.321, p. 103) that 15-20 are probably sufficient to overcome this.

Since many of our criteria were frequently inapplicable, for example, class of adjunct (see Section 4.3, p. 49), the effective number of them is probably close to the average number of points of comparison, which was between 20 and 25, rather than the average number of features, which was almost exactly 26. (The average number of points of comparison was greater for pairs of similar OTUs than for dissimilar pairs: see Appendix 2, pp. 232ff.). It will be seen that this number is too small, but not so small as to be absurd. Some of the numbers considered above cannot be specified in advance, but depend on the particular problem and the worker's common sense.

THE SIMILARITY MATRIX

7.1 COMPUTING THE SIMILARITY MATRIX

We use as our basic tool a similarity matrix, i.e. a set of numbers which are estimates of the similarity between the pairs of OTUs. The method divides into two halves: the computation of the similarity matrix, and the cluster analysis.

The use of a similarity matrix means immediately that the process of classification is polythetic (see Chapter 6, pp. 60f.), because after the computation of the matrix *all entries have been lost*, the cluster analysis proceeds without knowledge of the actual features associated with an OTU or even of those common to two OTUs.[1]

7.11 *Calculating the Similarity Coefficient*

The simplest interpretation of the similarity coefficient that we used is "the number of shared features", but this requires some discussion and modification. First of all, it will probably be clearer to make some distinctions, since certain devices with little intuitive

---

[1]   Later, in setting up the diagnostic key, we do use the entries (see Chapter 8, pp. 115ff.). There are methods whose main basis is the feature matrix instead of a similarity matrix (see, for example, papers by McQuitty in *Educational and Psychological Measurement* during the years 1957-62); and certain monothetic methods that involve finding overall key features, or combinations of features, such as factor analysis, or Williams' multivariate methods (see, for example, Williams & Lambert 1959). A potential weakness in monothetic methods may be mentioned: namely that an important feature may appear in quite different places in a classification. Thus the feature "No passive transform" may appear both in a group containing the sentence *Ice consists of water* (ex. 7, p. 15) and in a group containing the sentence *She came with his coat* (ex. 2, p. 11). It is also possible to derive a cline or a model of higher dimensions in a fairly straightforward way directly from the feature matrix. (This term will be defined immediately below. See also Appendix 1.)

meaning may be used to overcome such difficulties as hierarchies of criteria.

The linguist's data are criteria, responses to them (features), and OTUs. We may consider the data of the computer (whether electronic or human) as a matrix of ENTRIES, the entries being the *coded* form of responses. We shall call this matrix the FEATURE MATRIX or DATA MATRIX. There will usually be a straightforward coding of responses, but this may be changed if we so desire. If we think of the OTUs as entered one below the other, the columns of entries may be called TESTS.

We might, for example, have the following types of coding:

Criterion *P* (TR 1; see Section 4.3, pp. 42f.): Does the sequence admit passive transform?

Responses: "Yes"   "No"   "Query"
Entries: +   —   /
Feature: Allows passive transformation, Does not ... etc.

Criterion *At* (TR 4:3; see Section 4.3, p. 44): If there is a possibility of question-form with *wh*-adverb (Criterion *A*), can *when* be used?

Responses:	"Yes"	"No"	"Query"	Inapplicable
Entries: (1)	+	—	/	/
or (2)	+	—	/	—
or (3)	+	/	/	/
or (4)	+	/	/	—

We in fact used (3) for this criterion. It is possible to code one criterion as two or more tests (see for example Section 7.12, pp. 72ff.).

We first define the similarity coefficient in terms of the entries, bearing in mind that it is proposed as a measure of resemblance. We used two computer programs, and there is now a more elaborate program than either. We shall call them WHI, GOW, and CLASP respectively. The definitions of similarity coefficient for GOW and CLASP are identical, and hence we consider in this section only WHI and GOW.[2]

---

[2] WHI was written by H. Whitfield, now in the Department of English Language and General Linguistics, Edinburgh, who was then working for the

In all tests, entries are thought of as coding definite responses; we may write these entries as 0, 1, 2, ... (using the notation of GOW) and "NC" (for "no comparison"). "NC" is an entry which has become standard. It was designed to cover the case when information was lacking, but it can be used for other purposes.

The SIMILARITY COEFFICIENT between two OTUs is defined as the ratio of two numbers, which may normally be thought of as the number of resemblances (R) and the number of comparisons (K), so that

similarity coefficient of two OTUs $= R/K$

$$= \frac{\text{number of resemblances}}{\text{number of comparisons}}$$

or, effectively, $=$ proportion of resemblances

or $=$ proportion of shared features.

What matters is how resemblances and comparisons are counted in different types of test, and the nature of the test may conveniently be specified by showing the effect of each possible pair of entries, as exemplified in the coding of the WHI Dichotomy shown below.

There are two versions of WHI, distinguished by the type of test employed: the Dichotomy and the Alternative. In both cases, three entries are possible: $+$, $-$, and NC, orginally construed as "Yes", "No", and "Unknown" respectively.

DICHOTOMY: In this, the original similarity coefficient proposed by Sneath (1957b), a resemblance occurs when and only when a pair of corresponding entries are both $+$; and a comparison occurs both then, and also when one entry is $+$ and the corresponding entry is $-$.

Thus the similarity coefficient for the two OTUs below would be $\frac{1}{2}$:

Medical Research Council. This program is based directly on the suggestions in Sneath 1957b. GOW was written by J. C. Gower, Rothamsted Experimental Station, Harpenden, Herts; CLASP, a powerful descendant of GOW, by Gavin Ross and J. C. Gower.

	Test 1	2	3	4	5	6
OTU 1	+	+	−	+	−	NC
OTU 2	+	−	−	NC	NC	NC

There is comparison with agreement in Test 1, there is comparison without agreement in Test 2, and there is no comparison in Tests 3, 4, 5, 6.

The idea underlying the Dichotomy is that common failure to possess a feature should not be introduced into the calculations. (On the problem of negative features, see for example Sokal & Sneath 1963, pp. 128 ff., Ellegård 1959, and also Section 2.3, pp. 19 ff.

The dichotomy may be defined by the standard table of the contributions to R and K under all possible combinations of entries:

	+	+	−	+	−	NC
	+	−	−	NC	NC	NC
R	1	0	0	0	0	0
K	1	1	0	0	0	0

NC always leads to $R = 0$ and $K = 0$ and will usually be omitted from these tables.

ALTERNATIVE: The only difference between Dichotomy and Alternative is that − now counts as a resemblance, and therefore of course as a comparison. Thus, the relevant part of the table above would become:

R	1	0	1	0	0	0
K	1	1	1	0	0	0

and the similarity coefficient between OTU 1 and OTU 2 would be $\frac{2}{3}$ instead of $\frac{1}{2}$.

When using WHI, the tests can be either Dichotomies or Alternatives, but cannot be mixed. The choice must be made in advance: either all tests will be Dichotomies or they will be Alternatives.

We experimented with both options. The Dichotomy normally gives a wider range of similarity coefficients than the Alternative, and hence, to all appearances, a more refined output. In our case there were very few major differences between the outputs, and we imagine that this would commonly be so.

While we were using WHI, we found that the concept POSITIVE was very useful when we wished to note only the actual occurrence of some feature, without regard to the places where it was absent. For this purpose we recorded + for "Yes" and NC otherwise. It could, furthermore, be used under either option in WHI: the effects on the similarity coefficient are the same.

The choice between Dichotomy and Alternative is not an a priori weighting on the basis of the presumed relevance of a criterion, but is made on the basis of the nature of the question. When the choice has been available we have tended to use the Dichotomy for optional overt features, and the Alternative for both obligatory overt features and for covert features (see Section 4.3, p. 42). This distinction differs from another important and relevant one: namely, that between "symmetric" criteria such as "Is the subject animate or inanimate?", where the question can be framed as a "Yes/No" question in two equally sensible ways, and which generalises easily to a list type question; and asymmetric criteria such as almost all our covert criteria.

GOW may be regarded as an extension of WHI, in that there are three types of test; two go beyond what WHI is capable of; and each test can be of any one of these three types, so that it is not necessary to decide before the computation begins which is the most suitable. The three types of test are:

(1) DICHOTOMY, as in WHI.

(2) QUALITATIVE, which is a generalization of the WHI Alternative. Any number, say n, of different entries are admitted, named 0, 1, 2, and so on, and as usual there is NC. A resemblance is counted if and only if the two entries are the same and are not NC, and a comparison is counted unless one entry is NC. Thus, comparing two entries i and j, neither of which is NC, the standard table is:

	$i \neq j$	$i = j$
R	0	1
K	1	1

If $n = 2$, it reduces to WHI's Alternative.

If $n = 1$, it reduces to the Positive.

It would be possible, if it seemed necessary, to define a test which was a generalization of both the Dichotomy and the Alternative. It would have the entries + and NC, and a number of different entries corresponding to −. The extension beyond the Dichotomy would be in the comparing of two different type − entries, which would count as a difference: $R = 0$, $K = 1$. This might be useful in dealing with subordinate criteria (see Section 7.12) and also when a criterion gave more than one optional overt feature.

(3) QUANTITATIVE, which compares resemblance of numerical features, such as number of adjuncts in a clause or number of words in the subject. Suppose that the two entries which are being compared are the numbers i and j. The contribution to R (resemblances) is 0, if the difference between i and j is as large as possible; 1 if $i = j$; and is a number between 0 and 1 in the intermediate cases. The precise definition is given by:

$$\text{First entry} \quad i$$
$$\text{Second entry} \quad j$$
$$R \quad 1 - \frac{|i - j|}{\text{RANGE}}$$
$$K \quad 1$$

where "RANGE" is the maximum possible difference between entries and $|i - j|$ is the result of subtracting the smaller of i, j from the larger. (It is 0 if $i = j$.) It is probably sensible, in some cases (such as the number of words in the subject), to form entries by first taking logarithms. The base of logarithms is irrelevant. This will, for example, have the effect of making two subjects containing 9 and 18 words as close as another two containing 2 and 4 words. (Gaddum 1945 has remarked that the distribution of the logarithm of the number of words in the sentences of G.B. Shaw is approximately the normal distribution.)

7.12 *Coding and the Nature of Criteria*

We show in Tables 7:1-2 examples of the effect of different choices of coding in WHI. Table 7:2 is relevant when the criterion in question is surbordinate to another, so that the response "inapplicable" may occur ("=" stands for "is encoded as"). Table 7:2 is an extension of 7:1 where (2a) and (2b) are alternative extensions of (2).

The main difficulty we have encountered in our classification system is that the criteria are by their nature not independent. Compare, for example, the following (Section 4.3, pp. 41 ff.):

    (CON 4:1) Is N_1 animate?
    (TR 7:1)   Can N_1 be animate?

or again, somewhat differently:

    (TR 4:0)   Is adverbial *wh*-question possible?
    (TR 4:1)   If so, is it a place-adverb (*where*)?
    (TR 4:3)   Or is it a time-adverb (*when*)?
    (TR 4:4)   Or is it a manner-adverb (*how*)?

It should be noted that *any* classification method will have difficulty treating this situation. The solutions offered below are intended principally as illustrations of how these difficulties can be treated, and are not put forward as final solutions (see Appendix 1).

The "exclusive" type of relationship exemplified by TR 4:1, 3, 4 can be satisfactorily overcome by using the Qualitative of GOW. More difficult is the relationship between TR 4:0, on the one hand, and TR 4:1, 3, 4 on the other. If the coding is done in the obvious manner, treating the latter test as Alternatives and using NC as the entry when the answer to TR 4:0 has been "No", then the effect of including TR 4:1, 3, 4 is to decrease the similarity coefficients between many strings taking question-form with *wh*-adverb whilst leaving unaltered all other similarity coefficients (see Tables 7:1 (1) and 7: 2(1)).

TABLE 7:1

(1) When "Yes" = + and "No" = −		Yes Yes	Yes No	No No	Any response Query
		+ +	+ −	− −	Any entry NC
Alternative:	R	1	0	1	0
	K	1	1	1	0
Dichotomy:	R	1	0	0	0
	K	1	1	0	0
(2) When "Yes" = + and "No" = NC		+ +	+ NC	NC NC	Any entry NC
"Positive":	R	1	0	0	0
	K	1	0	0	0

TABLE 7:2

(1) When "Yes" = + "No" = − and "Inapp" = NC		Yes Inapp	No Inapp	Inapp Inapp
		+ NC	− NC	NC NC
Alternative: } { R		0	0	0
Dichotomy: ∫ { K		0	0	0
(2a) When "Yes" = + "No" = NC and "Inapp" = NC		+ NC	NC NC	NC NC
"Positive":	R	0	0	0
	K	0	0	0
(2b) When "Yes" = + "No" = NC and "Inapp" = −		+ −	NC −	− −
Alternative:	R	0	0	1
	K	1	0	1
Dichotomy:	R	0	0	0
	K	1	0	0

The situation is a little complex. The reason for grouping together the place-adverb, time-adverb, and manner-adverb question-
forms is that they are believed to be similar; indeed, what they are
conceived to have in common, namely the property of being *wh-*

adverb question-forms, is believed to be fundamental. This gives a slightly paradoxical situation. If this basic criterion TR 4:0 was felt to be of less importance, we should perhaps still include it, but we might not think of including the subordinate criterion "which *wh*-adverb?". In other words, TR 4:0 is liable to suffer because it is in some degree felt to be important. The direct effect of this feeling has been the use of additional criteria, which far from tending to draw the strings accepting TR 4:0 closer together, in fact force many of the strings farther apart, if they have been coded in the most natural way. It is true that, if TR 4:0 really is important, then provided the experiment is properly conducted and the classification method is adequate, it should appear relevant, that is, it should play a significant part in the classification. It is still obviously inappropriate that the effect of the linguist's bias in its favour is to *diminish* its importance in the classification.

When there are just two responses other than "Query" and "Inapplicable", typically when the responses are simply "Yes" and "No" as in TR 7:1 mentioned above, it may be satisfactory to treat the criterion as a single Positive or as a Dichotomy. In other cases, when the responses form a list, this treatment will necessarily be unsatisfactory even if the list has only two members. We have already considered the disadvantages of using the Qualitative of GOW, or, if the list has only two members, the special case of the Qualitative (the Alternative) available in the appropriate version of WHI. We may however code the criterion as a *number* of tests, and in particular we may use one Positive for each *response*. (In the experiment, this is what was done with the example we have been discussing.) The effect is to draw the strings accepting a place-adverb closer together, and similarly for strings accepting time-adverbs or manner-adverbs; that is, the similarity coefficients between OTUs of any one of these classes are increased, while all others are left unchanged. The same treatment may be given to any criterion for which the responses form a list, and may be useful if the Qualitative of GOW is not available. It is however liable to be wasteful.

We include two "feature-trees" in order to illustrate further some aspects of this type of problem (for the criteria, see pp. 48 f. and 43 ff.):

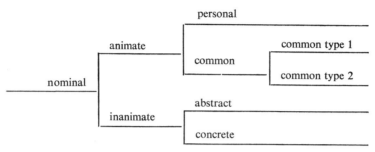

Figure 7:1

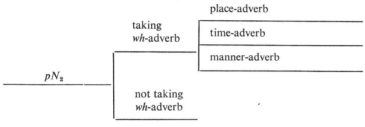

Figure 7:2

If we are using WHI, then for the animate/inanimate opposition we shall require the version employing the Alternative. With regard to the abstract/concrete branch of the tree, the most natural solution is that just suggested, that is to treat it as two criteria "is the nominal abstract?" and "is the nominal concrete?" and to code each as a Positive (see Tables 7:1 (2) and 7:2 (2a)). The effect will be that the similarity coefficients between all strings whose appropriate nominal is abstract will be increased, and so will the similarity coefficients between all strings whose appropriate nominal is concrete; no other similarity coefficients will be affected. (It might be convenient, in dealing with lists of several features, to have a test which only counted resemblance, ignoring all differences; this would result in more economical coding.) If GOW is used, we should probably code as in WHI, but if the subordinate criterion is of the "Yes/No" type, a possible solution is to employ the Dichotomy, coding "Inapplicable" by —, "No" by NC, and "Yes" by +, (see (2) and (2b)). This method is more extreme than the one just described; it increases similarity coefficients between OTUs for which the response is "Yes", decreases similarity coefficients between these and those to which the criterion is inapplicable, and does not affect the others. This method could also be employed in the case of subordinate criteria whose responses were lists of features, by using one Dichotomy for each feature. The disadvantage of doing this would be that one aspect of the superordinate criterion was overstressed. If, to counteract this effect, the superordinate criterion were itself omitted, the other aspects would be ignored, these being the resemblance between *all* the OTUs to which the subordinate criterion was applicable, and the similarity between all the remaining OTUs to which the subordinate criterion was inapplicable.

A feasible solution would be to treat the superordinate criterion as a number of Positives (one for each response of a list, or perhaps just one if the criterion is of the "Yes/No" type), while continuing to treat each subordinate feature as a Dichotomy. It might be useful to have available a more general test than either the Qualitative or the Dichotomy, one which was the Qualitative with entries 0, 1, 2, ... and NC, and with, in addition, an entry "—" which was treated as different from the remaining entries, but ignored when compared with itself:

	any entry other than NC or —	—
	—	—
R	0	0
K	1	0

The various entries 0, 1, 2, ... could be used for the subordinate features, and "—" could encode "inapplicable". The effect would be that similarity coefficients between OTUs to which the subordinate criterion was applicable would never be lowered more than those between these OTUs and those to which the criterion was inapplicable. The remaining similarity coefficients, those between the OTUs to which the subordinate criterion was inapplicable, would be unaffected. (This generalized Dichotomy is not that envisaged in Section 7.11, p. 68; both could be subsumed under a still more general definition.)

The proposals made above may not be the ideal remedies, but a still more difficult problem arises with the employment of criteria "nested" to a greater depth. An example occurs in Figure 7:1 (p. 73); much more complicated examples may be found in Svartvik 1966, and it seems that in the type of linguistic analysis discussed in this paper, such arrangements of criteria may be the rule rather than the exception. This hierarchical relationship may be characteristic of linguistic criteria. A possible solution is that of "counter-weighting", that is, duplication of the test corresponding to the superordinate criterion for each subordinate criterion, or less drastically, for each subordinate criterion beyond the first. This solution can only be considered as a makeshift device to avoid the worse errors of its alternatives. However, it seems worth examining counter-weighting a little more closely since there is no obviously better solution generally available. As an example we use Figure 7:1, naming the criteria $Q1$, $Q2$, $Q3$, and $Q4$ and naming *classes* of OTUs identical with respect to these criteria 1, 2, 3 and 4.

	$Q1$ Is the nominal animate?	$Q2$ Is the nominal personal?	$Q3$ Is the nominal common?	$Q4$ Is the nominal common type 1?
1	Yes	Yes	Inapp-licable	Inapp-licable
2	Yes	No	Yes	Yes
3	Yes	No	Yes	No
4	No	Inapp-licable	Inapp-licable	Inapp-licable

The obvious direct coding is shown in Table 7:3, and the coding using the maximum possible counter-weighting is shown in Table 7:4.

THE SIMILARITY MATRIX

TABLE 7:3

	Q1	Q2	Q3	Q4
1	+	+	NC	NC
2	+	−	+	+
3	+	−	+	−
4	−	NC	NC	NC

TABLE 7:4

	Q1	Q2	Q3		Q4
1	+ + (+)*	+	NC	NC	NC
2	+ + +	−	+	+	+
3	+ + +	−	+	+	−
4	—	NC	NC	NC	NC

*The bracketing of one entry in Table 7:4 is for identification purposes below.

We give four matrices, showing the effect on R and K of using only the primary criterion $Q1$; the effect on R and K of including $Q2$, $Q3$, and $Q4$ and coding as in Table 7:3; the combined effect of using $Q1$, $Q2$, $Q3$, and $Q4$ and coding as in Table 7:3; and the effect of coding as in Table 7:4. All the tests are considered to be WHI Alternatives.

The effect of using $Q1$ only:

		1	2	3	4
1	R	1			
	K	1			
2	R	1	1		
	K	1	1		
3	R	1	1	1	
	K	1	1	1	
4	R	0	0	0	1
	K	1	1	1	1

The effect of using Q2-4:

		1	2	3	4
1	R	1			
	K	1			
2	R	0	3		
	K	1	3		
3	R	0	2	3	
	K	1	3	3	
4	R	0	0	0	0
	K	0	0	0	0

The combined effect of using Q1-4, and coding as in Table 7:3:

		1	2	3	4
1	R	2			
	K	2			
2	R	1	4		
	K	2	4		
3	R	1	3	4	
	K	2	4	4	
4	R	0	0	0	1
	K	1	1	1	1

The effect of using the counter-weighting of Table 7:4:

		1	2	3	4
1	R	4			
	K	4			
2	R	3	7		
	K	4	7		
3	R	3	6	7	
	K	4	7	7	
4	R	0	0	0	3
	K	3	3	3	3

The disadvantage of using the maximum possible counter-weighting will be apparent: it results in overemphasising the superordinate criterion. If counter-weighting is used it seems advisable to use it less than in this example. But, in order to preserve objectivity as far as possible, whatever is done should be done only because of the structure of the hierarchy of criteria (and not because some criteria are felt to be important). It would also be defensible to replace the bracketed $+$ in Table 7:4 by NC, since there is an NC in the corresponding position under $Q4$. This has the disadvantage of making the relationship between inanimate and personal on the one hand, and between inanimate and common type 1 and type 2 on the other, no longer the same.

		1	2	3	4
1	R	3			
	K	3			
2	R	2	7		
	K	3	7		
3	R	2	6	7	
	K	3	7	7	
4	R	0	0	0	3
	K	2	3	3	3

We give, for comparison, the matrix that would be obtained by coding $Q2$ and $Q4$ as Positives, coding "common type 2" as a Positive and using no counter-weighting (this is what was actually done in the experiment). See Table 7:5. This has the disadvantage of not representing the branch "common", so that the resemblance between common type 1 and common type 2 is ignored. The coding has in fact failed to take account of the "depth" of the tree. It should be stated that $R = K = 2$ causes a greater increase in a similarity coefficient than $R = K = 1$, since it means adding a resemblance twice instead of once.

The effect of coding Q2-4 as Positives etc. (Table 7:5):

		1	2	3	4
1	R	2			
	K	2			
2	R	1	2		
	K	1	2		
3	R	1	1	2	
	K	1	1	2	
4	R	0	0	0	1
	K	1	1	1	1

An example of a possible solution would be to modify the program somewhat along the following lines. The program would first calculate a similarity coefficient on the basis of all superordinate and all isolated criteria. It would then consider the OTUs of one branch of the feature tree and modify the similarity coefficients amongst these OTUs in such a way that, in the case of maximum similarity within the branch, R and K were increased equally; in the case of maximum dissimilarity, they were altered so that R/K was not below some minimum (for example the average similarity coefficient before the branch was examined), and in all other cases the modifications were intermediate. J. C. Gower (1966) has proposed a more satisfactory remedy, also involving modification to the program. It is often true that if the user can decide exactly what effect he wants a criterion to have, on R and K, then he can obtain this effect by a careful choice of tests and coding. Indeed, in a subsequent experiment (described in Svartvik 1966) the GOW Quantitative was used to code one criterion not conceptually quantitative as the most economical way of obtaining the effect we required. However, it is not possible to simulate all *possible* tests in this way, using only the tests of GOW. In consequence it might be valuable to have a program which allowed the user to define his own tests if he so wished.[3]

By suitable repetition and encoding of Dichotomies, so that there are a number of tests for some criteria, any type of similarity coefficient so far dis-

With regard to the distinction between superordinate and sub-ordinate, which might be of great importance if it had to be supplied to the program, it should be noted that it may only be apparent. Consider, for example, the pair of criteria CON 4:1 and TR 7:1 already quoted, which could be expressed as

CON 4:1 Is N_1 animate?
TR   7:1 If not, can it be?

but which may equally well be phrased as

TR   7:1 Can N_1 be animate?
CON 4:1 If so, was it animate?

In Appendix 1 we consider the relationship between criteria to be simply the possibilities of co-occurrence of their features.

We give some references to other forms of "similarity coefficient" that have been proposed: Sokal & Sneath 1963, pp. 123 ff; Needham 1961; Dale 1964; Le Schack 1964. Needham 1961 and Rose 1964 use a similarity coefficient with only 2 values, viz. 0 and 1, for use with large volumes of data. In some of these the similarity coefficient cannot be calculated by adding the contributions to numerator and determinator arising through each test. The most radical difference that can be made is perhaps to have similarity coefficients defined relative to the whole set of data, so that the value of the similarity between two OTUs depends on the features exhibited by all the other OTUs (e.g. giving increased weight to co-occurrence of rare features, as in Sokal & Sneath 1963, pp. 135ff.). Such a change might be considered useful when taken in conjunction with an associated technique for cluster-analysis, but perhaps not consistent with a notion of absolute resemblance.

---

cussed in this paper can be simulated, though perhaps uneconomically. It is noteworthy, however, that in practice, this is not done. It seems to be very difficult, from a human point of view, to make adequate use of the facilities of two such programs during the same period. One's mode of thought is, in fact, conditioned by the programs. Thus, while we were using WHI, we found ourselves unable to make proper use of GOW's facilities presumably because we could not hold the work in two mental "channels" at once. On the other hand, we were able to make full use of these facilities in a later experiment.

The distinction between processes which when applied to a given set of OTUs depend on them only (local), and processes which necessarily depend on all the other OTUs also (global), can be made at various points (see Appendix 1, p. 229).

In cases such as that of the first tree (Figure 7:1), it may seem reasonable to consider the ways in which the various branches are identified (see Section 4.3, pp. 48f.) and then to replace the criteria by more basic ones in the hope of ensuring the correct degree of resemblance between common type 1 and common type 2, for example, or between abstract and personal. However, this would rapidly lead to diminishing returns (see "atomic features", Section 3.5, p. 37, fn. 11), and is not in conformity with our desire to use, and to form for future use, relatively elaborate concepts.

7.13 *Interpreting the Similarity Coefficient*

The most straightforward interpretation is "absolute resemblance", with the selected criteria considered as a random sample of all possible criteria.

Some of the implications of accepting this interpretation are:

(a) "Resemblance" can be measured by the "proportion of shared features".

(b) Features "felt" to be important are those which are associated with many others; hence weighting is unnecessary.

(c) By taking a sufficiently large random sample of criteria, we get a statistically reliable estimate of resemblance.

These seem broadly acceptable, but we might take into consideration the following comments. With regard to (a): as stated in Section 3.5, without a satisfactory notion of "atomic feature", this is difficult to place on a rigorous foundation (see fn. 11, p. 37). With regard to (c): we have not got a random sample, since both the finding and selecting of criteria are necessarily human.

It therefore hardly seems possible to define a strict measure of absolute resemblance; and so it seems essential, even theoretically, to start "in the middle" from where we are now. It might of course be true that this would give the same results as "absolute resemblance" and that this could be checked by using repeated classification and finding perfect consistency, but it seems simpler to admit a basis which is, in a broad sense, subjective.

An obvious way in which a subjective selection might be expected to differ from a genuinely random selection is in the omission of a very large number of features which are constant throughout. Another is perhaps the omission on non-binary criteria which have different responses for most pairs of OTUs.

If two OTUs had, in a subjective selection, m resemblances from n applicable criteria, reasonable measures of resemblance would be:

$m - n$ if a large number of resemblances have been omitted;
m if a large number of differences have been omitted;
m/n if the selection is really random.

Since n is not constant, these differences are not necessarily trivial; thus, if we have, for example, four similarity coefficients

$$A = \frac{16}{50} < B = \frac{20}{60} < C = \frac{32}{80} < D = \frac{50}{100}$$

and consider what happens as "yes"-responses are added steadily, we find that each similarity coefficient in turn becomes the least, and that, finally, the order is reversed after, say, 300 "yes"-responses have been added:

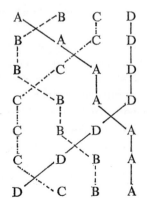

Another and more general way in which the selection of criteria is non-random is that we select in an order which is related to the order of relevance as we imagine it. Different linguists will select in different orders, but the divergence in the resulting set of criteria will be minimised by the use of a large number of criteria.

All in all, what we may hope for is not a random sample of all possible criteria, but a set of criteria approximately equivalent to a random sample of all conceivably relevant criteria — where the "conceivably" means "conceivably to the human mind, at least to the linguist's mind". As usual, we think of "important" criteria as in some way representing many others (see Section 3.6, p. 38).

We may imagine two graphs of the similarity coefficient of two OTUs against the number of selected criteria; the first (Figure 7:3) is valid if the idea of absolute resemblance holds strictly, the second (Figure 7:4) in the situation posited here. The shaded bands

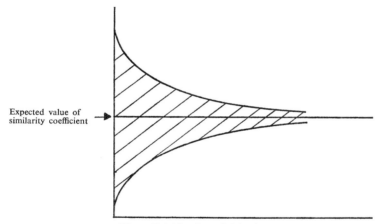

Expected value of
similarity coefficient

Figure 7:3 Number of Criteria

represent "confidence intervals", i.e., roughly, limits between which the similarity coefficient will usually lie, with the given number of criteria. The rise in Figure 7:4 is hypothetical; if it does not occur, Figure 7:4 will look like Figure 7:3, although the "limiting" value will presumably differ from that of the latter — if that can be defined.

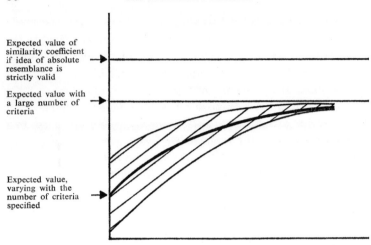

Figure 7:4 Number of Criteria, chosen naturally and hence not in
a perfectly random order

It will appear later (Section 7.32, pp. 97 ff.) that only the *order* of the similarity coefficients is fundamentally important in the method. If absolute resemblance could be theoretically defined, it might well be true that the order of our similarity coefficients was virtually the same as that of the "absolute" coefficients, and hence that the resulting classifications were almost identical; but the argument above suggests that this is not necessarily true. In a similar way, it is not obvious whether or not a classification using a truly random sample of criteria, including "irrelevant" ones, would be virtually identical to ours. The change in outlook is small, but of some interest. Our starting-point is now the subjective description of OTUs. This will still be true even if in another experiment we make use of the classifications resulting from earlier experiments. The procedure is then a heuristic device dealing initially with human descriptions, and perhaps later with descriptions which it has itself produced on the basis of them. Figure 7:4 has an interesting interpretation with regard to the manner of considering the similarity coefficient: it has been suggested that the coefficient is equal to the chance of getting agreement, if a randomly selected criterion is applied to the two OTUs in question.

It may be remembered that the word "resemblance" has never acquired a well-defined meaning in the way that certain terms in, say, statistics have.[4] Consequently we have been considering whether the definition we have used objectifies the notion of resemblance, and we may perhaps say that its achievement is instead to clarify the notion, and that, after all, this is all that can be hoped for except in precisely constructed model "universes". Other workers (see for example Needham 1961, Dale 1964, Le Schack 1964) have used other definitions of similarity coefficient and it is not in fact necessary that the similarity coefficient be considered as a satisfactory measure of resemblance; provided that, in conjunction with the cluster analysis or other classification technique, it results in a good classification.

7.2 INTERPRETING THE SIMILARITY MATRIX

It is customary to set out the similarity coefficients, expressed per cent, or per mil, or whatever is required, in a subdiagonal square array, or matrix, for example:

	A				
OTU B	95	B			
OTU C	49	51	C		
OTU D	78	69	50	D	
OTU E	24	32	48	30	E
	A	B	C	D	

As it stands, this particular matrix is not very informative. If we decide to put members which resemble each other close together, we might arrive at the following order: D, A, B, C, E; and the following display for the similarity matrix:

---

[4] For example "correlation" and "association". A particularly good example of a word whose meaning has been made quite precise is "continuous" in the context of mathematical analysis.

	D				
A	78	A			
B	69	95	B		
C	50	49	51	C	
E	30	24	32	48	E
	D	A	B	C	

This looks more sensible; the higher numbers are near the diagonal, and neighbours can be thought of as alike. It is usually possible using only common sense to rearrange small matrices — say for up to 12 or 16 OTUs — in such a way that there can be little doubt that the rearranged order is the best. However, this is not true for larger numbers, and it is necessary to devise a method which can be expected to give good results. It is perhaps not reasonable to expect to find a method of rearrangement for revealing structure which is simple to apply and which will, nevertheless, always give good results; nor is it easy to define "good". The data in which we are interested will normally be structured, and it may not be very sensible to look for a method which would describe everything fairly economically. (See Section 7.31, pp. 94 ff.)

A further aid in bringing out the structure of a similarity matrix is to shade it more or less densely according to the magnitude of the similarity coefficient (see Sokal & Sneath 1963, pp. 176 ff.).

There are terms commonly used to describe certain structures, and we first consider the appearance of sensibly rearranged similarity matrices when these structures are dominant. We consider artificially simple cases, and ignore any possible subtleties with regard to monothetic/polythetic situations.

7.21 Cline

This term (cf. Halliday 1961, p. 249) is used to mean that there is a gradual change from each OTU to its neighbour, such that the resemblance diminishes steadily as we take pairs of OTUs farther apart. The ideal appearance of matrices representing clines would be (we use a stepped diagonal when the individual OTUs are exhibited, and a straight diagonal otherwise):

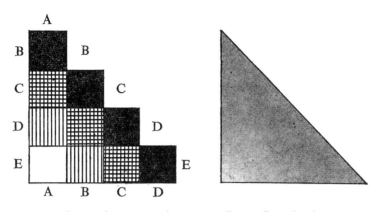

Geometric representation, necessarily one-dimensional:

A—B—C—D—E

A cline may be compared with a *cycle*, where the resemblance does not diminish steadily:

Matrix: Geometric model:

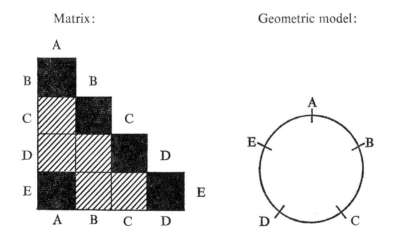

A cycle is not a common situation! However, it was encountered once unexpectedly when using a small number of OTUs in order to compare various processes. It is plain that there are no clear-cut divisions in the case of a cline, although some methods would produce them (see Appendix 1).

7.22 *Naturally Exclusive Classes*

The OTUs often fall into a number of classes such that members within a class have much higher similarity coefficients to one another than to non-members. This would give rise to a matrix as, for example, the following:

This means that there will be various combinations of features which commonly occur, while intermediate combinations will not occur. In the simplest case, a monothetic classification, if there were only two possible responses, we should have something like the following (where " ∼ A" indicates the converse of "A"):

A or ∼ A

or with geometrical representation, following Sneath:

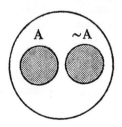

The OTUs with A resemble each other; those with $\sim$A also resemble each other; whereas members of the two sets are dissimilar from each other. More generally, there could be several features, such as "N_1 is name or pronoun or nominal group or zero", in which case it can again be pictured geometrically; no significance should be attached to the linear arrangement.

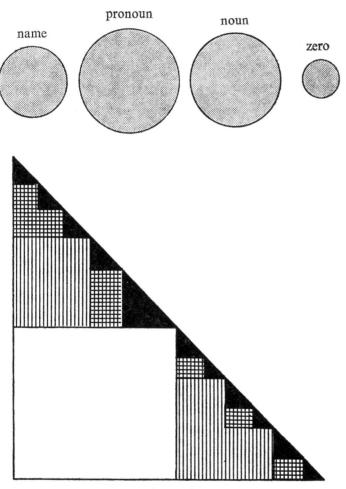

Figure 7:5

7.23 *Nested Hierarchy*

This is the simplest situation which is normally met, and is merely a "recursive" version of 7.22, each subclass being in turn broken down into naturally exclusive classes, as in Figure 7:5. Instructive diagrammatic illustrations of nested hierarchies and other types of classification may be found in Sokal & Sneath 1963, p. 172.

7.24 *Cross-Classification*

In terms of features, this means that there are a number of patterns of one set of features which are liable to occur, and a number of patterns of another set of features, and that the various occurring combinations of the first set all occur with various combinations of the second set. More generally, there could be several such sets instead of two; the most extreme case would be all sets of one

(1)

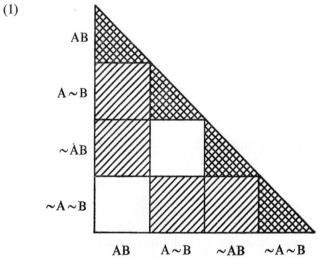

A, B represent a *set* of features; ~A, ~B represent the *set* of features opposed to those of A, B. Thus "A" might stand for children, i.e. for some set of features which characterize children. ~A would then be adults, B might then be males, ~B would then be females. And the OTUs would be a collection of human beings (as shown, about 25% boys, 25% girls, 25% men, 25% women).

Figure 7:6

feature only, which could mean that every possibility occurred equally frequently; in other words, we should have chaos.

The effect of cross-classification will be that the natural classes will be those associated with any of these sets of features, *and will overlap.* See Figure 7:6.

A cross-classification as simple as this can be represented in two dimensions thus:

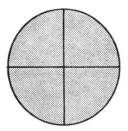

(2) This is more typical: ∼A B is not frequent, and there are two overlapping classes.

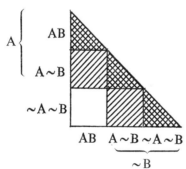

This can also be represented two-dimensionally:

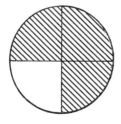

(3) This is more typical still:

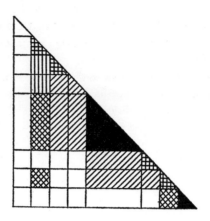

This cannot be represented in two dimensions!

7.3 OBTAINING A CLASSIFICATION FROM THE SIMILARITY MATRIX

7.31 *General Problems*

As we have stated already, if we have only a few OTUs, say 12-16, we can usually obtain a good, or even perfect order by common sense alone, although occasionally difficulties arise.

When there are a large number of OTUs this becomes impossible, and it is essential to have a well-defined process for obtaining a classification. There may, of course, be no *order* which is particularly enlightening.

Any method must be reasonably simple. Perhaps if the situation was perfectly understood, it would be reasonable to have very complex methods, but, at present, methods should be judged partly on their simplicity and on their effectiveness relative to their simplicity. When we state below the objects of a program, it is to be understood that noone believes the objects have been fully achieved.

If we do have a well-defined method, it may reduce the data to a form sufficiently simple to be improved by common sense. Thus, we might attempt to derive a better order, or even a number of orders for different purposes. We might, for example, wish to arrange the OTUs in what seemed to be the best possible cline; or to exhibit well-marked classes in the clearest way, even at the expense of having a small collection of unclassed OTUs, or "residue".[5] There are CLASP facilities relevant to manual investigation of the output. Some of these facilities are available also in GOW. We can for example name and define as many groups as we like by giving their members to CLASP in our chosen order. The groups may be of any size, from one member to the whole set; and of course may or may not be based on the groups originally suggested by CLASP itself. The program will print similarity matrices for these groups if this is desired; it can also print matrices for the resemblances between such groups, including in this case measurement of their internal homogeneity (see further "mean similarity" in Sections 7.321 and 8.23, pp. 99 and 125). An invaluable feature for the visual comprehension of the matrices is that CLASP will coarsen any matrix, first of all by reducing the accuracy from three significant figures to one, and, furthermore, replacing these figures by any symbols the user may choose. We may re-apply all these processes as often as we wish, with our choices assisted by "feedback" from earlier output; and since the intervals between applications may be as long or short as we please, the system is extremely convenient.

Methods, quite apart from their objectives, may be characterized by whether or not they are geometric, partially intuitive, or cluster-

---

[5] Two objective methods for obtaining clines were mentioned in fn. 1, pp. 59 f.; both of these would also enable a judgment to be made as to the reality of representing the data as a cline. It would be possible to measure the extent to which an order was a cline by measuring the closeness of the larger similarity coefficients to the diagonal. It would also be possible to measure the homogeneity of clustering (that is, how clearly marked the groups are) by measuring the extent to which both the high similarity coefficients are close to each other, and, simultaneously, the extent to which the low ones are close to each other. These are both fairly straightforward tasks.

producing. A geometric approach is one in which the OTUs are thought of as points in a space. Since we are starting from the similarity matrix, the number of dimensions is one less than the number of OTUs, if the representation is to be adequate (cf. fn.1, pp. 59-60). If the representation is reduced to two dimensions, the final assessment will probably be left to intuition. There are some useful two- and three-dimensional diagrams in Sokal & Sneath 1963 (pp. 143-4, 172, 203). Such diagrams enable one to see at a glance how realistic it is to think of the OTUs as a cline. Typically, classification involves clustering, and some of the geometric approaches have done this. We may look for natural clusters or for clusters derived from a natural partitioning. (See Section 2.1, pp. 15 ff., and Appendix 1, pp. 221 ff.). Having a natural cluster (or clusters), we may expand such a cluster or we may continue by applying the method by which it was obtained to the remaining OTUs, or ab initio to the whole set, which might yield overlapping clusters. Again, clusters might be formed by expansion from the most "central", or "typical" OTU, or from the least "typical" (see MacNaughton-Smith *et al.* 1964), or by a linkage system, as discussed in Section 7.321, pp. 98 ff.). This last alternative is not incompatible with the two previously discussed methods.

Groups may also be defined by some maximal condition, as for example in Appendix 1 (pp. 221 ff.). A numerical evaluation is defined for any proposed group or partition, and a group is accepted if it has a better evaluation than any other group with almost the same members. Successful methods of this type were proposed by Needham (1961) and have been further developed by, among others, A. and N. Dale (see Dale *et. al.* 1964). Another partitioning method has been given by Rose (1964). Both Needham and Rose have dealt with large volumes of data by sampling the similarity coefficients[6] (see also Appendix 1).

---

[6] A very interesting suggestion for defining a classification has been given (in a lecture) by Dr. R. Needham, who said that some work is being conducted along these lines. It is that if the columns of the feature matrix can be replaced by a set of columns (not extracted from the feature matrix) in such a way that, to some appropriate degree of accuracy, the resulting similarity coefficients are the same or almost always the same as those calculated from the feature

Since, in general, a classification experiment is performed without prior knowledge of the *type* of structure that exists, we may consider how far it is reasonable to expect a program to recover *any* structure latent in the data. A little reflection will show that there are a very large number of possible structures which might be present and worth recovering. By using a similarity matrix, the ability to recover some of these possibilities is lost. (Thus we could no longer hope to discover that, for example, "All OTUs answer 'Yes' to just one of the following three criteria: ...".) Nevertheless the total number of structures reflected in the similarity matrix remains large, and we believe it is unreasonable to hope to guarantee an optimum description of the data, even if such losses are allowed for. At the same time we feel that, within the fairly near future, classification programs will possess sufficient power and flexibility to achieve very good descriptions under almost all circumstances. It is also reasonable to hope for program capacity to discriminate between proposed structures (see Appendix 1).

7.32 *Cluster Analysis and Linkage Systems*

We used Sneath's method (1957b), which is designed fundamentally to obtain the best representation in the form of a nested hierarchy and, as a subsidiary aim, to obtain, *subject to this requirement*, the best linear order. This point is amplified a little in Section 7.321, pp. 100 ff. Even if the data do not fall happily into the form of a nested hierarchy, both the similarity matrix and the classes that have been obtained may be very informative.

A hierarchy may equally well be considered as a succession of divisions of larger groups into smaller, or as a succession of con-

---

matrix, then the new matrix *is* the classification. We might also say that the means of obtaining the new matrix *is* the classification. This approach is not likely to be useful to people who want groups as an aid to thought, as we do, but this consideration did not apply in the field for which the idea was devised. In this connexion we note that "simple", as used in Section 2.2, is not identical with "simple to use", as in Section 3.4.

flations of smaller groups into larger. If we use the terminology appropriate to the former viewpoint, we may say that the process tends to divide groups into smaller natural groups, leaving residues at each stage. The final divisions into very small groups are naturally seriously affected by sampling error, and are not likely to be useful.

7.321 — The method used is known as SINGLE LINKAGE, for reasons which will become obvious. The easiest way to explain single linkage is probably to describe a particular process which forms the groups, beginning with the individual OTUs. A set of LEVELS will have been assigned, say 95%, 90%, 85%, ... 60% (in WHI they need not be equally spaced). The process begins with the highest level, 95%. If there are two OTUs with a similarity coefficient greater than or equal to 95%, the two initiate the formation of a group at the 95% level. If there is any OTU which has a similarity coefficient greater than or equal to 95% with *either* of the preceding OTUs, it is added to the group, and the process is continued until no new member can be added. Repeating the process, a number of groups will be formed at the 95% level, and there will almost certainly be a residue of OTUs not drawn into any group; logically each of these constitutes a group containing one member.

So far as the definition of the groups is concerned, exactly the same could be said for the groups at the 90%, 85%, ... levels. It is also instructive, however, to consider part of the process of moving from the 95% to the 90% level. Any 95% group G must be at least part of a 90% group; if any OTU has a similarity coefficient greater than or equal to 90% with any member of G, it is added to G, and if it is already in a 95% or 90% group H, the whole of H is added to G.

The levels may be suggested by the user, and will normally be chosen so as to give a fairly smooth gradation between the whole set and the individual OTUs. The process of moving from one level to the next is sometimes known as SORTING.

The defining characteristic of groups at level $r\%$ is then that two OTUs are in the same group if and only if there exists a succession of LINKS between them, each link being a similarity coefficient of $r\%$ or more between the two OTUs at each end of the link. With a group of more than three members it is most unlikely that all the similarity coefficients will be the same, and the *average* similarity coefficient between the members of a group may be less than or greater than the level at which the group is formed. It is known as the MEAN INTERNAL SIMILARITY, and can be calculated by CLASP. It is theoretically possible for two members of a group formed at the 99 % level to have a similarity coefficient of O, but fortunately such a situation is unlikely to occur in practice!

The fundamental feature of a single linkage group is that any OTU outside the group is, at the level concerned, dissimilar to every OTU inside it. From this point of view such a "paradoxical" group as the one we have just envisaged would have no natural point or points of division, although from a broader standpoint it might be better to split it and to consider some OTUs as "bridges".[7]

For purposes of illustration we give some examples of single linkage groups, where the lines indicate similarity coefficients of *at least* the level at which the groups were formed:

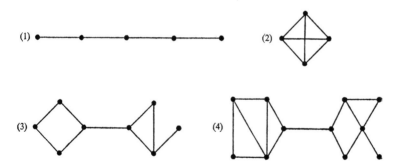

(1) is unusually cline-like; (2) is unusually homogeneous; (3) and (4) are perhaps more typical of the single linkage groups that one meets in practice. We might be tempted to divide (4) on other grounds; and in a case such as (4) it might well be that the group was the union of two groups formed at a higher level.

The most unsatisfactory features of single linkage are the tendency (which is not always manifest) to form straggling groups, and the high probability that one group will eventually "swallow" the rest. This is because an OTU is more likely to be drawn into a large group than into a small one, and the bias is cumulative. It is perhaps largely for this reason that there has been some effort to find methods that, for example, add OTUs to groups on the basis of *average* similarity rather than similarity to only one member.[8]

Throughout the execution of the sorting process the OTUs have an order, which is initially the input order and is gradually modified. The requirement is always made that *the members of a group formed at any level shall always remain together*, and this is generally all

---

[8]   There is a standard mathematical method for obtaining an important type of relation (the equivalence relation) from any symmetric relation, and, in turn, any equivalence relation defines, in a very natural way, a set of mutually exclusive classes (equivalence classes). If this method is applied to the inter-OTU relation "having a similarity coefficient at least $r\%$", it yields the groups formed by single linkage at $r\%$. This suggests, not so much that single linkage is the perfect method for forming groups, as that it is perhaps the simplest; which is in itself important, for execution, programming, and analysis. A complication that occurs with some other forms of group formation (including some not using a similarity matrix) is that there may be more than one legitimate continuation. This can mean either that rather trivially overlapping classes are formed, or that there are ambiguities needing to be resolved in some way. If the analysis is done by hand, it is often clear that some of the alternatives are not worth pursuing, but it is not easy to give general grounds for deciding this. There are also methods in which straightforward procedures suggest themselves both for building up the classes stage by stage from the OTUs, and for breaking down the whole set of OTUs into successively smaller components, but in which the results of the two approaches are different. This situation seems unsatisfactory.

In the case of single linkage it is reasonable to programme the process in either way, so that the initial description of a building-up process (given at the beginning of this section may or may not be what the computer actually does; it is irrelevant whether the computer proceeds by successive division or by successive agglomeration.

that is stated about the output order, everything else being considered fortuitous, and merely the result of an order being forced
on the OTUs and, implicitly, on the groups themselves (GOW,
but not CLASP, places the more homogeneous groups at one end).
Normally, however, if an OTU is added to a group because it resembles a member at one end of that group, it will be added at that
end. Consequently the final order is better than might be expected,
but not perfect: similar groups are not always neighbours (see Section 7.331, pp. 106 f.). GOW and CLASP permit reordering of the
OTUs after examination of the output, which is very useful, but
requires some care: it is surprisingly easy to be deceived by the
appearance of the similarity matrix in some cases, and it is advisable
to check the MEAN SIMILARITY BETWEEN TWO GROUPS, that is, the
average of the similarity coefficients between the OTUs in one group
and those in the other. This calculation can also be made by
CLASP. We give a simple illustration of the futility of demanding
that the order should always be illuminating — the problem of
placing the two groups below adjacent to each other, if they unite
solely because their "central" members are sufficiently alike:

where the linear arrangement merely indicates the links between
the members in their groups. It is also an illustration of the difficulty of writing an efficient program if we want the "best" order
subject to the requirement that all the groups be clearly displayed.

If instead we want the best order absolutely, we are then search-
ing for the best representation as a cline, and it would be advisable
to use a program expressly designed to find such a representation
(see fn. 1, pp. 59-60) (unless the OTUs happen to form a virtually
perfect cline, in which case they can easily be ordered by a single linkage program). The rearrangement from an order designed to display groups clearly into an order designed to display cline-relation
would generally involve a certain amount of reshuffling of the
groups, plus a large amount of interpolation of residual OTUs, and
would be difficult to do by hand. As suggested above, much of this

rearrangement would be necessary no matter how "clever" the original program had been.

Despite these reservations it is instructive to have the feature matrix retyped or reprinted in output order, or in a modified version of the output order; CLASP will do this. In our experiment, it sometimes happened that one block of features crossed the boundary of two groups, although they were not constant throughout both the groups.

The hope has been expressed that irrelevant features would play no fundamental part in the analysis, and it seems worth examining why this is likely to be the case. If a feature is irrelevant, either entirely or at some place in the classification, there should be a number of rather similar OTUs both with and without the feature; and some with it are likely to be particularly close to some without it, so that all the OTUs are drawn into one cluster. The situation needs further examination since, first of all, features are not merely relevant or irrelevant, but are more or less relevant. In addition, there will be distortion through sampling error, particularly when the numbers concerned are small. This can very easily happen even when the experiment is on a large scale through the rarity of a feature or through the small number of what we have called the "rather similar OTUs".

If the number of criteria is small, it will be relatively easy to find OTUs differing by at most one feature from any given OTU. Consequently all the OTUs will unite into one group at a very high level which, if NC is being used, might even be the 100% level. The transition from the unclustered OTUs to a single group containing all or almost all the OTUs would be abrupt, and the output would therefore be trivial. Hence *the method itself* imposes a lower limit on the number of criteria that must be used if the output is to have any chance of being useful. In a given case, however, it is difficult to estimate this limit in advance. The limit is not obvious even with the double simplification of calculating of the number of criteria needed to make it unlikely that all the OTUs agglomerate at a level representing just one difference in features, subject to the assumption that the criteria are independent. We naturally hope that this assumption of independence is untrue. With the present data, all the OTUs unite at the 100% level if only the seven criteria TR:1-7 are used. The number of criteria actually used was sufficient to form a reasonable number of groups, or (which is more fundamental since the type of data might never cluster into natural groups) these were sufficient criteria to give a satisfactory distribution of similarity coefficients (see Appendix 2, pp. 232 ff.). Perhaps 15-20 criteria would have sufficed for this purpose.

7.322 *Other Linkage Systems* — "Single linkage" can be described in various equivalent ways. It may be described as a process of adding OTUs to old groups: an OTU is added to a group if any relevant similarity coefficient is sufficiently high, and the process is repeated as long as possible. It may be described in terms of group union (where groups can have one member) or in terms of the nature of the resulting group. GROUP UNION is the formation of a new group whose members are precisely those of the former groups. It may also be described as a breakdown process. If, however, any one of these descriptions is modified, there will not usually be so many equivalent descriptions of the resulting set of groups, and the number of possible systems can thus be surprisingly large. It would be tedious to attempt to enumerate them, but we indicate some of the alternative lines of approach that can be followed.

Groups can be formed on the basis of their *resulting* nature. For example, the requirement can be made that *all* the similarity coefficients between members of a group should be at least $r\%$, or that their *average* similarity coefficient should be at least $r\%$. Such groups will be made as large as possible, but are likely to overlap in an unsatisfactory way, as stated earlier. (It is not the overlapping that is unsatisfactory, but the trivial way in which it tends to happen.)

Alternatively, groups may be built up by considering the relationship of old groups with either single OTUs or other groups outside them, or, similarly, they may be broken down in accordance with the relationship of old groups with either single OTUs or other groups inside them. Natural methods of this kind are, when working at the $r\%$ level, to add an OTU to a group if the *average* similarity coefficient between the OTU and members of the group is at least $r\%$ (AVERAGE LINKAGE) or if the minimum similarity coefficient is at least $r\%$ (TOTAL LINKAGE). The former suggestion appears very reasonable, but there are difficulties. On the one hand, it may be that many OTUs are worth admitting to a group, but that after one has been admitted the condition for admission no longer holds for some of the others; on the other hand, more cogently, an OTU may be a candidate for admission to a number of groups which, nevertheless, should not be united.

Various methods of the type outlined above have been used. It can easily happen in practice that groups formed at one level by one method will be almost identical with groups formed at a different level by another method, although some difference in the nature of the groups is to be expected (see Sokal & Sneath 1963, pp. 189-94). For the results of applying a similar method to part of our material, see below (Section 8.3, pp. 141 ff.) on "inter-groups analysis". Sneath has recently published the results of experiments to compare various linkage methods; single, average, and complete (total) linkage methods gave strikingly consistent clusterings (see Sneath 1966). An important factor that we have ignored in the discussion is the length of time needed to complete certain types of analysis; if this is prohibitively long (it is possible to devise schemes that would take millenia on any conceivable computer) some sort of sampling system may be used.

A rather different approach that has also been used is to consider posited groups in relation to the OTUs not in them. (See Needham 1961, Dale 1964, and Appendix 1.)

7.33 *Practical Considerations*

7.331 *Refined Levels.* — We are considering the similarity coefficient as a measure of resemblance within a definite context (see Section 7.13, pp. 83 ff.). If there are a sufficiently large number of points of comparison, the similarity coefficients should be moderately realistic, and their arrangement in order of magnitude should be still more realistic. Since it is only this ordering which affects the clusters formed, this seems fairly satisfactory. Now, suppose that two similarity coefficients are, for example, 16/19 and 17/20. Should they be treated as different? The natural answer is "No". The difference between them is small — less than 1/100 — and, quite apart from the degree of confidence we may have in the ratios as accurate similarity measures when the numbers involved are so small, it seems unjustifiable to work to one part in a hundred when there are only twenty comparisons. We may notice that, thinking of the selection of criteria as random, we would expect a similarity coefficient of 16/19 to become 17/20 if another criterion was added, since most criteria appear to agree for the two OTUs. We might say that, although, on average, similarity coefficients which are slightly greater than others will be realistically greater more often than not (this is trivial if we consider similarity coefficients from 20% to 100%, and if we imagine a fine gradation between them), it is not however worth treating this chance as significant in any particular case.

There are, however, some points in favour of giving the answer "Yes". The criteria are not selected anew for each pair of OTUs, and if we have

similarity coefficient between OTUs A and B = 17/20
similarity coefficient between OTUs A and C = 16/19
similarity coefficient between OTUs B and C = 16/19

then, in our experiment, it is likely to be true that A, B and C have 16 features in common and that, in addition, there is a Positive (see Section 7.11, p. 70) giving A and B an additional common feature, in which case we should be inclined to consider A and B as more similar than A and C, or than B and C. With WHI, we did in fact use very close levels, and this seemed in practice to give very satisfactory results. A partial explanation might be that in dealing with a fairly large number of similarity coefficients (as we do when considering the coalescence of a number of groups), we may have more confidence in differences of 1% between similarity coefficients than we have when there are just two similarity coefficients. Nevertheless, it seems difficult to justify the use of close levels.

It may be relevant to mention another surprising fact, namely that in a number of minor and unrelated experiments, satisfactory results have been obtained quite consistently using very few criteria and very few OTUs. The obvious explanation is that the criteria have been so carefully — albeit unwittingly — chosen that the results are forced. If this were strictly true it would presumably mean that the resulting analyses were exactly what had been expected, whereas in fact they were not — they merely seemed to make good sense. This still leaves unanswered the objection that they made sense because the criteria were powerful and carefully chosen, and that the results were not exactly those that had been expected because of sampling variation. This is perhaps not a very destructive objection. It is, instead, one which principally suggests interpreting such results with considerable caution. Returning to our main experiment, inasmuch as our procedures are not entirely objective and are therefore difficult to analyse in detail, it seems reasonable to say that, in work of this type, the employment of refined levels may be provisionally taken as useful, since it appeared to be so in this experiment. There were two ways in which it seemed useful, the first relating to the ordering and the second — more important — to the clustering:

a. The chance of having closely related OTUs placed contiguously was increased. Let us consider one particular group. If close levels are used, OTUs which are closely related to those in the group will be placed contiguously to this group at one level, and slightly less related OTUs (and perhaps groups containing such OTUs) will not be united with the original group until a lower level. If coarse levels are used, all these unions will take place simultaneously, so that a complete group may separate the original group from the OTUs most closely related to it. At the same time it should be emphasized that this favourable picture was not true in all cases, and that the ordering of groups and OTUs which united at one level was not always ideal.

b. There is only a small number of "outliers", i.e. OTUs which "should" belong to one group, but are not absorbed until this group is itself absorbed into a larger group. Furthermore, some of these outliers are adjacent to the appropriate group.

In the course of moving from high to low levels, groups tended to absorb outliers at some stages, and then to participate in a large-scale agglomeration. The refinement of the levels enabled the program to mark the points at which the change occurred very precisely.

This tendency is developed further in the diagnostic section by applying a well-defined process that had roughly the effect of retaining only these important points (see Section 8.22, pp. 120 ff). It may be true that some of the delicacy achieved is spurious, but the overall impression we formed was that it was useful. If coarse levels had been used, it might have been possible to achieve a similar result by visual inspection of the similarity matrix, though this is not certain.

7.332 *Some Practical Suggestions.* — Unless a coarsened similarity matrix is available, it is necessary to indicate the high similarity coefficients in some way: we used coloration. It is useful to draw lines between those groups which are of interest, and, if the matrix is large, to write OTU numbers along the diagonals. Any impressions formed by eye should be checked numerically if possible — an impression such as "this OTU ought to be here" can easily be mistaken. In considering where a particular OTU may best be placed, it should be remembered that if a large group and a small group are of comparable significance, the smaller group may be expected to have the higher mean internal similarity (see Section 7.321, p. 99). In order to be able to find quickly OTUs with any specified combination of features, it would be very useful to have the data on punched cards.

7.333 *Abbreviated Names for the Criteria.* — Henceforth, we shall find it convenient to use the following abbreviated names for the criteria presented and illustrated in Section 4.3 (pp. 41 ff.):

TR 1	P	potential passive transform
TR 2	C	potential coordination with transitive verb
TR 3	Q	potential question-transform with *wh*-pronoun
TR 4	A	potential question-transform with *wh*-adverb
TR 4:1	Ap	potential question-transform with *where*
TR 4:2	App	potential question-transform with *where* + preposition
TR 4:3	At	potential question-transform with *when*
TR 4:4	Am	potential question-transform with *how*
TR 5	D	potential deletion of $p\ N_2$
TR 6	M	potential mobility of $p\ N_2$ to front position
TR 7:1	$\rightarrow N_1 an$	potential animate N_1
TR 7:2	$\rightarrow N_1 in$	potential inanimate N_1
TR 8:1	$\rightarrow N_2 an$	potential animate N_2
TR 8:2	$\rightarrow N_2 in$	potential inanimate N_2

CON 1:1	$N_1 pron$	N_1 is pronoun
CON 1:2	$N_1 name$	N_1 is name
CON 1:3	$N_1 noun$	N_1 is noun
CON 2:1	$N_1 pre$	N_1 is premodified
CON 2:2	$N_1 post$	N_1 is postmodified
CON 3	$N_1 def$	N_1 is definite
CON 4:1	$N_1 an$	N_1 is animate
CON 4:2	$N_1 pers$	N_1 is personal
CON 4:3/4	$N_1 co$	N_1 is common gender
CON 4:5	$N_1 conc$	N_1 is concrete
CON 4:6	$N_1 abst$	N_1 is abstract

For CON 5-8, replace N_1 by N_2

CON 9:1	Ad	other adjunct present
CON 9:2	Adv	Adjunct is adverb
CON 9:3	$Vcon$	Adjunct is a verb construction
CON 9:4	$V+Ad$	$V + Ad + p + N_2$ order
CON 10	$p=$ *in*,	*at*, ... p exponence

In addition, certain other abbreviations are used.

$Ap(p)$ is used for "Ap and/or App"

$N_1 mod$ is used for "$N_1 pre$ and/or $N_1 post$"
(and similarly $N_2 mod$)

Qa and Qb: When it is desirable to distinguish between the responses of the two informant sources for Q (see Section 4.3, p. 43), one set of responses is denoted by Qa and the other by Qb. These names are also used as abbreviated names for the informants themselves.

All the abbreviated names except for those in the next paragraph can represent features as well as criteria. When they do so, a prefixed "$\sim$" indicates the converse feature. Thus, $\sim N_1 pron$ means "N_1 is not a pronoun". When a feature is prefixed by an arrow, the converse feature is prefixed by "$\nrightarrow$". In addition, the following special abbreviations are used:

$$N_1 in \quad \text{for } \sim N_1 an$$
$$N_1 indef \quad \text{for } \sim N_1 def$$
$$N_1 unmod \text{ for } \sim N_1 mod$$

and similarly for the corresponding N_2 features.

Certain additional criterion-complexes also have abbreviated names; these are exceptional in never representing features. They are:

TR 4, 4:1-4 $A+$
TR 7:1-2 $\rightarrow N_1$
TR 8:1-2 $\rightarrow N_2$
CON 1:1-3 $N_1 form$-$class$
CON 4:1-6 $N_1 gender$
(and similarly for $N_2 form$-$class$, $N_2 gender$)
CON 9:1-4 $Ad+$

Notice that the complex criterion $Nmod$ can represent a feature.

In conformity with TR 7-8, an arrow placed before the name of a CON feature is sometimes used to indicate a covert feature or criterion. Thus, $\rightarrow N_2 pron$ means "potential pronominal N_2". This convention is used to give names to certain additional criteria which are introduced at various points for purposes of comparison or because they seem potentially useful.

The term "criterion" is used for any question to which the response can be any one of a related set of features. The principal examples are the self-explanatory N_1 and N_2 *form-class*. If the context makes it clear that a set of CON features all apply to N_1 only (or to N_2 only) then the N_1 (or N_2) in the names may be omitted. This occurs in certain tables.

7.334 *An Illustrative Example.* — It may prove helpful to see the techniques applied to a small number of OTUs and criteria. We consider five OTUs from the corpus; they have been selected to cover a fairly wide range of types with respect to the criteria we have chosen.

(OTU 8)   *Emma* asked **for** her coat, ...   (b96)

(OTU 55)   *She* hurried **to** the gate, ...   (a24)

(OTU 84)   *Carfax sat down and began* to puff *militarily* **at** his pipe; ...   (b103)

(OTU 85)   *"He won't employ anybody who* trips up **on** his standards — of culture, *I mean*, and education."   (a20)

(OTU 112) ... *her face had* hollowed **underneath** the cheek-bones, ...   (a17)

We use six main criteria, *P, Q, C, D, A*, and *M*, and in addition the subordinate criteria *Ap, App, At*, and *Am*. The six main criteria are coded in the standard way as Alternatives, and the remaining criteria as Positives. This gives the following feature matrix:

	P	C	Q	A	D	M	Ap	App	At	Am
OTU 8	+	+	+	−	−	−	NC	NC	NC	NC
OTU 55	−	−	−	+	+	−	+	+	NC	NC
OTU 84	−	−	+	−	+	−	NC	NC	NC	NC
OTU 85	−	−	+	+	+	−	NC	NC	NC	+
OTU 112	−	−	−	+	+	+	+	NC	NC	NC

(This matrix could easily be rearranged by hand to give a more satisfactory appearance, by placing OTU 55 between OTU 85 and OTU 112; this would result in the sequences of $+$'s and $-$'s in the first six tests being unbroken).

In the case of OTU 8 and OTU 55, there are 6 comparisons ($K = 6$), one for each of the first six tests, and 1 resemblance ($R = 1$). Hence the similarity coefficient is 1/6. Continuing in this way, we obtain the similarity matrix:

	8				
55	1/6	55			
84	3/6	4/6	84		
85	2/6	5/6	5/6	85	
112	0/6	6/7	3/6	4/6	112
	8	55	84	85	

Writing the similarity coefficients as percentages, this matrix can be rewritten as:

	8				
55	17	55			
84	50	67	84		
85	33	83	83	85	
112	0	86	50	67	112
	8	55	84	85	

We show the links that are formed at all levels down to 50%, at which level the OTUs form one single-linkage group:

86% level 55 — 112
83% level 84 — 85 — 55
67% level 84 — 55 — 85 — 112
50% level   8 — 84 — 112

The groups at the same levels are then (we use double lines for old links):

86% level 55 — 112
83% level 84 — 85 — 55 = 112
67% level no change
50% level   8 — 84 = 85 = 55 = 112

We have placed new OTUs at the appropriate end of the pre-existing group; the example is very simple, and there have been no difficulties. The tree is:

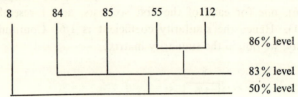

8	84	85	55	112

86% level

83% level
50% level

and the rearranged similarity matrix is:

	8				
84	50	84			
85	33	83	85		
55	17	67	83	55	
112	0	50	67	86	112
	8	84	85	55	

This matrix is a miniature cline, with OTU 8 rather separated from all the other OTUs. The cline can be further illustrated by a linkage diagram in which double lines indicate similarities of 83% or more, single lines indicate 67%, and dotted lines 50%:

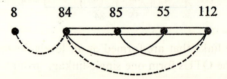

8	84	85	55	112

The cline is also clearly shown by the appearance of the feature matrix after rearrangement in accordance with the new OTU order; the tests have been rearranged for greater clarity, and the subordinate tests have been omitted:

	P	C	D	A	Q	M
8	+	+	−	−	+	−
84	−	−	+	−	+	−
85	−	−	+	+	+	−
55	−	−	+	+	−	−
112	−	−	+	+	−	+

It is noteworthy that when this experiment was repeated with thirteen criteria *not* used in the main experiment, a cline was again obtained, the only differences being that OTUs 8 and 84 were interchanged, and that the only OTU far removed from the rest was now OTU 112. Comparison with the similarity coefficients of the output is also of interest; the similarity matrix is:

	8				
55	666	55			
84	708	791	84		
85	727	909	909	85	
112	434	708	565	619	112
	8	55	84	85	

	8				
55	67	55			
84	71	79	84		
85	73	91	91	85	
112	43	71	57	62	112
	8	55	84	85	

At the 91% level one group is formed: $84 - 85 - 55$. At the 73% level OTU 8 is added by virtue of its similarity with OTU 85; if we wish to make the order significant, we observe that the similarity between OTUs 8 and 84 is greater than that between OTUs 8 and 55, and derive

$$8 - 84 = 85 = 55$$

The process is completed at the 71% level, at which there is a link between OTUs 55 and 112, and we obtain

$$8 = 84 = 85 = 55 - 112$$

	8				
84	71	84			
85	73	91	85		
55	67	79	91	55	
112	43	57	62	71	112
	8	84	85	55	

This order seems the best one; the ordered matrix is an almost perfect representation of a cline, with OTUs 84, 85, and 112 a relatively homogeneous centre. It may be helpful to use a shaded matrix, such as the following:

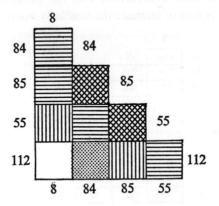

It is of interest to compare these results with the positions of the points representing these five OTUs in Figures A:8 and A:10 in Appendix 5 (see pp. 266, 269).

THE DIAGNOSTIC KEY

8.1 THE NEED FOR A KEY

It would be possible to describe the OTU classification (see Section 3.3, p. 32) in detail. Since this procedure would be extremely tedious, however, some form of diagnostic key will be very valuable in presenting its main points. In our situation we may go further and say that we are basically not interested in a detailed account of the output. Such an account would in any case have little apparent meaning. We are, rather, interested in making valid statements about the whole population, and in being able to classify easily, without recourse to a computer, any number of additional individuals (see Section 3.3) from the entire population. In this situation a diagnostic key is essential.[1]

---

[1] CLASP has facilities for referring new individuals to old groups. The groups are given to the program by the user, and they may be, but do not have to be, identical with groups suggested by CLASP on an earlier run. This facility is ideal if we are dealing with a finite population to which new members are added occasionally, provided there is no reason to expect the population to change in character as time passes.

We may mention here a relatively crude method with which we experimented for selecting key criteria without reference to the output. This was to classify the features by using the same program that was used for classifying the OTUs: the "properties" were "being possessed by each OTU" and each criterion became two "OTUs". Thus, for example, "Can N_2 be animate?" (TR 8:1) became two OTUs identifiable with the features "N_2 is animate" and "N_2 is inanimate". The features divided quite neatly into two groups. Each contained the opposites of the other. One contained, among others, $\rightarrow N_1 an$; $N_2 abst$ and related features, such as $N_2 in$ and $N_2 conc$; $\sim N_2 pron$; and M. All the members of this list were drawn in rapidly. In addition, the group contained $\sim P$ and $\sim C$, which united with each other early, and joined the group fairly quickly. The last feature to join this group was A, and the last but one, surprisingly, was Q! We may note that the similarity coefficient between A and

We have touched on two functions of a diagnostic key beyond mere description of the output. The first is that of being a practical tool for classifying OTUs rapidly. This is what would be required in the preparation of data for a further taxonomic experiment on a different type of material. Thus, if for example there had been a former satisfactory experiment on nominal groups, the principal classes could have been used in this present experiment.[2] It will be noticed that a bad key could have unfortunate effects here, and also that a key which was too dependent on unreliable criteria — that is, criteria over which informants often disagree — would be unsatisfactory unless means had been devised for obtaining more reliable results, perhaps from a group of informants (see the discussion in Section 4.4, pp. 51 ff. and Quirk & Svartvik 1966, Chapter 3). The second function of a diagnostic key is to help to establish categories of thought. For this purpose, minor weaknesses in the key are not so important, and indeed we might well expect a linguist using these categories to improve them by encounter with unusual situations (see Wexler 1966).

When setting up a diagnostic key, we may treat the groups of the OTU classification as fundamental and devise a system which would, always or almost always, place an OTU in the right group. Alternatively, we may devise a simple and probably monothetic

---

Q was 673, that between $\sim A$ and Q was 326, that between P and Q was 560, and that between $\sim P$ and Q was 439. The results do not seem very satisfactory, perhaps largely because the criteria are interdependent.

An estimate of the predictive power was made by adding all the similarity coefficients involving each feature of one group in turn; this gave the following ordering for the highest totals, where the features have been taken from this group only; the totals would be the same for the converse features:

N_2conc	M
N_2abst	N_1an
$\rightarrow N_1an$	$\sim N_1noun$
$\leftrightarrow N_2an$	$\sim P$
$\sim N_2pron$	$\sim C$

[2]   We find it convenient to use CLASS for any set of individuals defined by the diagnostic key. GROUP, OR CLUSTER, will be used for any set of OTUs, particularly those of the OTU classification (see Section 3.3).

key, which gives an approximation to the OTU classification, and then *define* the resulting classification to be the population classification. In our situation, a compromise between the two approaches is probably preferable. The first approach would result in a key that was much more complex than was either realistic or interesting, whereas the second would be too coarse. (See also Sections 8.21-2, pp. 118 ff., on the truncated tree and on predictivity). In addition, we might begin by modifying the OTU classification on other grounds, for example the appearance of the similarity matrix. There are two factors which tend to make a good key rather complex; one is that the output groups are likely to be polythetic, and the other that covert criteria are frequently unreliable.[3]

We give, for comparison, three diagnostic analyses arrived at by somewhat different methods, including a description of the principal groups of the tree. We also give a simplified version of the similarity matrix, together with some comments, and a few results obtained by very simple means, in order to compare them with results obtained more laboriously. The three methods were:

(a) A direct attempt to conform as closely as was realistic to the groups of the OTU classification. This was the method pursued in greatest detail (Section 8.2: A key based directly on the output).

(b) Classifying the groups themselves before looking for a key (Section 8.3: A key based on inter-group analysis).

(c) A feature-selection process (Section 8.4: A key constructed by a concept-formation process).

It will be seen that Section 8.2 is based on the unmodified OTU classification, whereas Sections 8.3 and 8.4 both alter it.

---

[3] It would of course be possible to use simple keys, and then to estimate the predictive power of classes by taking account of the fact that such criteria were not reliable; this would mean permitting classes to contain members which were much more like the members of some other class in which they should ideally be placed.

8.2 A KEY BASED DIRECTLY ON THE OUTPUT

8.21 *Numerical Tests for the Selection of Criteria*

A diagnostic key for the population must be based on the OTU classification, but this may be done in two ways. We may find a key for the OTU classification and leave open the question of extending it realistically to the population. Alternatively we may consider the population from the outset, in which case we shall be concerned with the statistical significance of the results as well as with an economical description of the OTUs and their features. We have attempted to use the latter approach, but, as explained directly below, the analysis was not adequate.

Two different numerical tests were used in the selection of criteria.

FIRST TEST. The values of χ^2 were calculated in the usual manner[4] for the contingency tables of features (i.e. the features of each criterion) against groups. Hence there was one table for each criterion; for example, for the criterion "form-class of N_2" (corresponding, unfortunately, to three tests), there is a contingency table of three features (N_2pron, N_2name, and N_2noun) against the appropriate set of groups. The only criteria considered as possible key criteria were those with particularly high χ^2 values.[5] In addition, those with fairly high values were provisionally retained as predictable from the groups.

This procedure is obviously not entirely satisfactory. A relatively minor point is that many of the numbers are likely to be so small that the test gives unreliable results; and, of course, the more structured the data are, the greater the proportion of small numbers, and the more serious this problem becomes.[6] Except for this, the

---

[4]   See, for example, Herdan 1964, pp. 37ff.,
[5]   Since the number of features corresponding to a criterion was not constant, the number of degrees of freedom varied. Hence the criteria were retained according to the *probabilities* corresponding to the values of χ^2, rather than to the actual χ^2 values themselves.
[6]   The high proportion of small numbers in the tables is to be expected if the data possess marked structure because there will commonly be clear correlations

procedure may be considered as normal and satisfactory where it rejects those criteria for which the χ^2 values are below, say, the 95% significance level. In practice, however, most of the χ^2 values are above the 95% level, and many are very much above it. There are indeed more serious objections to using the χ^2 values in order to grade the criteria and eliminate the low-ranking ones.

The groups do not exist independently of the features but, on the contrary, were constructed so as to bring together OTUs with many common features. In fact, they do not exist apart from the particular sample of OTUs, and there is no guarantee that, if the experiment were repeated with different OTUs, classes identifiable with the originals would again be formed. Our interpretation of χ^2 — and in particular of high values of χ^2 — is therefore un- orthodox and imprecise. On the one hand, we use it as a measure of intensity of association;[7] on the other, as simultaneously indicating the significance both of the association of a feature with a group and also of the *existence* of that group (and so of the group's stability if the experiment were repeated, and of its "reality" with respect to the population). The use of the χ^2 technique for this purpose would be difficult to justify, and it is doubtless not the best method.

It should be noticed that if we *knew* that the groups were stable, the question of their origins would be irrelevant, and we could work at the ordinary significance levels without reservations, and also use the χ^2 test to measure intensity of association in the usual manner.

It might be thought that the difficulty could be circumvented by *defining* stable groups through selected key features, but this is not so if the key features have been selected on the basis of the sample, because the sample has shown a bias towards those features, which might not be valid for the population.

The question of the stability of groups, or subgroups, is pre-

---

between the group and the features. The χ^2 test is not reliable when the numbers involved are small: see, for example, Kenney & Keeping 1954, p. 305 for a dis- cussion of a particular case.

[7] This is not in itself entirely unorthodox; see, for example Herdan 1964.

sumably related in some way to the significance of the association of features in the OTUs, but it would seem inappropriate to have a very complex method to test this, when the advantage of the procedure is largely its simplicity and directness.

SECOND TEST. Considerations of the diagnostic value of criteria. A precise definition of DIAGNOSTIC VALUE is given in Appendix 1, but we may attempt a brief explanation here. The diagnostic value of a criterion is a measure of that knowledge about the assignment of the OTUs to groups that is gained by learning which feature (from the choice that the criterion offers) the OTU possesses. Again, when we learn which group an OTU is in, we increase our knowledge of its features; and we can in a similar way measure this gain in knowledge. The analysis of the notions is of course identical, and the two quantities are simply related.

8.22 *The Tree*

There were 16 levels which could be distinguished in terms of the groups. The levels were numbered from 1 (75%), at which all the OTUs form one class, to 16 (100%) at which the smallest groups were formed. This is a complete list:

Level 16	100 %		Level 8	90.5%
Level 15	97 %		Level 7	90 %
Level 14	96 %		Level 6	88 %
Level 13	95.7%		Level 5	87 %
Level 12	95.4%		Level 4	86 %
Level 11	92 %		Level 3	82 %
Level 10	91.5%		Level 2	80 %
Level 9	91 %		Level 1	75 %

The major changes in clustering occurred between Levels 13 and 14, 12 and 13, 10 and 11. The chief characteristics of the clustering would have been shown by three levels situated at approximately 95.7%, 93%, and 91%. The groups were labelled by the level at which they were formed — i.e. the highest numbered level at which they exist — followed by a letter (A, B, C, ...) indicating their order in the set of groups formed at that level according to the order in which the OTUs were finally placed by the program. While it is useful to see the complete tree, a detailed description of it would be tedious, since it contains 61 groups. We therefore begin by simplifying it as follows, beginning from Level 1:

(i) We retain only subgroups whose number of members is not appreciably greater than $\frac{2}{3}$ the number of members of the immediately superordinate *retained* group; the only case where the ratio was greater than $\frac{2}{3}$ was that of 9A and 1A, where 9A was subordinate to 1A. The group 1A had 146 members (the complete sample) and 9A had 100.

(ii) We include only groups with at least 5 members.[8] This gives Tree I which has 13 groups; the number of members is shown in brackets. The most striking omissions are four small groups at Level 13 which are subgroups of 11A, indicating perhaps that a separate large scale analysis of the 11A type of string is desirable, and twelve additional small groups, not all independent, formed in the residue.

Most of the remaining omissions are groups which are almost identical with those shown, but slightly smaller. It will be shown in Section 8.23 that 15F and 15H do not differ significantly from 11B and 12E respectively, and this leaves Tree II, in which sets of OTUs not assigned to groups have slanting lines. This is admittedly a rather drastic simplification: over half the OTUs are left incompletely classified. Some of them do belong to small, probably viable groups; with the aid of the similarity matrix it is fairly easy to place them with respect to the remaining groups, and to see that some are close to these groups. In particular, a group of four should probably be assimilated to 13I, together with an isolated adjacent OTU.

We treat the "residues" — i.e. the sets of OTUs left over when a group subdivides — as themselves forming groups; this is the

---

[8] It may be of interest to remark that if there are 5 OTUs of some particular type in the sample, then it is reasonable to believe that there is a better than 95% chance that the true proportion for the population lies between 2 and 12 in every 146, and also that the chance of getting none in a second experiment is less than 1 per cent.

simplest course, and has the effect of reducing the diagnostic value and the value of χ^2.

The diagnostic key will to some extent re-absorb some of the omitted OTUs into proper groups, and it is of interest to find how successfully this is done. It may in some respects be more successful than the original output, since the program has the fault that once a fairly large group has been formed it tends to absorb everything else; and, since groups are never broken, all record is lost of what part of the group a newly joined OTU resembles most. There is no simple remedy for this; it would be rather bewildering to point out all the linkages and, as stated above, the similarity matrix

TREE I

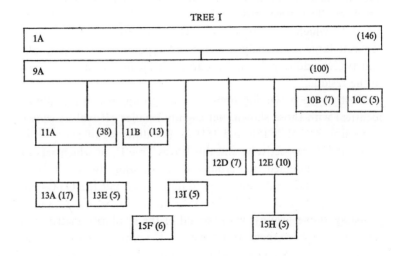

TREE II

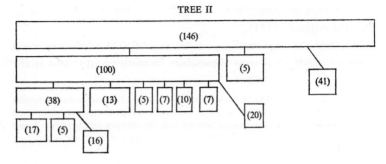

makes the situation fairly clear. The terms "high" and "low", as applied to levels, distinguish levels close to and distant from the 100% level respectively.

8.23 *The Analysis*

8.231 *Introductory.* — At each subdivision of a group, key criteria were selected by retaining those with high χ^2 values and then taking these in descending order of diagnostic value until a good approximation to the original groups was achieved. If there were no criteria with high χ^2 values or high predictive power, the subdivision was abandoned.[9] Since no information was available for gauging the reliability of criteria, the concept was not applied, except informally in subordinating C to P.[10] It may make the ensuing results clearer to give the most common features of each group, in general stating 100%, 75%, and 60% features, that is, features

---

[9] In fact, slightly more complex types of key are sometimes given, but it is clearer to discuss them as they arise. An alternative system, in general more economical to use when it is constructed, is to select what is apparently the most powerful criterion and to divide the OTUs into groups according to their responses to the criterion; then to test the remaining criteria against the division into the old groups separately for each of the newly defined groups of OTUs. This is a laborious process and the results can be complex to state. Since we were interested in drawing attention to the interesting criteria at each point, it did not on balance seem worth applying such a system with the possible exception of points where one criterion was very much superior to all others, and hence it did seem reasonable to split up the OTUs on the basis of that criterion alone, and then start afresh. Something like this does happen with the breakdown of 11A. We did use this system in Section 8.34, pp. 155 ff.

[10] A possible definition of "reliability of a criterion" is "estimated probability of getting the same (non-query) response twice in succession". This probability cannot be zero unless all the responses recorded have been queries. In the same way, reliability of a feature could be defined as the apparent probability of getting the same response. Reliability could be used in conjunction with diagnostic value; if the key is intended for stimulating thought rather than for analytic economy, reliability is less important. If a criterion is unreliable, and if single informants have been used for supplying the responses for the experiments, its usefulness will be less and hence its predictive power will be less than if many informants had been used. From the point of view of the solitary taxonomist, the unreliability of criteria is very unfortunate (see also footnote 3, p. 117).

which occur in 100%, in 75%, and in 60% of the OTUs; some features have been omitted because they were logically necessary, or at least linguistically almost necessary; or merely because it seemed unlikely that they would make the results clearer. C is omitted because it almost always co-occurs with P. We begin with the complete sample, giving 60% features:[11]

$$N_1pers, \; N_1pron$$
$$N_2in, \; N_2unmod, \; N_2def, \; N_2noun$$
$$\sim Ad$$
$$\sim P$$
$$Q$$
$$D$$
$$\sim M$$

There are some lists with the heading "Crude Predictivity". This is an extremely simple method of ranking criteria, sufficiently simple to be applied mentally; it is explained in Appendix 1. It has been used for purposes of comparison only, and has played no part in the selection of criteria.

In all the lists that rank criteria, that is, the χ^2 lists and the diagnostic value lists, the criteria are placed in descending order of

[11] The interpretation of the comma in, for example, $N_1pers, \; N_1pron$ is that the two features are independent, and *not* that more than 60% of N_1s were personal pronouns. In fact, just over 50% were so, indicating a slight positive association; in passing, there is also a positive association in the case of N_2, which is considerably stronger:

N_1	pers	$\sim$pers		N_2	pers	$\sim$pers
pron	79	15		*pron*	17	13
$\sim pron$	29	23		$\sim pron$	13	103

There is of course no reason why any OTU should manifest all the features below; indeed it could have happened that their co-occurrence was virtually impossible. There are no OTUs which possess all the most common features (that is, features which occur in at least 50% of the OTUs). The nearest to doing so are OTUs 81 and 48, in group 13E, and they do in fact possess all those quoted:

OTU 81 *She* fished **for** her handkerchief *and...*   (a 28)

OTU 48 *They* went **out of** the gate *and...*   (a 17)

but it would be injudicious to regard them as typifying the whole group!

value according to the test that is being applied. A single horizontal line indicates that there is a clear break between the criteria; a double line indicates a similar but much more striking division. The groups are labelled by a number, standing for the level (see Section 8.22, p. 120), and by a letter. The letters at any particular level correspond to the final order given by the program. The term "mean similarity" is sometimes used. This is an abbreviation (used in this section only) for "mean internal similarity" as defined in Section 7.321, p. 99, and is therefore the average of the similarity coefficients between the members of the group under consideration.

8.232 *Stage 1.* — The OTUs divide very asymmetrically into two groups, the central 9A containing 100 members, and 10C containing 5 members, leaving a residue of 41 members. ("Centre" is used for the expanding set of OTUs which begins as a group, 13A, formed at a high level, and increases to absorb all the remaining OTUs).

9A (100 members)
  100% feature: N_1def
  75% features: N_1pers, N_1pron
         N_2noun, N_2in
  60% features: N_2def
         $\sim P$
         Q

Most typical members: OTUs 48 and 81 quoted above in fn. 11, p. 124.

10C (5 members)
  100% features: N_1indef, N_1conc, N_1noun (i.e. N_1 is always an indefinite concrete noun)
         N_2def, N_2conc, N_2noun (i.e. N_2 is always a definite concrete noun)
         $\sim P$
         Ap (including some App)
  Mean similarity $= 92\%$

Most typical member: OTU 61: ... *and a few bright discs spun down and* settled **round** their feet. (a 26).

Residue (41 members)
    75% feature: $\sim P$
    60% features: N_2def, N_2in

Criteria ranked by χ^2:
    N_1def
    N_1an
    N_1mod
    $N_1form\text{-}class$
    ————————
    M
    P
    C
    Ad
    A
    $N_2form\text{-}class$
    Qa
    Qb
    ————————
    all remaining criteria

Criteria ranked by diagnostic value (as in all subsequent diagnostic value lists, asterisks indicate criteria not listed in the corresponding χ^2 list):
    $N_1form\text{-}class$
    N_1an
    N_1def
    N_1mod
    ————————
    P
    A
    $N_2form\text{-}class$
    C
    Qb
    Qa
    N_2def*

$N_2 mod*$
$N_2 an*$
M
Ad
$D*$

It is obvious that only the N_1 criteria are worth considering. It is easy to distinguish 10C from 9A (N_1 is animate for all 9A and inanimate for all 10C) but there is no way to mark off the residue reasonably clearly nor does it seem reasonable to expect that there should be. In passing to Stage 2 we therefore retain all the criteria except $N_1 an$ and $N_1 def$ which are almost invariant for 9A (and, in fact, 10C). The residue has no very clear characteristics of its own, although there are significant differences between it and 9A, or between it and 9A and 10C combined. The striking difference between the χ^2 ranking and the diagnostic value ranking of M may be explained by the rarity of the feature M.

8.233 *Stage 2.*

11A (38 members)
100% features: $N_1 def$, $N_1 an$
          N_2 *noun*
 75% features: $N_1 pers$, $N_1 pron$
          $N_2 in$
          $\sim P$
          D
 60% features: $N_2 conc$
          A

Most typical members: OTU 85: "*He won't employ anybody who* trips up **on** his standards — of culture, *I mean*, and education."   (a 20)
OTU 59: "*Besides, he's* gone **to** the football match."   (a 26)

Notes: *Am* is unusually frequent; *Qa* often differs from *Qb*.

11B (13 members)
100% features: $N_1 def$, $N_1 an$, $N_1 pron$
$N_2 def$
P
Q
$\sim A$
75% features: $N_1 pers$
$N_2 pers$, $N_2 pron$
Mean similarity = 91%
Most typical   OTU 7: *he should be* thinking **of** her. (b 96)
members: OTU 31: "*And the way he* looks **at** me *some-times.*"   (b 104)

13I (5 members)
100% features: $N_1 pers$, $N_1 name$
$N_2 abst$, $N_2 noun$
$\sim P$
D
At or *Am*
Notes: *M* in 4 cases, and queried in 1 case; $\sim Q$ with the exception of *Qa* once.
Mean similarity = 93%
Typical   OTU 87: *Watching him, Madeleine* con-
members: tinued **in** a vague and level manner: ... (a 20)
                 OTU 123: *Dr Adrian Carfax happened* **at**
                 that moment *to be* passing by, ...   (b 100)

12D (7 members)
100% features: $N_1 pron$
$N_2 pron$
$\sim P$
75% features: $N_1 an$
$N_2 pers$
Q
$\sim A$
Mean similarity = 91%
Most typical
member: OTU 62: "*Should we* run **for** him?" (a 26)

12E   (10 members)

100% features: N_1pron

N_2indef, N_2noun

Q

75% features: N_1pers

N_2unmod, N_2abst

P

$\sim A$

Mean similarity $= 94\%$

The most typical OTUs are the 5 members of 15H, identical in features save for their prepositions, e.g. OTU 10: "*... and I* talk **about** life, *as I told you.*"   (b 95)

10B   (7 members)

100% features: N_1def, N_1pers

N_2def

P

Q

$\sim A$

75% feature: N_2noun

Note: The preposition is *at* in 4 cases: *look at* (3 times) and *stare at* (once).

Mean similarity $= 91\%$

Most typical   OTU 8: *Emma* asked **for** her coat, ...   (b 96)

members: OTU 9: *Emma* looked **at** his face *and said* ....

(b 96)

Resi-   (20 members)

due   100% features: N_1def, N_1an

75% features: N_1pers

N_2noun, N_2def, N_2in

60% feature: $\sim P$

Most typical   OTU 94: "*But if she* worked **in** Woolworth's

member: *you wouldn't call her a saint, ...*"   (b100)

Naturally no member is very typical; the residue also includes: OTU 30: "*Have you* talked **to** this man Bates?*"*   (b 107)

10B and 11B appear similar; the only important differences are

the form-classes of N_1 and N_2. It is interesting to compare the
*Vp*s in these two groups. Each group has *look at* three times,
stare at once, and *deal with* once. 10B has, in addition, *refer to*
and *ask for* once each; 11B has *think of* three times, *talk to* twice,
and *talk about*, *live with*, and *look after* once each. The inter-group
similarity of 10B and 11B is 79% (see Section 8.3, pp. 141 ff.).

Criteria ranked by χ^2:

C

N_2*form-class*

N_1*form-class*

P

N_2*def*

Qb (compare the position of Qa)

N_2*an*

A

M

Qa

Criteria ranked by diagnostic value:

P

C

N_1*form-class*

N_2*form-class*

N_2*an*

A

Qb

Qa

N_2*def*

M

Criteria ranked by "crude" predictivity (for comparison only):

N_2*form-class*

P

C

N_2*an*

N_1*form-class*

These results suggest initially that the key criteria should be P, C, N_1form-class, N_2form-class, and possibly N_2an and N_2def. N_2def is clearly conditioned by the higher ranking N_2form-class and may be omitted since it is unlikely to be useful. C almost always co-

TABLE 8:0

	N_1form-class					N_2form-class			P	C
	pron	Øa	—b	name	noun	pron	name	noun		
11A (38)	35	2	1	—	—	—	—	38	—	1c
11B (13)	13	—	—	—	—	11	—	2	13	13
13I (5)	—	—	—	5	—	—	—	5	—	—
12D (7)	7	—	—	—	—	7	—	—	—	—
12E (10)	10	—	—	—	—	—	—	10	8d	10
10B (7)	—	—	2	4	1	1	—	6	7	7
Residue (20)	11	2	1	1	5	1	4	15	5	4e

a Ø form-class was used for clauses with shared subject, as in: ... *the dog emerged and* bounded off **in** another direction. (OTU 88, a19).

b "—" was used for imperatives without subject: "*Come in and* look **at** it /*the effigy*/" (OTU 21, a23).

c (OTU 125) "*It* /*the rat*/ *'s* got **inside** this damned ..." (a25).

d The two OTUs which accept C but not P are:

∼P: (OTU 146) "*I* believe **in** scrupulousness in the face of action" (b94). (There are three other OTUs with verb + preposition "believe in", such as: "... *that I don't* believe **in** public philosophies, ..." (OTU 12, b94), and informants accepted P for all three.)

?P: (OTU 27) "*He's only six; and not allowed* to play **with** rough children" (a26).

e The OTU which accepted P but not C was: (OTU 35) ..., *and you feel honoured that, when they* live **in** such a thoroughly amiable world, *they should* ... (b101).

occurs with *P* but is not easy to apply; it might perhaps be better to use it as a backing criterion for *P*.

If we are seeking to *partition* the data, then it is fairly obvious with the aid of the similarity matrix that some OTUs in the residue should be placed with groups we have retained, and in particular that 5 OTUs should be added to 13I. However, in order to keep to straightforward methods, we continue to treat the residue as a group; it will then be interesting to see whether OTUs that are placed in the wrong groups by any proposed key are placed sensibly or not. Some appear to be close to two groups.

With regard to the four principal criteria, the situation is as set out in Table 8:0. (In 9A, N_2an almost always co-occurs with N_2pron an therefore makes a negligible additional contribution.) With the exception of the residue, it is normally possible to identify a class by the criteria N_1form-*class*, N_2form-*class*, *P* &/or *C*. The table below indicating the divisions made by the criterion may make this clearer:

N_1	13I / 10B / remainder
N_2	11B, 12D / remainder
P &/or *C*	11B, 12E, 10B / 11A, 13I, 12D

The situation is more fully set out in Table 8:1 (p. 133); "*P/C*" means "*P* or, if in doubt, *C*".

At least five of the residue in 9A with Pattern 6 should, in a partitioning, be placed with 13I; this would make the overall success proportion 79/85, with, in addition, 21 unplaced or misplaced. The eleven successfully-placed members of 11B are in a group (12B); the remaining two have Pattern 3, and are adjacent to one of the residue with Pattern 3. Pattern 6 could be subdivided by N_1noun/N_1name and for those OTUs not in 9A, by N_2form-*class*. In Patterns 3 and 4, the restriction N_2noun may be omitted without much loss, which would place three of the residue in 11A. This would give the "diagnostic tree" on p. 133.

TABLE 8:1

Pat-tern	N_1pron	N_2	P/C	Proportion of 9A				Re-main-der	Over-all total
				TAR-GET	Target success-fully placed	Others	Total		
1	+	pron	+	11B	11/13	1	1		12
2	+	pron	−	12D	7/7		7	5	12
3	+	noun	+	12E	9/10	6	15	1	16
4	+	noun	−	11A	35/38	4	39	7	46
5	−		+	10B	7/7	1	8	3	11
6	−		−	13I	5/5	11	16	26*	42
7	+	name	+					1	1
8	+	name	−			3	3	3	6
					74/80	26	100	46	146

* (including 10C)

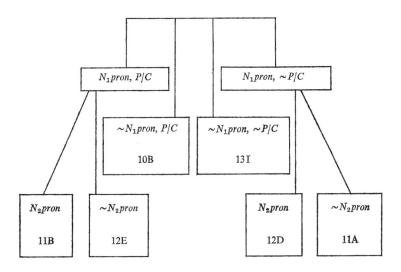

The order of these branches is arbitrary. The repetition of questions suggests cross-classification. If we wished to construct a tree for serious use, it would be desirable to investigate each branch individually; we have tested the criteria for importance *simultane-*

ously, whereas the importance of N_2pron, for example, might be different on different branches.

The relationship between the groups may be made clearer by a 3-dimensional figure plotting the groups against three axes representing the oppositions P & $C/\sim P$ & $\sim C$, $N_1pron/\sim N_1pron$, and $N_2pron/\sim N_2pron$. The axes are:

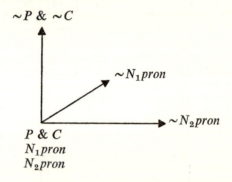

In the group diagram below, 13I and 10B are placed against edges joining adjacent points, since the opposition $N_2pron/\sim N_2 pron$ is irrelevant.

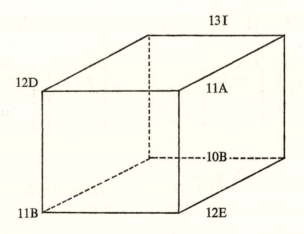

This diagram might be simplified to:

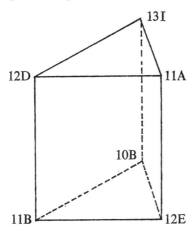

The relative distances in these diagrams are *not* intended to correspond in any way to similarities between groups.

In addition, it may be helpful to include the internal mean similarities and the inter-group similarities for these groups (see Section 8.3, pp. 141 ff.).

	12D	11B	10B	12E	11A	13I
Internal Similarities	91	91	91	94	84	93
Number of OTUs	7	13	7	10	38	5

The similarity matrix, firstly in the order suggested by single linkage, and secondly with 12D and 11B interchanged to give a possibly more natural order:

	12D	11B	10B	12E	11A	
11B	82	11B				
10B	67	79	10B			
12E	69	62	82	12E		
11A	67	62	65	71	11A	
13I	50	45	60	57	77	13I

	11B					
12D	82	12D				
10B	79	67	10B			
12E	62	69	82	12E		
11A	62	67	65	71	11A	
13I	45	50	60	57	77	13I
	11B	12D	10B	12E	11A	

It may also be interesting to show two drawings of a three-dimensional model in which the distances between the points do correspond approximately to the inter-group similarities given in the matrices above.

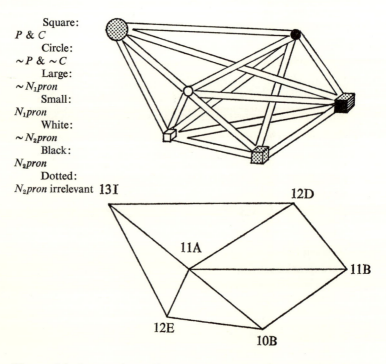

Square:
P & C
Circle:
$\sim P$ & $\sim C$
Large:
$\sim N_1 pron$
Small:
$N_1 pron$
White:
$\sim N_2 pron$
Black:
$N_2 pron$
Dotted:
$N_2 pron$ irrelevant

If we wished to make a dichotomy by using one criterion chosen from one of the three we are using, these diagrams would suggest choosing *P* and *C*. $N_2 pron$ appears to be useful at some points, but it is irrelevant in 13I and 10B. N_1pron divides the OTUs into 13I + 10B + 11B, and 12E + 11A + 12D; the first of these groups does not form a reasonable geometrical unit, since 13I does not resemble 10B and 12E. Consequently it would not be sensible to make a dichotomy on the basis of N_1pron. A is consistent for all groups save 11A, where it varies considerably; Q is almost consistent for all except 11A, where again it varies considerably; indeed, between Qa and Qb disagreement is frequent:

	Qa	$\sim Qa$
Qb	12	2
$\sim Qb$	6	18

$Qa = Qb$ 30
$Qa \neq Qb$ 8

See also Section 8.23.

The differences between some of these groups do not amount to very much, indeed to any more than the key features and the features that almost inevitably follow from them. The material is too coarse to make it worth looking for a perfect polythetic key. The key given is on the whole satisfactory, since even misplaced OTUs are in groups with which they have considerable affinity.

8.234 *Stage 3.* — (We consider the groups of the truncated tree, and not those given by the diagnostic key for Stage 2.)

(i) BREAKDOWN OF 11A INTO 13A, 13E, AND A RESIDUE.
    11A has the following 100% features:
        N_1def, N_1an
        N_2in, N_2noun

13A (17 members)
    100% features: N_1def, N_1an, N_1pron
        N_2in, N_2noun
        $\sim P$
        A
    75% features: N_1pers
        N_2def, N_2conc
        $\sim Q$

Notes: 13A shows a concentration of disagreement between Qa and Qb.

	Qa	$\sim Qa$
Qb	0	2
$\sim Qb$	5	10

$Qa = Qb$ 10
$Qa \neq Qb$ 7

The table below shows that, in general, residues have more dis-agreement than the rest of the material between Qa and Qb, but that 13A shows greater disagreement than any residue:

←——————————— 9A ———————————→
←————11A————→

	13A	Remainder of 11A	Other 9A groups	Remainder of 9A	Remainder	
$Qa = Qb$	10	20	40	14	36	120
$Qa \neq Qb$	7	1	2	4	10	24

(There were two $?Qa$, which have not been included.)

13A is the largest group at this level, and may be considered as the group which grows to absorb all the other OTUs in the material.

Mean similarity = 90%

Most typical members:

OTU 128: *She* strolled back **on** her tracks *and* ...   (a 21)

OTU 137: *He* pulled **into** the kerb *and* ...   (b 90)

OTU 41: *She hurried to the gate,* looked **up** *and down* the road.   (a 24)

13E   (5 members)

100% features: $N_1 pers$, $N_1 pron$
$N_2 in$, $N_2 noun$
$\sim P$
Q
$\sim A$

75% features: $N_2 def$, $N_2 conc$

Mean similarity = 91%

Most typical members: OTUs 81 and 48 already quoted as, in a naive sense, the most central in the material (see fn. 11, p. 124).

Residue (16 members)
    100% features: $N_2 in$
                $\sim P$
    75% features: $N_1 pers$, $N_1 pron$
    60% features: $N_2 mod$, $N_2 indef$, $N_2 abst$
                Ad

Notes: One discarded group (13D) has A and Q, e.g. OTU 59 quoted above, and OTU 70: *She* stopped *again* **on** a small bridge with white wood railings *to watch a pair of swans glide from the main stream into a ... backwater.*   (a 21)

    Most typical   OTU 145: *She said something to her companion, who* turned **from** a vague survey of the landscape *and ...*   (a 17)
    members: OTU 117: *She* flushed *darkly,* **to** her forehead.   (a 21)

Criteria ranked by χ^2:

A
$\overline{}$
$N_2 conc$
Ad
$\overline{}$
Remaining criteria

Criteria ranked by diagnostic value:

A
$\overline{}$
Qb
Ad
$N_2 conc$
$\overline{}$
Remaining criteria

The weakness of the criteria must principally be attributed to the large residue. In turn, the residue is large because there are not many OTUs in 11A, so that most of the groups that were formed were too small to have much confidence placed in them and hence have been discarded. It seems very probable that if the experiment were conducted on a larger scale, this part of the classification would be highly structured.

    Returning to an earlier point (see Section 7.321, p. 100, the group

that eventually engulfed the rest (13A) began as a group accepting
A. This group is typified by low cohesion between V and p. A
partially subjective confirmation of this statement may be obtained
by relating this group to an intuitively derived five-point scale of
"degrees of cohesion", in which "1" represented the least cohesion,
"5" the most (see Appendix 3, pp. 247 ff.). 13A had 17 OTUs;
seven had been given Degree of cohesion 1, another seven 2, and
the remaining three, 3. The group expanded to 11A with 38 members — eighteen 1s, ten 2s, seven 3s, and three 4s. By way of
contrast, the most strikingly homogeneous group was 13H, which
had ten members — three 4s and seven 5s. It expanded to 11B, with
three new members, all 5s. (13A and 13H were groups at the 95.7%
level, and 11A and 11B were groups at the 92% level.) Needless
to say, the degrees of cohesion had played no part in the classification. Our data give:

	A	N_2conc	Ad
13A (17)	17	15	2
13E (5)	0	4	3
Residue (16)	8 plus 2 Queries	5	12

(All the members of 13E have Q.)

N_2conc serves principally to distinguish the residue from 13A and
13E. In the output, 11A divided into seven groups with a residue
of one OTU. There were no inconsistencies in these groups with
regard to A, although there were two queries. Q is also consistent
with the groups except for one disagreement between Qa and Qb
and, in addition, the striking disagreement shown in the largest
group of all, 13A. A and Q would have appeared more important
if all these groups had been considered, and A would have continued
to be the most important criterion. It is interesting that, at this
point in the classification, A has become so clearly superior to
Q; this is entirely due to the equivocal position of the latter in

13A. The significance of the unreliability of criteria is shown here. If the only informant had been Qa, A would have remained clearly superior, but in the case of Qb the superiority would have been slight, whether or not all the groups were considered.

(ii) The remaining breakdowns, those of 11B and 12E, yield no criteria of significance, and hence are not considered.

We have found it necessary to confine the diagnostic key to the tasks of describing the truncated tree, and selecting and ranking important criteria; it appears, for example, that A is important, but that it should rank beneath P. The 46 OTUs outside 9A have been left almost entirely uninvestigated, although we could provisionally draw them into the 9A groups.

8.3 A KEY BASED ON INTER-GROUP ANALYSIS

8.31 *Introductory*

If a measure of resemblance is proposed for pairs of groups, it is reasonable to form matrices of the similarity coefficients between the member groups of a collection of groups, and also to form new groups by uniting the old ones on the basis of these coefficients. The most obvious measure of resemblance between two groups is the INTER-GROUP SIMILARITY or the average of all the similarity coefficients between OTUs in one group with OTUs in the other. (As usual, CLASP will calculate this, and provision has been made for extending the facilities to include other possible measures.)[12] It is then natural to consider the average similarity coefficient of all the members of a group, which gives a measure of the "general likeness" between the group members; this we have used before, in the preceding section.

---

[12] As a group expands, even when it remains equally "natural", one may expect its mean similarity to diminish. We might correspondingly argue that the similarity measure between groups should be increased slightly, whether directly or indirectly, as the groups increase. It might be said that single linkage favours the increase of the large groups, and that approaches such as this favour the increase of the small, very slightly.

We might consider such a process as "classifying groups", although this term might be more appropriately applied to Section 8.4 (pp. 174 ff.); and we might use exactly the same technique as before, i.e. single linkage.

An obvious technique would be to consider OTUs as groups containing one member, and to consider inter-group similarity as the similarity coefficient between groups; in the case of two OTUs this similarity coefficient would reduce to the original similarity coefficient. At each level, new groups could be formed in any way (e.g. by single linkage) but at the next level, any new groups that had been formed would replace their old subgroups. This process would be extremely laborious to execute by hand, and would mean effectively processing the data by another program — the only stage of the original sorting process that was used being the easily effected formation of groups at the highest level.

In fact, we used any *non-linguistic* considerations that occurred to us, provided they did not take into account the individual features. The analysis is thus not purely "objective". The groups to be analysed were chosen in a fairly mechanical way, however. It seemed apparent to the eye that Level 13 was the most interesting; by this stage, 86 OTUs had been gathered into 22 groups (the largest number of groups at any level), 18 formed at Level 13 itself (95.7%), and 4 consisting of pairs of OTUs identical save for features which are encoded as Positives, or for query responses, so that their similarity coefficients were 100%. We included all these groups, even those with only two members, and no others.

We abbreviated the names of the groups to A ... R in the case of the Level 13 groups, and S, T, U, V for the others (15I = S, 15M = T, 15N = U, 15O = V).

The groups were situated as shown in Tree III, based on that of Section 8.22, pp. 120 ff. Groups that are neither in the original truncated tree nor considered in this section have been omitted from this tree unless they helped to reveal the degree of separation between two of the groups considered here. The inclusion of some such groups, for example, helps to show that R is remote from the centre, and V even more so.

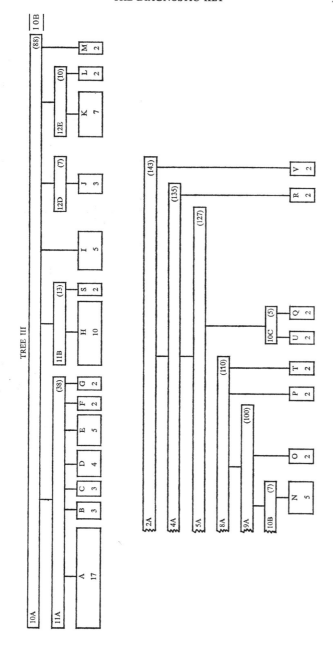

	T	J	H	N	O	S	K	L	G	D	F	E	A	M	B	C	I	P	R	Q	U	V	
T	100																						T
J	86	94																					J
H	79	85	95																				H
N	68	66	76	94																			N
O	73	72	76	84	96																		O
S	73	67	81	86	85	100																	S
K	83	69	78	85	86	90	97																K
L	72	68	76	79	82	80	89	96															L
G	87	70	64	71	83	77	85	73	96														G
D	83	71	66	72	78	81	82	69	89	94													D
F	78	75	69	75	78	87	78	70	80	91	96												F
E	82	73	69	77	80	85	81	70	88	88	89	91											E
A	74	65	57	64	78	70	70	60	84	86	82	80	90										A
M	66	67	55	55	72	66	56	50	70	75	75	69	83	96									M
B	64	56	44	60	69	60	64	57	76	75	73	70	82	78	94								B
C	69	54	48	53	68	70	68	55	70	75	72	78	80	71	81	97							C
I	61	49	42	62	63	59	60	47	75	74	68	70	79	69	81	82	93						I
P	61	61	48	56	56	59	61	64	74	65	65	69	78	73	76	77	67	96					P
R	38	38	26	45	45	41	38	38	54	57	52	54	69	59	66	64	70	73	96				R
Q	57	56	44	63	63	58	56	55	68	75	64	71	71	59	63	53	63	64	80	96			Q
U	55	56	45	65	38	55	56	63	57	68	72	64	64	56	65	43	52	66	73	90	100		U
V	76	56	46	54	69	56	66	71	76	68	64	69	64	54	65	61	49	76	63	72	74	100	V
	T	J	H	N	O	S	K	L	G	D	F	E	A	M	B	C	I	P	R	Q	U	V	

The order of the groups has been principally determined by the formation of single linkage clusters, but there has been some rearrangement. No claim is made that this is the best order, but it is a convenient order. The terms above the heavily drawn stepped diagonal are mean internal similarities, and are omitted in the shaded versions of the matrix.

Figure 8:1.

INTER-GROUP SIMILARITY MATRIX: LEVEL 13 GROUPS

The matrix contains all the groups which existed at Level 13 (the 95.7% level).

Inter-Group Similarity Matrix
Level 13 Groups, Shaded Version

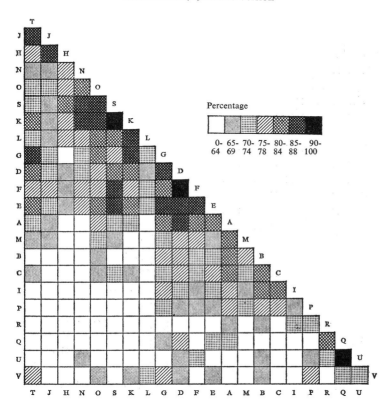

Notes: T is close to J, which is in turn close to H; otherwise T is anomalously placed. Thus G-D-F-E is closer to T than to L. T-J-...-F-E is more homogeneous than G-D-...-I-P. A is related to G-D-F-E and to M-B-C-I-P.

Part of the most natural single-linkage ordering would be ...L-A-G...; V is not close to any other group, but it slightly resembles a number of scattered groups.

Figure 8:2

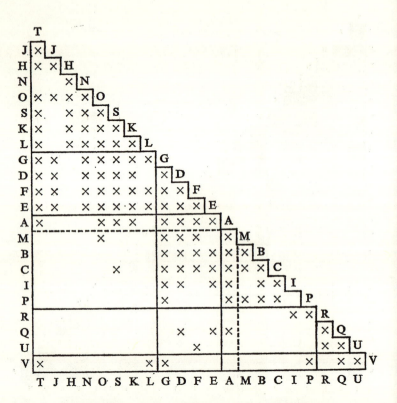

Inter-Group Similarity Matrix: Level 13 Groups. The marked cells are those corresponding to similarities of 70% or more.

Figure 8:3.

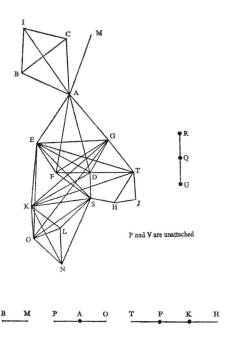

Figure 8:4. Linkage Diagram, showing all Links of 79% or more.

The first direct link, CE, between the two "groups" MBIC and GDFEKLON SHJT, is formed at 78%, together with the other links shown below:

B	M		P	A	O		T	F		K	H

"First Group"   "Second Group"

No attempt has been made to give a good two-dimensional representation: distance should not be interpreted in terms of similarity.

The groups were chosen as a manageable and well-defined sample; it is apparent that, as they unite, they ought also to be united with several other groups, and to absorb various OTUs. This is easy to see from the similarity matrix, and is also in part obvious from the tree: for example, when K and L unite, it is obvious that the united group should either be 12E, or contain it. However, it seemed probable that most of the essentials would be revealed from these 86 OTUs alone.

8.32 *The First Union*

We begin by showing the inter-group similarity matrix for these groups, both in the standard numerical form and in two shaded versions (see Figures 8:1-3). We also give a linkage diagram for the groups (see Figure 8:4). In the numerical form of the matrix, numbers are expressed as percentages.

From the inter-group similarity matrices, it appears that:

G + D + F + E form a homogeneous group (13 members)

S + K + L form a homogeneous group (11 members)

(This is the group 12E, excluding of course the OTUs outside the 86 we are considering, but including, in addition, S. Under single linkage S was absorbed by 13H, with another OTU, to form 11B.)

R + Q + U form a group, which however is not very homogeneous (6 members). Q and U are very alike, and formed most of 10C originally; 10C and R were absorbed by the central group referred to in Sections 7.321, 8.232, and 8.234 (pp. 100, 125, and 139 ff.) which engulfed all the others. This happened at Level 4, at which point this group had 135 members.

Single linkage unites the groups T to A as marked down the axes of the similarity matrix (see Figure 8:2) in a single group at the 85% level. The similarity matrix also suggests a group from T to E or A, and, as a less important group, G to P. The linkage diagram suggests G + D + F + E together with 15M ... L; M + B + C

+ I together with P; and A as a bridge (or "cutpoint"). (It is interesting that the separation of I and the similar 12C from 12A — containing A, B, C, D, E, F, G — by the "Passive" group H was considered a failure on the part of the program when the output was first inspected.) In view of all the considerations we have adduced, we first define the following new groups. They are defined largely in order to study their relationships rather than because they are all natural groups:

	A	(17 members)
B_2	T + J + H + N + O + S + K + L	(33 members)
B_1	G + D + F + E	(13 members)
B_3	M + B + C + I + P	(15 members)
B_4	R + Q + U	(6 members)
	V	(2 members)

recognising that B_3 in particular is *not* a natural group.

We obtained the following similarity matrix:

	A					
A	90	B_1				
B_1	83	89	B_2			
B_2	65	75	82	B^s		
B_3	80	72	56	79	B_4	
B_4	68	64	48	56	84	V
V	64	69	58	59	69	100
	A	B_1	B_2	B_3	B_4	V

B_3 was not designed to be a natural group, and it will be seen that the inter-group similarity between B_3 and A is higher than the internal mean similarity of B_3. The internal mean similarity of A + B_3 is 83%.

Using double lines for links above 80%, we give two link diagrams, the first showing links of 70% or more, and the second showing links of 65% or more.

(1)

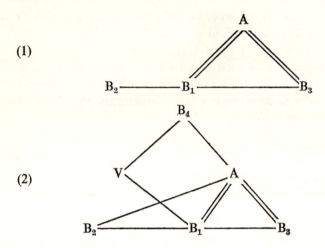

(2)

The diagram in Figure 8:5 is very accurate in representing the similarities as distances (low similarity = large distance, and vice versa), except that A should be nearer to B_1 than to B_3. The fit is

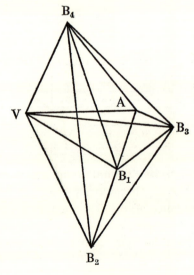

Figure 8:5

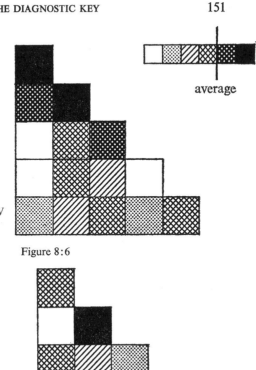

average

B₃					
80	A				
72	83	B₁			
56	65	75	B₂		
56	68	64	48	B₄	
59	64	69	58	69	V
B₃	A	B₁	B₂	B₄	

Figure 8:6

B₄					
68	A				
56	80	B₃			
69	64	59	V		
64	83	72	69	B₁	
48	65	56	58	75	B₂
B₄	A	B₃	V	B₁	

Figure 8:7

accurate in the sense that the ascending order of the similarities is almost the same as the descending order for the distances. There has been no attempt to find anything more precise. If a precise correspondence is defined between similarity coefficients and distances (a *metric*), then we could hope for greater refinement.[13]

13 J. C. Gower's method (Principle Component Analysis), referred in fn. 1, pp. 59f., and described Gower 1966, seems to be the perfect method for defining a suitably high dimensional map when any metric is given, and also of finding the

There is evidently no good representation as a cline. At the same time, if we ignore the small and less central groups B_4 and V, the remaining groups do form a miniature cline, with B_2 as the homogeneous end. It may be recalled that A was the group which expanded to absorb the rest, and also that it was much the largest group at Level 13. B_1 contains the "average" OTUs mentioned in fn. 11, p. 124. A further point to note is the relationship of Q with group A, mentioned in Section 8.234, pp. 137f.; the interest of this will appear when the features of these groups are discussed. The best order for the matrix is perhaps that shown in Figure 8:6, in which B_4 and V are displayed outside the central group. This order could be rather artificially considered as the cline given by the "E. — W." direction in Figure 8:5; it is interesting to see the cline given by the perpendicular direction "N. — S." shown in Figure 8:7. This is not so satisfactory, but notice the improved position of the coefficient 48 in Figure 8:7.

8.33 The Second Union

Various groups suggest themselves, and in particular we may define the following:

$$C_1 = B_3 + A + B_1 \qquad \text{(45 members)}$$
$$C_2 = B_1 + B_2 \qquad \text{(46 members)}$$
$$D_1 = B_3 + A + B_1 + B_2 \quad \text{(78 members)}$$

and, without much confidence in its naturalness,

$$C_3 = B_4 + V \qquad \text{(8 members)}$$

C_3/D_1 is then a partitioning of the 86 OTUs in the Level 13 groups. The groups might perhaps be diagrammatically represented thus:

---

best one- and two-dimensional projections of that map. J. Doran's method has as its objective, as we had here, the correct *ordering* of the distances as calculated from the figure, and requires no metric (see Gower 1966, Kruskal 1964, and Shepard 1962).

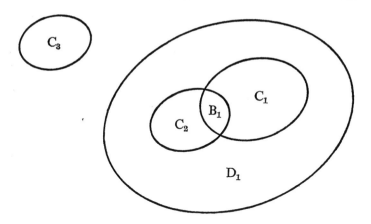

It may seem unreasonable to form $D_2 = A + C_2 = A + B_1 + B_2$ without adding B_3 to give D_1; but B_2 and B_3 are particularly dissimilar. In fact D_2 has a mean similarity of 76.3%, which is lower than that for C_2 but higher than that for D_1. We also define $C_4 = A + B_3$, which is A ... P inclusive, in the original inter-group matrix (Figure 8:1, p. 144). The relationships between these groups are shown in a set of diagrams on p. 157.

	45 C_1	46 C_2	8 C_3	78 D_1	63 D_2	32 C_4
15 B_3		61	56		66	
17 A		70	67			
13 B_1			65			78
33 B_2	65		50			61
6 B_4	63	52		56	57	62
2 V	64	61		61	62	62
45 C_1	81*		63			
46 C_2	X	79*	55			66
8 C_3	X	X	78*	58	58	62
78 D_1	X	X	X	73*		
63 D_2	X	X	X	X	76*	
32 C_4	X	X	X	X	X	83*

* = internal similarities
Numbers placed at the extreme top and left represent the number of OTUs in the corresponding group.

The blank cells correspond to two overlapping classes; the crossed cells would duplicate others.

The mean similarity of the 86 OTUs we have considered (i.e. the average similarity coefficient between them) is 70.6%. As observed in Appendix 2, this number is virtually determined by the feature inventories of the particular OTUs, and so has little intrinsic interest; however, it is useful as a reference point. We may note that every internal similarity in the table above is greater than 70.6%, and every external similarity is below, although the similarity coefficient between A and C_2 is only just below.

It is to be expected that the mean similarity of all the OTUs will be appreciably below 70.6%; it is in fact 68.0%.

The complement of a group is the group containing those OTUs of the 86 under consideration which are not in the group concerned. The first column in the table below contains the mean internal similarity of the group indicated; the third contains the mean internal similarity of its complement; and the second the inter-group similarity between the group and its complement. If the partitioning is efficient we should have the numbers in the first and third columns high, and the numbers in the centre column low. A complement is generally denoted by a bar over the symbol for the group it is complementary to.

				Number of group members	Number of complement members
C_1	81	64	71	45	41
C_2	79	63	76	46	40
C_3	78	58	73	8	78
C_4	83	65	73	32	54
D_2	76	63	68	63	23
B_2	82	63	76	33	53

$D_1 = C_3$; hence there is no row for D_1. The best partition here is, with little doubt, $B_2/\overline{B}_2$, if we ignore differences in the proportion of OTUs in each group. Under the same conditions, the next best partitions are $C_3/\overline{C}_3$ and $C_4/\overline{C}_4$, which are quite similar to each other in quality. Since the partition of OTUs into $C_4/\overline{C}_4$ is in virtually the same proportions as that into $B_2/\overline{B}_2$ — in fact one OTU worse — and since the partition $C_3/\overline{C}_3$ is too extreme to be satisfactory, the partition $B_2/\overline{B}_2$ is probably the best (see Figure 8:8). (It should be noted that the method of selection we have employed will lead to biassed results — since the homogeneous "passive type", for example, is likely to be over-represented in the sample, while the more variable kinds of OTU will be under-represented. In fact we have:

	P	$?P$	$\sim P$	
Present Set	26	1	59	86
Remainder	12	2	46	60
	38	3	105	146

Hence the importance of "passive" will be exaggerated here.)

$C_4/\overline{C}_4$ is, *very roughly indeed*, a division into $A/\sim A$; $C_3/\overline{C}_3$ cannot be specified by any feature, but the nearest is $N_1 in$. B_2 is almost co-extensive with both P and C:

	P	$?P$	$\sim P$	C	$?C$	$\sim C$
B_2	26	1	6	28	0	5
$\overline{B}_2$	0	0	53	0	0	53
	26	1	59	28	0	58

8.34 *The Diagnostic Key*

We now consider the problem of finding a diagnostic key for the groups of this section. We shall consider only the six groups A, B_1, B_2, B_3, B_4, V, and the groups we have formed from these. It is unfortunate that these groups only comprise 86 OTUs, and that B_4 and V are unsatisfactorily small. There is one point especially at which the order of value of the criteria may be expected to be different from that for the whole sample: it is obvious that $N_1 form$-$class$ will be of very little value, since it is almost constant ($N_1 pron$) in these OTUs. This is discussed in Section 8.41, p. 177. It also seems likely that $N_2 form$-$class$ will be less important than in the last section; every example of $N_2 pron$ (15 in all) is in B_2

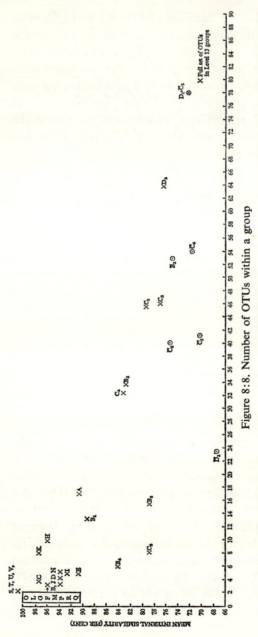

Figure 8:8. Number of OTUs within a group

In this graph points corresponding to every group considered in Section 8.3 have been plotted by mean internal similarity against number of members. The groups are marked by crosses unless they were defined as complements, in which case they are marked by circles.

C_1 appears to be a "good" group, $\overline{D}_2$ a poor one; and in general the groups defined as complements appear to be inferior to the others.

Since at Levels 12 and 11 OTUs similar to members of Level 13 groups are added to these groups, it is likely that rather better groups than those shown here could be obtained by including these OTUs. In particular it is likely that some of the Level 12 and Level 11 groups have mean internal similarities approximately the same as those of the groups plotted on this graph, and also have more members.

(the remaining 18 members of which have $N_2 noun$). The $N_2 pron$ OTUs are precisely those of H, J, and N.

Before commencing the diagnostic study of these groups, we give diagrams which show the relationships between the various groups, the number of members they have, and some of their typical features.

No. of members

RQU	A	MBCIP
V	GDFE	
	SJHN OTKL	

B_4	A	B_3
V	B_1	
	B_2	

6	17	15
2	13	
	33	

C_3	C_4
C_2	

C_3	B_3
	D_2

C_3	C_1
	B_2

C_3	
	D_1

We add a simple feature diagram, in which "$\tfrac{1}{2} D$" means "approximately half the members of the group accept D", "Q" means "all or almost all the members of the group accept Q", and similarly for other features:

Q $\tfrac{1}{2}D$ $N_1 conc$ $N_1 indef$ $N_2 conc$	A $\tfrac{1}{2}D$ $N_1 def$ $N_1 pers$ $N_2 conc$	$\tfrac{1}{2}A$ $N_1 def$ $\tfrac{1}{2}D$ $N_1 pers$ $\tfrac{1}{2}M$ $N_2 abst$ $\tfrac{1}{2}Ad$
Q A $N_1 in$ $N_2 in$	Q $N_1 def$ D $N_1 pers$ $\tfrac{1}{2}Ad$ $N_2 in$	
	P $N_1 pers$ C $\tfrac{2}{3}N_2 pron$ Q $\tfrac{1}{2}N_2 an$ $\tfrac{1}{2}D$	

To these diagrams we add the following notes, some of which have been mentioned above:

B_2 is very nearly the group of OTUs possessing the features P and C. The exceptions are the three OTUs of J, the two of T, and for P only, one of K. This last was OTU 146, quoted above, p. 131.

B_1, B_2, and hence C_2 (which has 46 members) are almost 100% Q; B_1 is 100% D; and most of the Ms are in B_3.

Rather fancifully, we may represent the situation with respect to the features in a diagram based on the "map" in Figure 8:5 (p. 150), where the features shown are thought of as strongest in the centres of their groups.

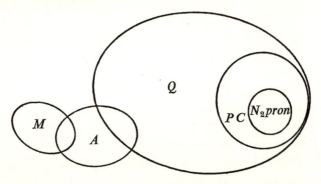

The procedure we should adopt in finding a diagnostic key is not quite obvious, since the groups we are considering overlap, and since B_3 was never meant to be a natural group. (See Section 8.32, p. 149.) We therefore begin by considering, as in Appendix 1 (pp. 221 ff.) the merits of various partitions first, after which we apply the diagnostic system of Appendix 1.2 (p. 224) to the best of these in turn. In doing this we do consider criterion-complexes (see Section 3.3, pp. 32f.) such as $N_1gender$ (CON 4; see Sections 4.3, pp. 48f. and 7.333, p. 107 ff). The most difficult of these to analyse was $Ad+$, in which there are independent subordinate criteria, for which it seemed unreasonable to assume knowledge of the actual *co-occurrences* of the features. We also include a numerical estimate of the quality of groups, again using the methods of Appendix 1.

The "gains" of the various partitions are set out in Table 8:2, and represented graphically in Figure 8:9. The best partitions for each number of groups are marked with double circles. The curve joins these, and is included merely as a visual aid. ("Gain" is defined in Appendix 1, p. 222.) We select as the best partitons:

B_2, $\overline{B}_2$ B_2, C_1, C_3

C_4, $\overline{C}_4$ B_1, B_2, C_3, C_4

C_2, C_3, C_4 A, B_1, B_2, B_3, B_4, V

The relationships between them may be displayed in two trees. The percentage gain for each partition has been included.

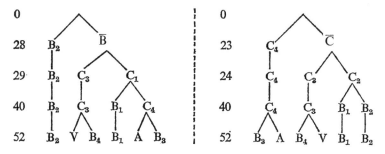

TABLE 8:2

Gains for various partitions (expressed as percentages)

Partition						Gain
		No Partion				0
		A	$\overline{A}$			11
		B_1	$\overline{B}_1$			6
		B_2	$\overline{B}_2$			28
		B_3	$\overline{B}_3$			15
		B_4	$\overline{B}_4$			3
		V	$\overline{V}$			3
		C_1	$\overline{C}_1$			15
		C_2	$\overline{C}_2$			16
		C_3	$\overline{D}_1$			10
		C_4	$\overline{C}_4$			23
		D_2	$\overline{D}_2$			12
		C_2	C_3	C_4		24
		C_3	B_3	D_2		20
		B_2	C_1	C_3		29
	B_1	B_2	C_3	C_4		44
	A	B_3	C_2	C_3		30
A	B_1	B_2	B_3	B_4	V	52

From these trees, and from Fig. 8:9, it will be seen that we have not found a useful partition into three groups..

In Tables 8:3-12 we give the diagnostic values of the criteria for various partitions. "Diagnostic value" is defined in Appendix 1:2 (p. 224). Both $A+$ and A are given; the A is included to enable it to be compared both with $A+$, and with other "simple" criteria. For the same reason N_2an is given in Table 8:12 in addition to the normal $N_2gender$. In all such cases the simple criterion is bracketed.

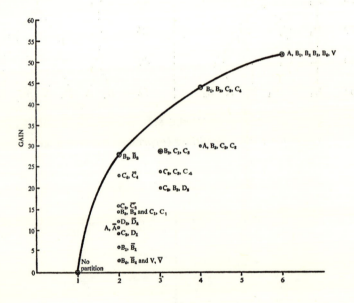

NUMBER OF GROUPS

Figure 8:9

The partition B_2, $\overline{B}_2$. The results are set out in Table 8:3.

Diagnostic Values of Criteria for the partition B_2, $\overline{B}_2$
(expressed as percentages)

Criterion	Diagnostic Value	Criterion	Diagnostic Value
C	72	$\rightarrow N_1$	13
P	68	M	12
$A+$, A	52	$Ad+$	10
N_2form-class	51	N_1gender	8
$\rightarrow N_2$	50	N_1form-class	7
N_2gender	37	N_1def	6
Qa	32	D	6
Qb	30	N_2def	3

We divide by C; any further division will be statistically un-reliable, although it may be noticed in passing that one criterion, N_2form-class, will suffice to complete the partition:

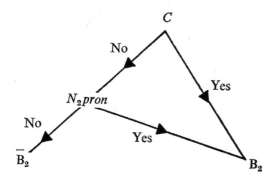

The partition C_4, $\overline{C}_4$. The results are set out in Table 8:4.

TABLE 8:4

Diagnostic values of the criteria for the partition C_4, $\overline{C}_4$

Criterion	Diagnostic Value	Criterion	Diagnostic Value
Qb	63	*M*	14
Qa	57	N_1*form-class*	10
A+	47	*Ad+*	9
$\rightarrow N_2$	39	N_1*gender*	9
(A)	39	$\rightarrow N_1$	9
C	31	N_1*def*	6
P	28	N_2*def*	4
N_2*form-class*	25	*D*	3
N_2*gender*	16		

It is obvious that *Q* is much the best criterion here; the situation may be compared with that of Table 8:3. There is no criterion which will satisfactorily complete the partition.

The tendency is:

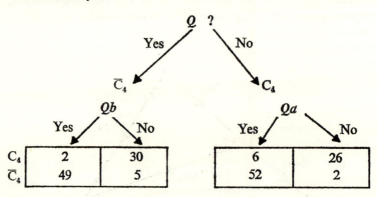

There are no query responses to *Q* in this set of OTUs, but there is disagreement between *Qa* and *Qb*:

The two "exceptional" OTUs (p. 163), those in $\overline{C}_4$ which have $\sim Qa$ and $\sim Qb$, are the members of 13 R; they are probably misplaced. The 11 with disagreement between *Qa* and *Qb* can, as it

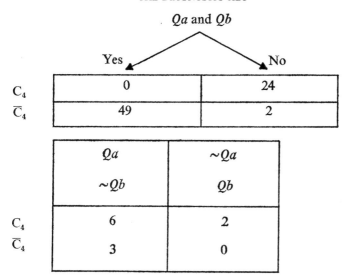

happens, be correctly assigned by putting those with *A* in C_4, and the remainder in $\overline{C}_4$; no other criterion could be used with complete success.

The partition B_2, C_3, C_1. This can be considered *ab initio*, or from the initial partition B_2, $\overline{B}_2$ (i.e. as a partition of $\overline{B}_2$ into C_3 and C_1).

We begin by setting out the results for the first case (the *ab initio* analysis) in Table 8:5.

TABLE 8:5

Diagnostic value of the criteria for the partition B_2, C_3, C_1

Criterion	Diagnostic Value	Criterion	Diagnostic Value
C	52	*Qb*	27
P	49	*Qa*	27
A+	44	→ *N₁*	26
→ *N₂*	38	*Ad+*	12
N₂form-class	37	*N₁form-class*	7
(A)	33	*D*	6
N₂gender	30	*N₂def*	4
N₁gender	28	*M*	4
N₁def	27		

The Table closely resembles Table 8:3; the numbers are however lower, corresponding to the evident fact that a criterion is not likely to be as good at diagnosing OTUs into 3 classes as into 2 classes. The main differences are in $N_1 def$, $N_1 gender$, both of which are good in distinguishing C_1 from C_3; and M, which is virtually useless for this purpose.

The best criterion is C. We therefore place OTUs with $+C$ in B_2 (no exceptions) and re-analyse for the OTUs with $\sim C$. This yields Table 8:6.

TABLE 8:6

Diagnostic value of criteria for the partition B_2, C_1, C_3: OTUs with $-C$ only. None of these have $+P$; the value of P here is therefore 0.

Criterion	Diagnostic Value	Criterion	Diagnostic Value
$N_1 gender$	52	Qb	18
$N_1 def$	49	Qa	17
$N_2 form$-$class$	44	$Ad+$	13
$\rightarrow N_1$	38	D	13
$N_2 gender$	34	$N_2 def$	7
$A+$	31	M	6
$\rightarrow N_2$	27	$N_1 form$-$class$	6
(A)	20		

C_3 is distinguished by the feature $N_1 in$ (2 exceptions)

and the feature $N_1 indef$ (1 exception)

B_2 is distinguished by the feature $N_2 pron$ (no exceptions)

Only limited confidence can be placed in these results; however, by using $N_1 def$ and $N_2 form$-$class$, we have achieved almost complete success.

Since the initial criterion we used was C, which was almost equivalent to marking off B_2, and since we used the same criterion to set up the partition B_2, $\overline{B}_2$, there is little point in considering the deduction of B_2, C_3, C_1 from B_2, $\overline{B}_2$.

The partition C_2, C_3, C_4. This may again be considered *ab initio* or from the partition C_4, $\overline{C}_4$.

The diagnostic values *ab initio* are given in Table 8:7.

TABLE 8:7

Diagnostic Values of the criteria for the partition C_2, C_3, C_4

Criterion	Diagnostic Value	Criterion	Diagnostic Value
Qb	49	N_1def	27
$A+$	47	$N_2form\text{-}class$	24
Qa	46	$N_2gender$	21
A	38	M	15
C	31	$Ad+$	9
$N_1gender$	30	$N_1form\text{-}class$	9
$\rightarrow N_2$	29	N_2def	4
$\rightarrow N_1$	29	D	4
P	28	Qb and A	83

It will be seen that it is not possible to give an order of preference to $A+$, Q; and we include at the foot of the table the value for the two criteria Qb, A in combination. This combination gives:

	Qb $-$ $\;A$ $-$	Qb $+$ $\;A$ $-$	Qb $-$ $\;A$ $+$	Qb $+$ $\;A$ $+$
C_2	2	43		1
C_3		2		4
C_4	4		26	2

It would be pointless to attempt to analyse the situation further since so few OTUs are involved. If instead we consider the partition of $\overline{C}_4$ into C_2, C_3, the criterion ranking begins:

$$N_1gender\ 84$$
$$\left.\begin{array}{l}N_1def\\ \rightarrow N_1\end{array}\right\}\ 81$$

with a long gap before $A+$ 49

and another gap before the next criterion ($N_2gender$)

The partition B_1, B_2, C_3, C_4. The *ab initio* rankings are given in Table 8:8.

TABLE 8:8

Diagnostic values of the criteria for the partition B_1, B_2, C_3, C_4.

Criterion	Diagnostic Value	Criterion	Diagnostic Value
$A+$	42	N_1gender	23
C	39	$\rightarrow N_1$	22
Qb	37	N_1def	20
P	37	M	11
(A)	36	$Ad+$	10
Qa	35	N_1form-class	8
$\rightarrow N_2$	34	N_2def	8
N_2form-class	29	D	8
N_2gender	24		

The situation is not clear; $A+$ cannot be confidently asserted to be significantly better than A, since the number of cases on which the difference depends is small; P and C are known to be almost the same; Qb and Qa are variants. The approximate effect of these criteria can be shown in the figure; B_1 and C_3 can be distinguished by N_1gender (C_3 has N_1in, B_1 has N_1an).

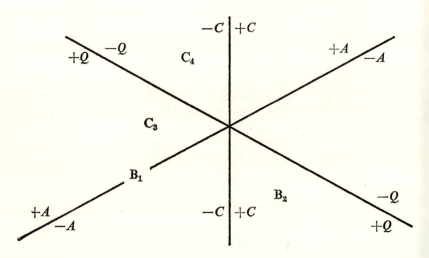

We may also derive the partition B_1, B_2, C_3, C_4 from both B_2, C_3, C_1 (by considering the division of C_1 into B_1, C_4) and C_2, C_3, C_4 (by considering the division of C_2 into B_1, B_2). Alternatively we might prefer to derive it from B_2, $\overline{B}_2$ (see above p. 161) on the grounds that the divisions into three groups were not profitable.

Deriving the partition B_1, B_2, C_3, C_4 from B_2, $\overline{B}_2$. This is the same as deriving B_1, C_3, C_4 from $\overline{B}_2$. The diagnostic values are set out in Table 8:9.

TABLE 8:9

Diagnostic values of criteria for the partition B_1, C_3, C_4 of $\overline{\overline{B}}_2$. None of the OTUs have P or C, whose diagnostic values are therefore zero.

Criterion	Diagnostic Value	Criterion	Diagnostic Value
Qb	46	D	11
$N_1 gender$	42	M	11
Qa	38	$N_1 form$-$class$	10
$N_1 def$	37	$N_3 gender$	9
$\rightarrow N_1$	32	$N_2 def$	6
$A+$	31	$Ad+$	3
(A)	17	$N_2 form$-$class$	2
$\rightarrow N_2$	15		

If we select Qb and $N_1 gender$ we have, roughly:

	$N_1 an$	$N_1 in$
Qb	B_1	C_3
$\sim Qb$	C_4	

or more precisely

		$N_1 an$		$N_1 in$
Qb	B_1	12	B_1	0
	C_3	0	C_3	6
	C_4	2	C_4	0
$\sim Qb$	B_1	1	B_1	0
	C_3	0	C_3	2
	C_4	28	C_4	2

The inclusion in the table of the refinements of $N_1 gender$ into $N_1 pers$ etc. does not seem useful; nor is it realistic to take the analysis further.

Deriving the partition B_1, B_2, C_3, C_4 from C_4, $\overline{C}_4$. This is the same as deriving B_1, B_2, C_3 from $\overline{C}_4$. The diagnostic values are set out in Table 8:10.

TABLE 8:10

Diagnostic values of criteria for the partition B_1, B_2, C_3 of $\overline{C}_4$. Q was the best criterion for predicting the partition C_4, $\overline{C}_4$; it is therefore natural that here Q is poor.

Criterion	Diagnostic value	Criterion	Diagnostic value
C	49	$\rightarrow N_2$	29
P	46	D	13
$N_1 gender$	40	$Ad+$	12
$A+$	37	M, Qa	9
$N_1 def, \rightarrow N_1$	37	Qb	6
$N_2 gender$	33	$N_2 def$	6
$N_2 form\text{-}class$	33	$N_1 form\text{-}class$	6
(A)	32		

C and P are the best criteria, and distinguish most of B_2 from B_1 and C_3, e.g.:

	C	$\sim C$
B_1 & C_3	0	21
B_2	28	5

N_1 *gender* is sufficient to distinguish B_1 from C_3. Comparing these results with the derivation of the complete partition B_1, B_2, C_3, C_4, through the partition B_2, $\overline{B}_2$, we find we have in each case used the criteria P or C, Q, and $N_1 gender$; whereas in deriving the partition *ab initio* we used P or C, Q, and $A+$.

The remaining partitions to be considered are those that lead to the division into six groups; there are the partitions of C_3 into B_4 and V, of C_4 into A and B_3, and of course the *ab initio* division into the six groups themselves.

The partition of C_3 into B_4 and V. This is a partition into groups with 6 and 2 members respectively, and is not worthy of serious investigation. Despite these low numbers, there is no single criterion which will effect the division.

The partition of C_4 into A and B_3. The results are given in Table 8:11.

TABLE 8:11

Diagnostic values of the criteria for the partition of C_4 into A, B_3.

Criterion	Diagnostic Value	Criterion	Diagnostic Value
N_2gender	53	N_1gender	12
$A+$	49	Qa	11
N_1 form-class	37	D	9
$Ad+$	31	N_2 form-class	8
M	26	$Qb, \rightarrow N_2$	6
N_2def	17	$\rightarrow N_1$	5
(A)	16	P, C, N_1def	0

The division by N_2gender is fairly efficient, and is in fact entirely between N_2conc and N_2 abst, all N_2's in C_4 being inanimate:

	N_2conc	N_2abst
B_3	2	13
A	15	2

$A+$ ranks much higher than A; this is partly because there are a large number of At, Am in C_4, and would not be so if the test embodied a significance test. (See Appendix 1.2, p. 221.) It is not obvious whether this division is realistic; several features seem to be associated with the two groups, but the material is too small to base any definite conclusions on.

We conclude this analysis by giving Table 8:12, showing the diagnostic values for the *ab initio* division into the six groups. For purposes of comparison we include N_2an as well as N_2gender, and we also include a "compound criterion", Qb & $A+$, which can be

considered as a general question-form criterion. The table includes
a heading "Number of features", which states the number of
features needed to answer the criterion or criterion-complex (not
including the "query" response). The greater this number is, the
greater the diagnostic value is likely to be, and, also, the labour of
using the criterion. This is exemplified by the pairs N_2an, $N_2gender$
and A, $A+$; and also by Qb, $A+$ taken separately and taken
together. In the analysis of this section, N_1form-$class$ has been
treated as a five feature criterion, but since two of the features were
rare and were not distinguished in the original feature matrix
analysed by WHI, "4" has been entered in the table.

TABLE 8:12

*Diagnostic values of the criteria for the partition into six groups, A,
B_1, B_2, B_3, B_4, V.*

Criterion	Diagnostic value	Number of features
$A+$	45	6
(A)	33	2
Qb	32	2
Qa	30	2
C	30	2
$N_2gender$	29	4
P	28	2
$\rightarrow N_2$	26	3
N_2form-$class$	25	3
$N_1gender$	21	4
$\rightarrow N_1$	20	3
N_1def	17	2
$Ad+$	15	4
M	13	2
(N_2an)	13	2
D	12	2
N_2def	9	2
N_1form-$class$	1	4
Qb and $A+$	60	12

Many of the important results are summarized in Figure 8:10.
P is always close to C, and normally slightly inferior; hence it has
been omitted.

It appears that if a succession of useful divisions is required, then it is best to begin with C (or P). On the other hand, if we are interested only in the final groups, Q and A are both better, and, in addition, can usefully be used together. Even in this case, how-ever, we should need C to complete the process. It is interesting here to consider the Level 13 groups which accept A; they are A, R, Q, U, D, F, I, B, and M. The similarity matrix (Fig. 8:1, p. 144) shows clearly that this collection is far from being a natural group, or even two natural groups; it is, very approximately, C_4:

	C_4	$\overline{C_4}$
Groups which accept A	A I B M (27 OTUs)	B_4 D F (12 OTUs)
Groups which reject A	CP (5 OTUs)	B_2 V G E (42 OTUs)

B_1 and B_3 are far from consistent with regard to A, but, apart from two query responses, all the Level 13 groups are consistent with regard to A, which indicates that it continues to be a valuable criterion at a slightly more refined stage.

Some of the criteria not given in Fig. 8:10 are moderately useful, some are probably almost or quite useless, while others do correlate with the groups and other criteria despite having low diagnostic values. The outstanding example of such a criterion is probably M, which marks off a small and rather extreme type of OTU (see also Appendix 5). Its low diagnostic value is because of the rarity of the feature M (19 cases out of 146) rather than the heterogeneous nature of the OTUs possessing it. Those which do *not* accept M are of course heterogeneous.

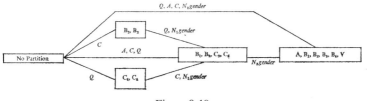

Figure 8:10

We conclude this section with Table 8:13 and Figure 8:11, which give some indication of the value of groups (as opposed to partitions). "Ignorance" is defined in Appendix 1, p. 221. It depends on the size of the group, and so the numbers can only be considered relative to each other. The lower the number is, the better the group. The numbers in column 4 are closer to being absolute measures of the values of the groups; it is in theory approximately true that if two groups are made up of the same types of OTUs, but have different numbers of members, then the column 4 evaluation gives the same result for both, especially if the groups are large. However, when OTUs are selected from a given set, the larger groups will vary more internally than the smaller groups, and so

TABLE 8:13

GROUP	NUMBER OF MEMBERS ($= n$)	IGNORANCE ($= U$)	$100 \times U/n$
All OTUs in Level 13 Groups	86	383	446
A	17	34	199
B_1	13	22	173
B_2	33	74	226
B_3	15	44	294
B_4	6	8	141
V	2	1	30
C_1	45	181	403
C_2	46	174	377
C_3	8	17	213
C_4	32	101	315
D_1	78	328	420
D_2	63	246	390
$\bar{C}_1$	41	143	349
$\bar{C}_2$	40	150	374
$\bar{C}_4$	54	195	361
$\bar{A}$	69	306	443
$\bar{D}_2$	53	201	380
$\bar{B}_2$	23	93	403
$\bar{V}$	84	371	441
$\bar{B}_4$	80	367	458
$\bar{B}_1$	73	336	461
$\bar{B}_3$	71	283	399

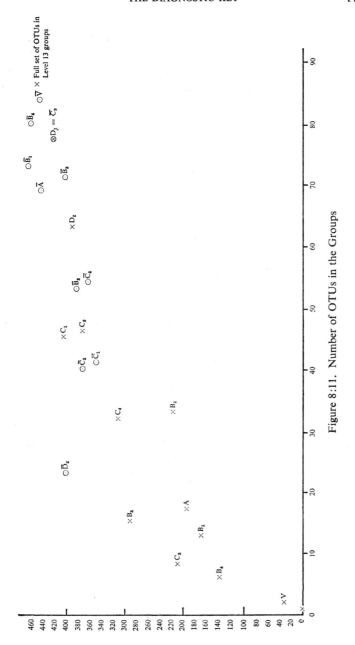

Figure 8:11. Number of OTUs in the Groups

it is still true that the larger groups will in general have higher numbers. Fig. 8:11 plots 100 U/n against n, the number of OTUs in a group; it should be compared with Fig. 8:8 (p. 156), where groups high on the graph are good, whereas in Fig. 8:11 groups low on the graph are good; thus Fig. 8:11 suggests that B_2 is the outstandingly good group, and D_2 the outstandingly poor one.

8.4 A KEY CONSTRUCTED BY A CONCEPT-FORMATION PROCESS

8.41 *Introductory*

This is perhaps an ambitious name to choose for what was intrinsically a fairly simple process, though one laborious to execute. Part of the motivation for employing the process was to refine the output, since, as stated a number of times above, the original output had one group engulfing the others, beginning by absorbing seven groups (13A-13G) without revealing any structure among them. The notion behind it was that in human thought only certain aspects of the "observable" universe (including all that can be experienced) are actually used, and that these aspects are associated with a variety of concepts, which *may* be named, these being in turn associated with further aspects.[14] We wished to think of groups as objects in their own right.

The process was basically to take groups provided by the output, to associate with each a description in terms of its predominant features and then to use these descriptions to define similarity

---

[14] For comparison we quote some ideas about concepts. A. Church, *Introduction to Mathematical Logic*, Vol. 1 (1956), paraphrased by Hunt & Hovland (1964), p. 313: "Church's argument is that any given symbol (or *name*) can be attached to the members of a set of objects. For any arbitrary object there exists a rule concerning the description of the object, a rule which can be used to decide whether or not the object is a member of the set of objects to which the name applies. The decision rule is the concept of the name, the set of objects is the denotation of the name." The authors continue by describing features typical of psychologists' concept-learning experiments: the emphasis is on selection of features (the decision rule) that correspond to the names given to various objects (i.e. enumerations of the sets of objects possessing the names). See also Michie (1965, pp 58-61), who equates, operationally, concept-formation and feature-selection.

coefficients and hence a new similarity matrix between the groups, from which clusters of the groups were obtained by single linkage. The process was then repeated *ab initio* on these clusters, selecting only from the features included in previous descriptions. In each cycle, including the first (which had been performed by the program), the clustering was stopped when a number of groups was about to amalgamate into one large group. The whole process was stopped when the descriptions became vacuous.

Speaking in Church's terms (see fn. 14), the denotation was given by the cluster analysis, and the search for the decision rule was merely the choosing of a description. The justification for calling the process concept-formation is that new denotations arose from the old descriptions: the selection of features (i.e. of a diagnostic key) was linked with the building of groups. The *object* was thus to move towards describing a set in terms of concepts formed earlier rather than in terms of the individual features.

Viewing the matter differently, the process could accurately be called "the classifying of descriptions". It may be compared with the inter-group analysis of Section 8.3, to which it is obviously related. The size of a group now makes little difference (a large group will of course tend to have fewer predominant features). We may say that all groups worth considering (or concepts worth forming) start on equal terms; this makes reasonable sense in terms of economical description. Notice that if a large group is united with a smaller, the features are not weighted by the size of the groups.[15]

[15] There is a temptation to weight features by their frequency, attaching higher weights to infrequent features. It becomes stronger in this section, for, in the case of criteria which are usually answered in only one way, the rare answer tends to play no part in the analysis, even if it is *relatively* common in some of the groups. If there were weighting, it might best be according to the "surprise value" of a feature, that is, we could (as in information theory) expect one feature and feel either that we had learnt little when it duly appeared, or that we had learnt a good deal when it failed to appear. This can lead to useful linkages; thus, after applying the classification methods of Appendix 1.6 (pp. 228 ff.) to a small test example, we found that such a similarity coefficient gave results in closer conformity with the classification than a normal similarity coefficient. At the same time it seems a dubious measure of resemblance; it is a measure of resemblance relative to a norm.

In Section 8.31 we suggested that this process might be considered as classifying the groups themselves. If we rephrase this to "classifying the group-concepts" this seems accurate; the features of the OTUs in a group may happily be said to be the features of the group-concept, but it is rather illogical to call them features of the group. It would seem appropriate to say that two groups of OTUs, each cline-like, each of 40 members, and each having one end more homogeneous than the other, were in some sense alike, even though their members were in sharp contrast; we can do this by saying that the groups as groups have much in common, but that their concepts have not.

The detailed procedure was as follows. The groups chosen were those formed at Level 13 (95.7%) which had coalesced at Level 11 (92%) into 11A (see Tree III, p. 143). This was the groups A ... G of the last section, together with two isolated OTUs. (The reason for the choice was that this was the first large-scale amalgamation, and that the process is too laborious to make it feasible to apply it to the whole of the data at once; it was therefore applied to the expanding central portion.) At the completion of this stage the scope was broadened to include groups and OTUs from the 88 members of 10A, i.e. the OTUs which had amalgamated into the central portion at 91.5%. This was 9A with 10B, 13O, and 4 unattached OTUs subtracted.

The process of concept-formation was repeated on this set of OTUs a number of times. The scope was then enlarged to the whole of 9A (91%), and the process was taken to the final stage, in which the scope was 6A, with 113 members. At this stage the process had exhausted itself, as might be expected. The only features remaining were those that were almost universal. In fact the process had now been taken too far, and it was necessary to go back to 10A when forming a diagnostic key (which is in fact a "feature-tree"). However, it is of interest to show the complete tree of the groups (see Section 8.42, pp. 181-182).

When a group or concept absorbed one or two OTUs (or even a small lower level concept), it seemed more reasonable to enlarge the scope (or denotation) of the higher level concept, absorbing the new OTUs without forming a fresh concept. The grounds for drawing the line at a particular place were not formulated; the decision was a matter of judgment each time. The reasons could be formulated if necessary, e.g. for a computer program.

From the point of view of this process, there were 33 OTUs not considered, and in the formation of the key there were 60 not considered. (The first "residue" of the original diagnostic analysis, see Tree II, p. 122, had 41 members, while the inter-group analysis, ignored 60 of the OTUs.) Their "oddness" seemed to lie in N_1 features and in M, which did not seem relevant in the centre (see Section 8.232, p. 127), and the key that was constructed seemed to give satisfactory results when applied to the 60 not used in its formation (see Section 8.43, pp. 183-193). Nevertheless our earlier results in Section 8.2 (pp. 118 ff.) suggest that, perhaps largely independently of the other criteria, the N_1 criteria are significant. Among the 46 OTUs outside 9A there are 30 different patterns of N_1 features; the crucial factor is probably the extraordinary uniformity of N_1 patterns in the central part of the classification, which means, basically, the high frequency of occurrence of certain patterns in the whole data. In fact there were only 15 patterns in 9A, one of which (*virtually* that for "personal pronoun"; and by far the most frequent) occurred 64 times. In 6A, with 113 OTUs, there were 17 patterns, this frequent pattern now occurring 72 times, while the 33 remaining OTUs yielded 27 patterns! The frequent pattern occurs altogether 73 times: exactly 50%. The situation was therefore as follows. There were 73 OTUs which all had in common 8 N_1 entries, not including NC, and a further 73 of which few members had many N_1 entries in common with either each other or the first 73. Consequently, high similarity coefficients would occur very infrequently between a member of the second 73 and *any* other OTU, whereas among the first 73 there would be several high similarity coefficients so that groups could be expected to arise principally among these 73. In addition, we may remember that a group once formed tends to grow (see Section 7.321, p. 100).

With regard to M, we have:

	M	$\sim M$	
5A	7	119	126
outside 5A	12	7	19 (There is one query M in 5A)
	19	126	145

Also striking is the comparison between realised and potential M,

	Realised	Not realised	
5A	4	8	12
outside 5A	5	2	7 (The two outside 5A which
	9	10	19 are not realised form 13R)

although it is not statistically significant. 5A has been chosen to make the difference as striking as possible, which to some extent reduces the value of the first table. (*Realised* mobility was not a criterion in this experiment.)

Because of the unreliability of individual features, the reduction in the number of features could occasionally cause increased misplacement of absorbed OTUs. However, this danger was probably of no significance at the level of delicacy of this experiment. As stated earlier, if the OTUs had been tested by a large number of informants we could have had more confidence in the features attributed to them, but, in any case, the unreliability is a serious difficulty in some applications of diagnostic keys. It is of course reasonable to set up monothetic keys, and to find the degree of variation for each criterion in the resulting groups. This method will, to a great extent, take into account the occasional misplacement. We have tended to do this because of the simplicity of the approach, but it is not the perfect solution. If we have a classification based on unreliable responses — surely not in itself a good thing — we might at least hope that the responses not conforming to normal judgment would help to show us the magnitude of variation that we could expect in groups when a single worker uses a monothetic key. However, even this is not certain; one of our most relevant criteria, C (p. 43), is difficult to apply and almost certainly unreliable, and it is very probable that another informant would have given less relevant responses (for the use of the term "relevant" see Section 3.3, p. 32). In other words, if we find the apparent predictive power of this criterion on the basis of our data, it will probably be misleading as a guide to its predictive power when used by an average informant. A possible remedy might be to use the responses of several informants to estimate the reliability of a criterion, defining this as the chance of receiving the same response twice. This could also be divided into components for each feature:

reliability of P feature = chance of second, independent informant giving the response P, if we know that it was given by a first informant; and then

reliability of P criterion = reliability of P feature *times* chance of getting response P + reliability of $\sim P$ feature *times* chance of getting response $\sim$ P.

Such measures could be used as an aid in calculating the effective predictive power of criteria, and would be worth applying if we had great confidence in the groups. We should of course have had somewhat more confidence if the data had been prepared on the basis of reactions from many informants. (On the problem of informant reactions, cf. Section 4.4, pp. 51 ff. See also Note 1 in Section 8.43, p. 189.)

8.42 *Execution*

The group descriptions, or characters, were arrived at as follows. For each test, that is in each column, the entry "+" was chosen if and only if it occurred at least three times as often as "−", *and* if and only if it occurred in at least $\frac{2}{3}$ of all the cases, including NC. The entry "−" was chosen in an exactly corresponding manner. NC was chosen otherwise, that is if neither "+" nor "−" could be chosen.

STAGE 1. Comprising 13A ... 13G and the OTUs 138 and 117.

Similarity Matrix:

	138	13A	13B	13C	13D	13E	13F	13G	
13A	67	13A							
13B	78	83	13B						
13C	67	50	67	13C					
13D	67	86	57	38	13D				
13E	56	75	29	50	88	13E			
13F	70	67	43	38	88	100	13F		
13G	64	75	63	70	88	88	63	13G	
117	67	80	63	83	56	80	70	70	117
	138	13A	13B	13C	13D	13E	13F	13G	

We stop at the single linkage group formed at the 88% level; all links drawn are 88% except 13E-13F.

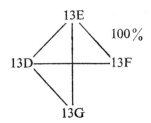

(At 85% we should add 13A, at 83% 13B, and at 80% 13C and OTU 117). We name 13D + 13E + 13F + 13G "Q1", choosing this letter because the feature Q is almost universal in this group. This group is the B_1 of the last section.

For purposes of comparison we show coarsened forms of this matrix and the inter-group matrix (for 13A-13G only):

	C	B	A	D	G	F	
B	8	B					
A	8	8	A				
D	7	7	8	D			
G	7	8	8	9	G		
F	7	7	8	9	8	F	
E	8	7	8	9	9	9	E
	C	B	A	D	G	F	

Inter-group matrix

	C	B	A	D	G	F	
B	7	B					
A	5	8	A				
D	4	6	9	D			
G	7	6	7	9	G		
F	4	4	7	9	6	F	
E	5	3	7	9	9	10	E
	C	B	A	D	G	F	

Concept matrix

It will be seen that the concept matrix resembles an exaggerated version of the inter-group matrix.

STAGE 2. The groups are the output from Stage 1 and those Level 12 (95.4%) groups which unite eventually into 10A. The first matrix has 210 cells, and is omitted. It is instructive however to see the formation of groups by the single linkage system: at 94% 12E and Q1 unite (12E is approximately 13K + 13L). At 88% there are four sets of linked groups, reducing to three at 87%, one of which proceeds to absorb the rest; complete union is achieved at 78%. We therefore stop at 88% with new groups:

$$12E - Q1 \quad 136 - 13A - 91 \quad 12D - 11B \quad 13B - 35$$

We form new concepts from 12E and Q1, named Q2, and from 12D and 11B, named Q3, and let 13A and 13B absorb the OTUs shown, without altering the names or the associated features. 13A accepts A throughout and 13B fails to accept Q.

OTU 35 does not accept A and does accept P, despite not accepting Q, or C. It is:

... *when they* live **in** such a thoroughly amiable world ... (b101)

It is probable that many informants would not accept P, and the OTU seems to have some slight affinity with those accepting Am.

Finally we consider lower levels and form the concepts "A1" from 13A and 13B, and "D1" by letting 13C absorb OTU 117. The letters "A" and "D" are chosen because the features A and D are conspicuous in these groups.

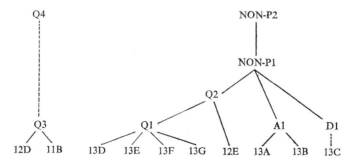

We omit the remaining details and give the tree we obtained when the final stage was completed; dotted lines indicate absorptions. The tree is shown in two halves, the first (p. 181) being the part used for the formation of a key. It was based on 86 OTUs.

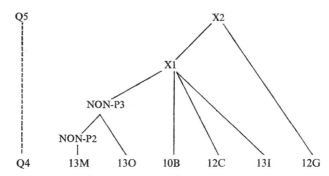

We show the second part of the tree to emphasise the separateness of Q3 — Q4 — Q5. The only possible criteria left to distinguish Q5 from X2 are N_2pron and $\rightarrow N_2an$, and over the whole set of OTUs there is not a very convincing agreement between these two criteria, even though the table below is statistically significant.

	$\leftrightarrow N_2an$	$\rightarrow N_2an$	
N_2pron	5	24	29
$\sim N_2pron$	60	52	112
	65	76	141

(There are 5 ? $\rightarrow N_2an$)

We therefore confine ourselves to the first tree. The features used are taken from the group characters.

The remainder of the process takes place in a few simple steps. We first add to the tree at each point the features which are lost at the stage above; these features serve to distinguish the branches. For simplicity, we have used only the features which appeared to be most important in this respect. This gives Tree IV. Where P is queried, we use C; an alternative would be to use P and/or C. We have, again for simplicity, used a straightforward monothetic key, without reinforcing for unreliable criteria except in this one case.

TREE IV

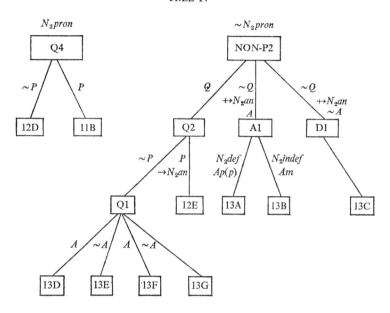

From this tree we derive the next, Tree V, which continues to
mark the "targets"; the arrangement has been altered from Tree IV
for graphical convenience. The division of Q1 into 13D, 13E, 13F,
and 13G is not very efficient if A is used, since it merely separates
13D (4 OTUs) and one OTU of 13F. N_2def and N_2conc would
be the best choices to separate 13E and 13F, but would each
misplace the same two members of 13D. There is no convincing
evidence that the division of Q1 into the four groups 13D ... F is
realistic. We therefore tentatively leave Q1 undivided. (See p. 184.)

8.43 *The Key Compared with the Data*

The diagnostic version of Tree V, with the end-points labelled by
new names which designate classes applicable to the whole population, is Tree VI. This tree is thus a diagnostic key.

We give a few miscellaneous notes on the Tree before proceeding.

TREE V

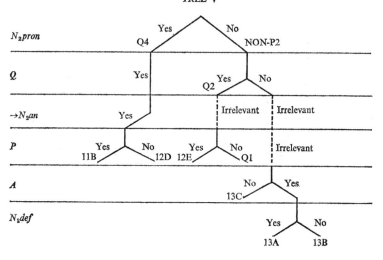

TREE VI

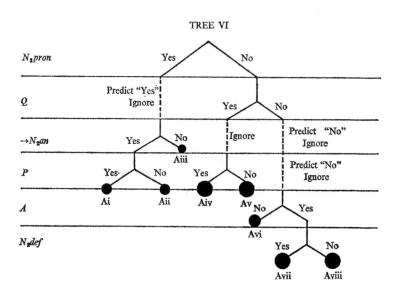

We notice that the same question is once asked on different branches; this indicates cross-classification. Aiii had no target. The OTUs of Aiii taking N_2pron are of interest; four members of Aiii are quoted below when examples of all the groups are given, and the remaining example is:

OTU 86 "*they have a code they can, and ought to,* live **by**."

(b 95)

If we have ?Q we then check $\rightarrow N_2an$ and P:

	P	$\sim P$
$\rightarrow N_2an$	Aiv	Av
$\leftrightarrow N_2an$	Aiv	?

In our data we include cases of disagreement between Qa and Qb as ?Q. Where the tree has "Predict 'no', Ignore" (which means that the response is usually 'no', but that the criterion is not to be applied), we should, ideally, investigate the exceptions, but there are not enough in the material for valid conclusions to be drawn. We do however add some additional classes for what may be exceptional OTUs:

N_2pron, $\sim Q$	Bi
$\sim N_2pron$, $\sim Q$, $\rightarrow N_2an$, $\sim P$	Ci
$\sim N_2pron$, $\sim Q$, $\leftrightarrow N_2an$, P	Cii
$\sim N_2pron$, $\sim Q$, P, $\rightarrow N_2an$	Ciii

We now have 6 unclassified OTUs, and 140 classified. The relationships between the groups Ai-Aviii and the principle features are presented in Table 8:14 (p. 186).

The members of Bi, Ci—Ciii are included in the eight primary classes Ai—Aviii. Where there are two columns of figures under one feature name, the left hand column gives the number of OTUs with the feature, and the right hand column gives the number without it. If there is in addition a central column, this gives the number of query cases. The entries "YES" and "NO" indicate that the group was *defined* by the presence or absence of the feature named in the column. Bi has 3 members, Ci 8, Cii 2 (both without C), and Ciii 1. Av invites splitting, either by a previous $\rightarrow N_2an$ or

TABLE 8:14

	N_1pron		P		C			D			M		A			Ap(p)	~Ap(p)	→N_1in			Qa	Qb	N_2an			Total
	+	-	+	-	+	?	-	+	?	-	+	-	+	?	-			+	?	-	+	+	+	?	-	
Ai	12	1	YES		13	—	—	6	3	4	—	13	—	—	13	—	—	—	—	13	13	13	YES			13
Aii	10	3	NO		—	—	13	6	1	6	—	13	4	—	9	3	1	1	1	12	11	9	YES			13
Aiii	2	3	—	5	1	1	3	4	—	1	1	4	4	—	1	2	2	3	—	2	3	3	NO			5
Aiv	17	8	YES		23	—	2	13	2	10	—	25	1	—	24	1	—	—	—	25	YES		22	—	3	25
Av	18	13	NO		1	—	30	23	1	7	2	29	14	2	15	11	3	7	—	24	YES		18	3	10	31
Avi	8	7	3	12	1	—	14	6	2	7	5	10	NO			—	—	6	—	9	NO		4	—	11	15
Avii	15	9	—	24	—	1	23	16	—	8	7	17	YES			17	7	6	—	18	NO		2	—	22	24
Aviii	7	7	—	14	—	—	14	9	2	3	3	11	YES			7	7	3	—	11	NO		3	1	10	14

by A; but there is no direct evidence that this would be useful. We have:

	$\to N_2an$	$? \to N_2an$	$\leftrightarrow N_2an$
A	7	3	4
$?A$	2	0	0
$\sim A$	9	0	6

This certainly does not suggest that both criteria are relevant. $\to N_2an$ would split four of the computer groups, 13D, 13E, 3B, and 10C that are contained within Av.

In order to make the classes more meaningful, we quote 4 OTUs from each class:

Ai   OTU   14 *and he* looked *severely* **at** them; ... /them = her words/   (b93)

     OTU   21 *"Come in and* look **at** it */the effigy/."*   (a23)

     OTU   25 *"He asked me if I could* look **after** him *till he came out, so ..."* /him = the dog/   (a18)

     OTU   33 *"We want* to talk **to** you, *Stuart."*   (b102)

Aii   OTU   54 *The dog* went **after** it */the rat/;* ...   (a24)

     OTU   69 *"I thought you were* agreeing **with** us?"   (b104)

     OTU   77 *He* kneeled down **in front of** her *and* ...   (b96)

     OTU   113 *... the tremendous vitality of her youth had faded out ...no, rather* sunk down **in** her.   (a17)

Aiii   OTU   49 "Come **out of** it, *there's nothing there."*   (a18)

     OTU   58 *The branches of the ancient yew* **under** which *they* stood *enlaced them with serpentine malevolence.*

     OTU   64 **From** it */the spade/ the tail* hung down, *swinging.*   (a28)

     OTU   130 *...: only young people and innocent countries could afford* to play about **like** this.   (b98)

Aiv   OTU   9 *Emma* looked **at** his face, *and* ...   (b96)

     OTU   17 *"Do you like* talking **about** life?"   (b92)

     OTU   26 *"Mr Bryce* deals **with** the bibliophiles — ..."   (a20)

OTU   39 *"I wondered if I could* trespass **on** your time and
          good nature." (b91)

Av   OTU   53 *A group of poplars, still topped with lemon-*
          coloured turbans, stood **beside** the gate; ...
                                                        (a23)

OTU   66 *afternoon rain* dripped **off** the roofs, ... (b93)

OTU   76 *A waitress* came **with** a cloth. (b96)

OTU 100 *He* looked up **at** Viola; ... (b101)

Avi OTU 103 *"One /objection/ is ... that you* weigh *intellectually,*
          instead of being a moral being and acting and
          letting your morality come out in your actions."
                                                        (b95)

OTU 117 *She* flushed *darkly,* **to** her forehead. (a21)

OTU 134 *The swans* slid **out of** sight, *making for some known*
          evening haunt in the creek's upper reaches.
                                                        (a21)

OTU 139 **Beneath** its cursing throat, *its midget hands* hung
          pink, useless, as if in supplication: ... /it = the
          rat/ (a25)

Avii OTU   94 *"But if she* worked **in** Woolworths *you wouldn't*
          call her a saint, ..." (b100)

OTU 102 *after a while she stopped dead close to the church*
          door and stood **with** her head poked forward.
                                                        (a27)

OTU 123 *Dr Adrian Carfax happened* **at** that moment *to*
          be passing by, ... (b100)

OTU 128 *She* strolled back **on** her tracks *and* ... (a29)

Aviii OTU 72 *"I* work **in** a bookshop." (a19)

OTU   88 *At once, all simple optimism and goodwill, the dog*
          emerged and bounded off **in** another direction.
                                                        (a19)

OTU 120 Rest **in** peace. (a29)

OTU 142 **Like** one moving in a barbaric rite of dedication
          towards some altar *she* stepped *onward and* ...
                                                        (a29)

Comparison with Target.

Ai contains 11B except for two OTUs (the last to join 11B), which are in Aiv.

Aii contains 12D.

Aiv contains 12E.

Av contains 13D, E, F, and one of the two members of 13G; the other is in Aviii.

Avi contains two of 13C; the third is unplaced, being ?*A*:

> OTU 119 **From** some distance *she* waved and nodded, *calling greeting and encouragement to Gwilym.* (a29)

If *A* had been rejected, it would be placed in Avi, otherwise in Aviii.

Avii contains most of 13A; but four members are in the adjacent Aviii, and two are unclassified. They have disagreement between *Qa* and *Qb*; if *Q* is accepted, they are placed in Av, otherwise in Avii:

> OTU 41 *She hurried to the gate*, looked **up** *and down* the road.
> (a24)
> OTU 42 *She hurried to the gate*, looked *up and* **down** the road.
> (a24)

Aviii contains 13B.

This comparison represents 85% success, if we treat partially unplaced OTUs as failures (even though they may be in the right region of the tree).

Notes

(1) One sequence was entered twice in the data, but coded independently (OTU 5 and OTU 83: ... *the woman he was* living **with**). Different responses were given for P, C, $\rightarrow N_1 in$. Here they are placed as "neighbours" (Ai and Aii) although Ai and Aii do not appear alike.

(2) The results suggest that other possible useful criteria are $\rightarrow N_2 pron$, $\rightarrow N_2 def$. We tested $\rightarrow N_2 pron$; those OTUs accepting the criterion were drawn from all groups, but those rejecting (or

querying) it were usually in Avi, vii, or viii, *not* Aiv or Av (2 exceptions in 28 cases). The criterion was rather difficult to apply, and could perhaps be subdivided into several pronominal types. Another possible criterion, which might perhaps stand in the same relation to →N_2*pron* as *A* does to *Q*, is "can *p* N_2 be replaced by an adverb ?" or even just "can N_2 be replaced by an adverb?".

(3) The method lends itself to a procedure based on recommendations in Wexler (1966). He suggests that one looks for rules, then notes the exceptions, and then searches for the rules governing the exceptions; and, again, that one should modify criteria to give better results. We can interpret the latter suggestion in two ways: the "better results" may be according to the linguist's belief, or according to the groups produced by the program.

(4) It is interesting to classify some "concocted examples" by this key:

(a) Ice *consists of water*   : Av
(b) They *slept in the bed*   : Aiv
(c) They *talked to themselves* : Av
(d) They *talked to the class*   : Aiv
(e) He *looks like a weasel*   : Av

All these examples represent high cohesion. From this point of view, (b) and (d) are satisfactorily classified as Aiv, whereas (a), (c), (e) are not. These last three are instances of conflict between *P* and *C* (see Section 2.3), and it might therefore be advantageous to use "*P* and/or *C*" in all cases. Notice that *C* need only be used when *P* is not satisfied. The reason why *P* is rejected in these examples is that co-reference obtains between N_1 and N_2, in which case we may talk about "exponential restriction" (see Section 2.2, p. 18) as opposed to "systemic restriction". Compare the same type of restriction in transitive verb clauses:

They admired *her.*   → She was admired (by them).

They admired *themselves.*→ *Themselves were admired.
?They were admired by themselves.

$$\text{They behaved } \textit{themselves.} \rightarrow \begin{cases} \text{*Themselves were behaved.} \\ \text{*They were behaved by themselves.} \end{cases}$$

Notice that the agent is obligatory in the transform *They were admired by themselves* whereas it is normally optional, as in *She was admired*.

(5) All Aiii reject *P*.

Conformity with Other Groups

The key was compared with five other groups of the output; it was consistent with them except for OTU 139 quoted as an Avi, for which *A* had been unacceptable; if *A* had been acceptable, the OTU would have been in Avii in common with the other members of 5B. Since it may be useful to give some idea of the external regions of the original classification, we give the OTUs in these groups, together with the last eight OTUs to be absorbed into groups. The percentages quoted with these eight OTUs and the four groups are the levels at which they were absorbed into the central groups.

Av 75% OTU 124 *and* **after** the dog went *the frantic voice* of Dinah, repeating ... (a24)

Aii 75% OTU 113 *... the tremendous vitality of her youth had faded out ... no, rather* sunk down **in** her. (a17)

Avi 75% OTU 133 *"I wanted to ask you what* happened **about** Mr Eborebelosa." (b92)

Aiii 80% OTU 64 **From** it |*the spade*| *the tail* hung down, *swinging.* (a28)

Avi 82% OTU 135 *A medley of disagreeable noises* broke **upon** their ears: *whimperings, moans, maniacal hoarse growls ...* (a23)

Aiii 82% OTU 130 *...: only young people and innocent countries could afford* to play about **like** this. (b98)

Aii   82%   OTU 110 *"Who* lived *here* **before** you?"   (a17)
Aiv   82%   OTU 11 *"But* ... *if people can* believe **in** God, *so much the better; ..."*   (b95)

Group 3B 80%

Av   OTU 67 "... *and how does this* apply **to** other people?"
                                                                    (b94)
Av   OTU 68 *What* goes **with** shishkebab?   (b97)
Av   OTU 52 *"It* comes **to** a bit more than that."   (a22)

Group 5B 86%

Avii   OTU 144 *weak sun drew out of the damp ground a haze*
                     within whose grained iridescence *shapes and*
                     colours combined *to create ...*   (a18)
Avii   OTU 129 *"A lot* happens **in** this cemetery."   (a27)
Avii   OTU 112 ... *her face had* hollowed **underneath** the
                     cheekbones, ...   (a17)
Avi   OTU 139 **Beneath** its cursing throat, *its midget hands*
                     hung *pink, useless, as if in supplication:* ...
                     /it = the rat/   (a25)

Group 12H 87%

Av   OTU 76 *A waitress* came **with** a cloth.   (b96)
Av   OTU 71 *The dog* bounded back **with** a stick, ...   (a22)

Group 10D 87%

Aiii   OTU 58 *The branches of the ancient yew* **under** which
                     they stood *enlaced them with serpentine*
                     malevolence.   (a26)
Aiii   OTU 49 "Come **out of** it, *there's nothing there."* (a18)

Group 10C 87%

Av   OTU 66 *afternoon rain* dripped **off** the roofs, ...
                                                                    (b93)

Av   OTU 61   *A sigh came out of the poplars and a few bright discs spun down and* settled **round** their feet.   (a26)

Av   OTU 53   *A group of poplars, still topped with lemon-coloured turbans,* stood **beside** the gate:...
                                                        (a23)

Av   OTU 75   *vodka* splashed **in** his glass; ...   (b107)

Av   OTU 60   *A* sigh came **out of** the poplars *and a few bright discs spun down and settled round their feet.*   (a26)

CLASSIFICATION OF THE OTUs

In this section we give a final classification of the OTUs, and with it both the OTUs themselves and their associated concept groups (see Section 8.4, pp. 174 ff.). The procedure used in constructing this classification was roughly the following:

We first attempted to form the best groups and to place the OTUs in the best order without splitting up the groups. We did not attempt to include all the OTUs in these groups. As a basis, we used the results of the inter-group analysis (see Section 8.32, pp. 148 ff.) and also visual inspection of the similarity matrix. The original groups were augmented by the addition of OTUs taken to be similar on the basis of the similarity matrix. We also added Group 12C, which is similar to 13A and 13I. Table 9:1 shows the order given in the inter-group analysis without reference to the features. The second column indicates the number of OTUs in each group. The third column shows the corresponding concept-formation groups (see Section 8.4, pp. 174 ff.). Table 9:1 accounts for 120 out of the total 146 OTUs. The "kernel" of this set of OTUs extends from 12B to 5B inclusive. Of the two groups at the top of the matrix, 12D is like its neighbour, 12B, but it is closer to 13E, F, D, and G than it is to 12E, 15I, 13O, and 10B; 15M has some similarity with all the groups that follow it, down to and including 13E. At the bottom of the matrix, 3B resembles various dissimilar groups in the kernel, and also, particularly, 15M; 10C is somewhat like 5B and also 13A, E, D; 5B is somewhat like 13P, and especially like 12C.

So far, the group-order had been determined by the overall similarity of their OTUs. Next, we arranged the groups according to the following TR-criteria which, though few in number, were found to be powerful (see Section 8.23, p. 123f., and Appendix 2,

TABLE 9:1

Group	No. of OTUs	Level 13 groups contained by the first column groups	Associated inter-group analysis groups (see Section 8.33)		Concept-formation groups	Features P A Q M D
15M	2	T	B_2 C_2	D_2	ii	− − + − +
12D	7	J	B_2 C_2	D_2	ii	− − + − ±
12B	13	H	B_2 C_2	D_2	i	+ − + − ±
10B	8	N	B_2 C_2	D_2	iv/i	+ − + − ±
13O	2	O	B_2 C_2	D_2	iv	+ − ± − −
15I	2	S	B_2 C_2	D_2	iv	+ − + − +
12E	11	K, L	B_2 C_2	D_2	iv	+ − + − ±
13G	3	G	B_1 C_2 C_1	D_2	v	− − ± − +
13D	4	D	B_1 C_2 C_1	D_2	v	− + + − +
13F	3	F	B_1 C_2 C_1	D_2	v	− ± + − ±
13E	6	E	B_1 C_2 C_1	D_2	v	− − + − +
13A	21	A	C_4 C_1	D_2	vii	− + ± − ±
12C	5				vii	− + ± − ±
13M	6	M	B_3 C_4 C_1		vii	− + − − −
13B	4	B	B_3 C_4 C_1		viii	− + − − −
13C	4	C	B_3 C_4 C_1		vi	− − − + +
13I	5	I	B_3 C_4 C_1		vii/viii	− + ± + +
13P	2	P	B_3 C_4 C_1		vi	− − − − ±
5B	4	R	B_4 C_3		vii	− + − + +
10C	5	Q, U	B_4 C_3		v	− + + − ±
3B	3	V	C_3		v	− − + − ±

pp. 232 ff.): P and C (which, as is shown in Appendix 2, almost invariably agree and hence may be given here simply as P), A, Q, M. In accordance with the results of Section 8.2, we ranked the criteria in the order P, A, Q, M (see also Appendix 3, pp. 247 ff.). This yielded a group-order which is only partially consistent with the order in Table 9:1. If, instead, A and Q are taken together, it is possible to produce an order that corresponds much more closely with that of Table 9:1. The groups are ordered by reference to Columns 1, 2, 3, and 4 in turn as follows: Column 1 begins with $+P$ followed by $−P$; the next pair of columns begin with $−A$,

TABLE 9:2

Sets	Groups/OTUs	No. of OTUs	P A Q M	Related groups and OTUs in the kernel
I	12B + 10B + 15I + 12E	34	+ − + −	
II	130	2	+ − ± −	
III	15M + 12D + 13E	15	− − + −	
IV	13G	3	− − ± −	
V	13F	3	− ± + −	
VI	13D + 10C	9	− + + −	
VII	13A + 12C	27	− + ± −	
VIII	13I	5	− + ± +	
IX	13B + 13M	9	− + − −	
X	5B	4	− + − +	
XI	13P	2	− − − −	
XII	13C	4	− − − +	
	3B	3	− − + −	13G 13N 10C
	12G	4	± − ± −	12D 12B
	10D	2	− ± + −	12D 13E (77)
	12H	2	− − + −	13E 13G 13F 10C 10B 12E
	122	1	− + ± −	13A 12C 13I
	78	1	− − ± −	12C (80)
	79	1	− + + −	10C 13F
	90	1	+* + ± −	12C 13A 10C
	101	1	−* − ± −	12E 13A 13D 13F 13G
	108	1	− − − −	13I 13B
	43	1	− − + −	12G
	54	1	− + + −	12D
	114	1	− + + +	12C 12H
	131	1	− + ± −	13A
	11	1	+ − + −	12G 10B 13H
	110	1	− + − −	12D (77)
	130	1	− + − −	12C 13B 13I
	135	1	− − − −	10C 5B
	64	1	− + + +	10C 5B
	133	1	− − − −	
	124	1	− − ± +	
	113	1	− − − −	

*   Here, *C* conflicts with *P*.

$+Q$, then $-A$, $\pm Q$, then $\pm A$, $+Q$, then $+A$, $+Q$, then $+A$, $\pm Q$, then $+A$, $-Q$, and finally $-A$, $-Q$; in the last column, $-M$ precedes $+M$. This gives Table 9:2 with 12 sets in the order I, II, ... XII. After Set XII are listed those groups and single OTUs which have not been included in the sets.

We list below all the OTUs in the order given in Table 9:2, attempting to achieve within each set (and the groups not placed in the sets) the most reasonable order suggested by visual inspection of the similarity matrix: The concept groups have been added in their simplest form, Ai-Aviii only; OTUs 41, 42, and 78 have been placed in Av rather than Aviii, giving Qb precedence over Qa (see Section 8.43, p. 189). Other doubtful cases were dealt with by treating $?A$ as $+A$, and by considering the predictions of Tree VI (see Section 8.43, p. 184). The Residue here is smaller than the collection of OTUs called "the Residue" in Chapter 8.

Set	Group	Con-cept	OTU	Text	Ref
I	12B	i	40	"*He'll* deal with it, *won't he?*" /he = the dog, it = the rat/	a24
		i	32	"*Must we* talk about him?"	b102
+P	(B₂)	i	31	"*And the way he* looks at me *sometimes.*"	b104
+Q		i	19	"It /*the rat*/ looked at me."	a27
		i	7	*he should be* thinking of her.	b96
		i	5	*They also looked benevolently on a morose, barrel-chested artist named Herman, and the woman he was* living with.	b99
		i	29	*and still they all* stared at each other *as if each had been the victim of a great betrayal.*	b107
		i	25	"He asked me if I could look after him *till he came out, so ...*" /him = the dog/	a 18
		i	33	"*We want* to talk to you, *Stuart.*"	b102
		i	16	"*..., because I've been wanting* to talk to you."	b 92
		i	14	*and he* looked *severely* at them;... /them = her words/	b 93
		iv	30	"*Have you* talked to this man Bates?"	b107
		i	3	"*But she's giving herself because of something she* believes in, *his work, and because she loves him.*"	b100

Set	Group	Con-cept	OTU	Text	Ref
	10B	i	21	*"Come in and* look at it *|the effigy|*."	a 23
		iv	26	*"Mr Bryce* deals **with** the bibliophiles- ..."	a 20
	(B₂)	iv	28	*The other* stared **at** the windows, *thinking they looked uncommunicative.*	a 17
		iv	20	"Look at its eyes, *just look.*"	a 25
		iv	9	*Emma* looked at his face *and said:* ...	b 96
		iv	15	*Emma was* referring **to** the fact that she had received two letters from Louis Bates, in which he had confessed his mad passion and sought to drag her some way towards the altar.	b 92
		iv	8	*Emma* asked **for** her coat, ...	b 96
		vi	37	"Look at this situation."	b100
	15I	iv	22	*...,* *Madeleine* thought *ruefully* of the hundred a year.	a 22
	(B₂)	iv	2	*he was* thinking, *specifically,* of the heavy bag of potatoes which he was carrying; ...	b 91
	12E	iv	4	*They also* looked *benevolently* on a morose, barrel-chested artist named Herman, and the woman he was living with.	b 99
		iv	1	*here in my universe there is someone who* talks **of** believing*!*	b 94
		iv	6	*they* prayed ... **to** To Whom It May Concern.	b 99
		iv	10	"*... and I* talk **about** life, *as I told you.*"	b 95
		iv	17	"*Do you like* talking **about** life?" "*... when you* talk **about** life."	
		iv	18	"*I won't* ask **for** details."	a 29
		iv	12	"*All I'm saying is that I don't* believe **in** public philosophies, ..."	b 94 / b 94
		v	146	"*I* believe in scrupulousness in the face of action."	b 94
		iv	27	"*He's only six; and not allowed* to play **with** rough children."	a 26
		iv	24	"*It |the bookshop| does* cater **for** what's called the cultivated reading public — *and for* specialists."	a 20
		iv	23	"*It |the bookshop| does* cater *for* what's called *the cultivated reading public* — *and* **for** specialists."	a 20

Set	Group	Con-cept	OTU	Text	Ref
II	130	iv	13	"*You know, I did* go **over** the whole thing *very carefully and seriously.*"	b 93
+*P* ±*Q*	(B₂)	iv	39	"*I wondered if I could* trespass **on** your time and good nature."	b 91
III +*Q*	15M (B₂)	ii	47	"*Truly,* what *do we* live **for** *?*"	b107
		ii	51	"*That's not all you* — what *you've been* living **on** *?*"	a 22
	12D	ii	62	"*Should we* run **for** him *?*"	a 26
		ii	83	*They also looked benevolently on a morose, barrel-chested artist named Herman, and the woman he was* living **with**.	b 99
	(B₂)	ii	105	"*I don't* know **about** you, *but I've enjoyed this.*"	b 95
		ii	69	"*I thought you were* agreeing **with** us*?*"	b104
		ii	46	"*It doesn't* worry **about** you, *you know.*" /it = your conscience/	b106
		ii	56	"*It* went **for** him *again and again — screeching.*" /it = the rat/	a 25
		ii	77	He kneeled down **in front of** her *and* ...	b 96
	13E	v	63	*She walked away ... and presently* returned **with** a large garden spade.	a 27
	(B₁)	v	45	"*You should stop* worrying **about** your conscience *so much.*"	b106
		v	84	*Carfax sat down and began* to puff *militarily* **at** his pipe; ...	b103
		v	81	*She* fished **for** her handkerchief *and* ...	a 28
		v	48	*They* went **out of** the gate *and* ...	a 17
		v	50	"*He said I must* stay **with** the children."	a 21
IV	13G	v	44	"*What Carfax means ... is that he's psychotic, that he* suffers **from** schizophrenia, *and is ...*"	b104
±*Q*	(B₁)	viii	145	*She said something to her companion, who* turned **from** a vague survey of the landscape *and* ...	a 17
		vi	35	*..., and you feel honoured that, when they* live **in** *such a thoroughly amiable world, they should* ...	b101
V	13F	v	57	"*At least we'd better* make **for** the Jeyes Fluid *as soon as possible.*"	a 25
±*A* +*Q*	(B₁)	v	74	*after a while she* stopped *dead* **close to** the church door *and* ...	a 27
		v	80	*professors nibbling cheese straws* peered **over** the tops of them *to see what was happening.*	b107

Set	Group	Con-cept	OTU	Text	Ref
VI	13D	v	59	"*Besides, he's* gone **to** the football match."	a 26
		v	85	"*He won't employ anybody who* trips up **on** his standards — of culture, *I mean*, and education."	a 20
+*A*	(B₁)	v	82	*they practically* lived **on** wheat germ.	b 99
+*Q*		v	70	*She* stopped *again* **on** a small bridge with white wood railings *to watch a pair of swans glide from the main stream into a ...* backwater.	a 21
	10C	v	66	*afternoon rain* dripped **off** the roofs, ...	b 93
		v	61	*A sigh came out of the poplars and a few bright discs spun down and* settled **round** their feet.	a 26
	(B₄)	v	53	*A group of poplars, still topped with lemon-coloured turbans,* stood **beside** the gate: ...	a 23
		v	75	*vodka* splashed **in** his glass; ...	b107
		v	60	*A sigh* came **out of** the poplars *and a few bright discs spun down and settled round their feet.*	a 26
VII	13A	vii	104	"*All I'm saying is that ..., that I want* to live **according to** my own lights, *and that ...*"	b 94
+*A*		vii	125	"*It /the rat/ 's* got **inside** this damned ..."	a 25
+*Q*		vii	137	*He* pulled **into** the kerb *and ...*	b 90
		v	41	*She hurried to the gate,* looked **up and down** the road.	a 24
		v	42	*She hurried to the gate,* looked *up and* **down** the road.	a 24
		vii	109	*They* went out, **down** the garden path.	a 16
		vii	128	*She* strolled back **on** her tracks *and ...*	a 29
		viii	73	"*/I/* Worked **in** rest centres *mostly*."	a 21
		viii	89	"*Sometimes I wish I could just go away and* start *again* **in** another town."	b 96 / b 96
		vii	55	*She* hurried **to** the gate, *looked up and down the road.*	a 24
		viii	143	*She* smokes **like** a chimney.	a 21
		viii	72	"*I* work **in** a bookshop."	a 19
		vii	93	**From** this wired stronghold *they* looked out *and ...*	a 26
		vii	99	"*They* fought **down in** that ditch — ..."	a 25
		vii	102	*after a while she stopped dead close to the church door and* stood **with** her head poked forward.	a 27
		vii	140	*What made them* stand **out of** the ordinary run *was that ...*	b 99

Set	Group	Con-cept	OTU	Text	Ref
		vii	127	*Like one moving in a barbaric rite of dedication towards some altar she stepped onward and* disappeared **below** the brow of the slope.	a 29
		vi	136	..., *Madeleine went slowly ... and* started **up** the road.	a 28
		vi	107	"*I* believe, *I suppose*, **in** my way; ..." (NB ambiguous)	b 94
		viii	142	**Like** one moving in a barbaric rite of dedication towards some altar *she* stepped *onward and ...*	a 29
		v	65	*Emma* looked **out of** the window, *feeling shaken and disturbed.*	b 93
	12C	vii	126	*The dog* sat down **on** his haunches *and ...*	a 27
		vii	98	*But the rat began* to run along the bottom of the ditch, *blood on its back,* ...	a 24
		vii	95	*The dog was no longer* sitting **in** the porch.	a 23
		viii	88	*At once, all simple optimism and goodwill, the dog emerged and* bounded off **in** another direction.	a 19
		vi	134	*The swans* slid **out of** sight, *making for some known evening haunt in the creek's upper reaches.*	a 21
		vi	36	"*His master had to give up his job and go and* live **in** the country — ...	a 18
VIII	13I	viii	115	*Turning over in her mind rumours that had reached her ...,* Madeleine paused **before** asking in a delicate way: ...	a 19
+*A*	(B₃)	viii	121	*and at once,* **with** automatic briskness, *Dinah* turned *and advanced to stand beside her.*	a 28
±*Q*					
+*M*		viii	87	*Watching him, Madeleine* continued **in** a vague and level manner: ...	a 20
		vii	123	*Dr Adrian Carfax happened* **at** that moment *to be* passing by, ...	b100
		vii	111	*Could Madeleine really have* retired **in** her prime, ...?	a 17
IX	13B	viii	138	*Observing what they took to be a bull in the next field, they* turned **for** home.	a 22
+*A*	(B₃)	viii	106	*Carfax ...* talked *jovially but* **with** a somewhat officers-to-men attitude, *and ...*	b103
		viii	120	Rest **in** peace.	a 29
		viii	141	*Madeleine walked forward and* stood **at** a little distance, ...	a 27

Set	Group	Con-cept	OTU	Text	Ref
	13M	vii	97	*Presently they* retired **to** the Kardomah Café *and ...*	b 92
		vii	94	"*But if she* worked **in** Woolworths *you wouldn't call her a saint, ...*"	b100
		iii	86	"*they have a code they can, and ought to,* live **by.**"	b 95
		vii	92	"*/If only I could/* Go **to** Oxford or Cambridge."	a 22
		vii	91	..., *for as he* chugged off **down** the High Street, *who should he see ...*	b 90
X +A +M	5B (B₄)	vii	144	*weak sun drew out of the damp ground a haze* **within** whose grained iridescence *shapes and colours* combined *to create ...*	a 18
		vii	129	"*A lot* happens **in** this cemetery."	a 27
		vii	112	*... her face had* hollowed **underneath** the cheekbones, ...	a 17
		vi	139	**Beneath** its cursing throat, *its midget hands* hung *pink, useless, as if in supplication* :... /it = the rat/	a 25
XI	13P (B₃)	vi	116	"*You do the proper moral thing, as it* appears **under** the gaze of the *New Statesman* or whatever the proper moral agencies are these days."	b105
		vi	132	"*With Mr Eborebelosa it's his colour, and with this other one it's his class that* come **into** the picture."	b 92
XII +M	13C (B₃)	vi	103	"*One /objection/* is ... *that you* weigh *intellectually,* **instead of** being a moral being and acting and letting your morality come out in your actions."	b 95
		vi	118	*and he* sprang *backwards* **with** a yelp, *nipped in the lip.* /he = the dog/	a 25
		viii	119	**From** some distance *she* waved and nodded, *calling greeting and encouragement to Gwilym.*	a 29
		vi	117	*She* flushed *darkly,* **to** her forehead.	a 21
	3B +Q	v	67	"*... and how does this* apply **to** other people?*"*	b 94
		v	68	*What* goes **with** shishkebab*?*	b 97
		v	52	"*It* comes **to** a bit more than that."	a 22

Set	Group	Con-cept	OTU	Text	Ref
	12G	v	100	*He* looked up at Viola ; ...	b101
	±*P*	v	96	*She* turned back to Carfax.	b101
	±*Q*	iv	38	*she could* look at Machiavelli or La Roche-foucauld *and find them innocent.*	b 98
		iv	34	... *and he* smiled *benevolently* at Viola.	b102
	10D	iii	58	*The branches of the ancient yew* **under** which *they* stood *enlaced them with serpentine malevolence.*	a 26
	±*A* +*Q*	iii	49	"Come **out of** it, *there's nothing there.*"	a 18
	12H	v	76	*A waitress* came with a cloth.	b 96
	+*Q*	v	71	*The dog* bounded back with a stick, ...	a 22
RESIDUE		v	122	*She handed the lead to Madeleine and* strode towards the church.	a 26
		v	78	... *and people* went by in their raincoats, *looking enclosed and self-contained.*	b 93
		v	79	*Outside the dusk was* creeping up **between** the market stalls, ...	b 93
		iv	90	Strike **on** the back of its head, *don't waver.*	a 28
		v	101	"*He just doesn't* respond to the terms on which we have him here."	b106
		vi	108	*Treece realised that Carfax and Viola had already* met **on** this point, *and* ...	b103
		v	43	*Treece* turned to Viola.	b104
		ii	54	*The dog* went after it /*the rat*/ ; ...	a 24
		v	114	**With** intermittent yelps of hysteria, *Dinah's dog* tore along *full pelt,* ...	a 18
		vii	131	"*It doesn't* show **under** the coat ; ..." /it = the stain/	b 96
		iv	11	"*But ... if people can* believe in God, *so much the better* ; ...	b 95
		ii	110	"*Who* lived *here* before you?"	a 17
		iii	130	...: *only young people and innocent countries could afford* to play about **like** this.	b 98
		vi	135	*A medley of disagreeable noises* broke **upon** their ears : *whimperings, maniacal moans, hoarse growls* ...	a 23
		iii	64	**From** it *the tail* hung down, *swinging.* /it = the spade/	a 28
		vi	133	"*I wanted to ask you what* happened **about** Mr Eborebelosa."	b 92
		v	124	*and* **after** the dog went *the frantic voice of Dinah, repeating on a full chest note* : ...	a 24
		ii	113	... *the tremendous vitality of her youth had faded out ... no, rather* sunk down **in** her.	a 17

10

LINGUISTIC ASSESSMENT

In Chapters 7, 8, and 9, the classification problems have been discussed regardless of the linguistic content of the features and of the nature of the OTUs. The discussion has been entirely based on the feature matrix and, especially, the similarity matrix derived from it. OTUs have been quoted for illustrative purposes only. In Chapter 9, the OTUs were classified by a two-fold process. Firstly, groups were defined with both the groups and the order of the OTUs within them determined by the similarity matrix (Table 9:1). Secondly, these groups were themselves ordered according to the four powerful criteria P, Q, A, and M (Table 9:2) in the way which seemed to give the best results obtainable by such a method. The ordering of the groups by criteria was adopted because the resultant order appeared to be at least as good as any other, and because the method was easily intelligible and a step towards a simple diagnostic key. The groups were in no way monothetically defined, and it is not always true that all OTUs in a group gave the same responses to these four criteria. Thus the presentation of Chapter 9 is essentially polythetic (see Chapter 6, pp. 60-61).

The linguist is, naturally, chiefly interested in finding a few key criteria, i.e. weighted, ordered criteria by means of which the classification, arrived at via a large number of unordered, unweighted criteria and a small number of OTUs, can be used for classifying new instances of strings of the same structure as the OTUs. The linguist's key may differ considerably from the taxonomist's; in our case, a coarser version of the taxonomist's key seems most realistic.

Table 9:2 gives us the four powerful criteria P, A, Q, M. For a preliminary classification, M may be omitted, since it is much the least powerful of the four, applying positively for only nineteen

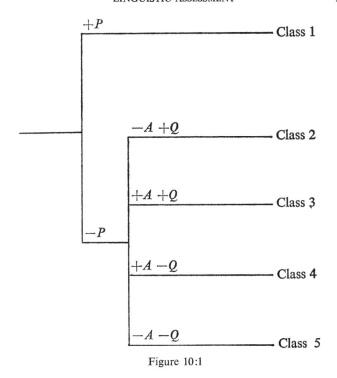

Figure 10:1

OTUs. Applying the remaining three criteria as in Table 9:2, we get the simple diagnostic key of Figure 10:1, where "$\pm$" and "?" features have been grouped with "$-$" features. This seems realistic, if we want a diagnostic key with maximum linguistic reliability; especially as we shall advocate the re-examination of OTUs with no positive key features.

We shall now use "class" to mean "the collection of representatives of a class in our data"; thus, statements about the relative sizes of the classes refer only to our corpus.

There are certain deficiencies in Figure 10:1; some can be overcome. First of all, cases of ?P may be re-examined by C; when the response is +C, the OTUs are placed in Class 1, otherwise they are treated as $-P$. (It might also be advantageous to use C rather than P when N_1 and N_2 are co-referent; see examples (7) and (9) in Chapter 2. However, there were no examples of this type in our data, and so it would confuse the issue to introduce this refinement here.)

A more fundamental difficulty is Class 5, which is the least satisfactory class both computationally and linguistically. Computationally it corresponds much less well with the sets of Chapter 9 than do the other classes; and linguistically there is both th e empiric objection that it has the worst correspondence with the degrees of cohesion (see Appendix 3) and the theoretical objection that it is defined entirely by negative features (cf., p. 19 and pp. 34f.). We quote three OTUs from this class to illustrate its diversity:

OTU 101: *"He just doesn't* respond **to** the terms on which we have him here." (b 106)

OTU 139: **beneath** its cursing throat, *its midget hands* hung *pink, useless, as if in supplication:* ... /it = the rat/ (a 25)

OTU 134: *The swans* slid **out of** sight, *making for some known evening haunt in the creek's upper reaches.* (a 21)

This class should be re-analysed. To a certain extent we could attempt to do this on the basis of our present data, using C and M as in Figure 10:2. This would transfer one OTU (101) to Class 1; and seven OTUs to Class 4, reducing Class 5 from 21 to 13 members. Nevertheless it is probable that other criteria not used in our experiment would be more efficient for this purpose (see Appendix 3, pp. 247ff.). The modified diagnostic key is given in Figure 10:3.

It will be observed that C has been used twice; in a small proportion of cases (none in our data) it will be used twice on the same OTU. The majority of cases using the second C node will however be for OTUs with $-P$, and so the two uses are almost independent; and the value of a criterion varies considerably according to context. Consequently the tree is not uneconomical, despite first appearances. The situation with regard to C may be summarized as follows:

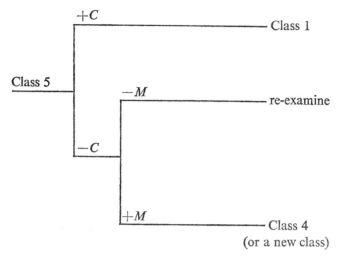

Figure 10:2

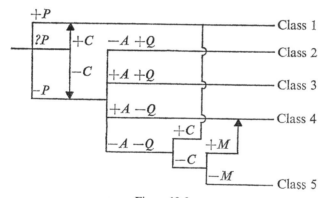

Figure 10:3

a) it is powerful as a first criterion, almost identical to *P*, but less reliable.

b) it is very weak after +*P*, probably very powerful after ?*P*, and weak after −*P*.

c) it is not very powerful in the context −*P*, −*A*, −*Q*, but it may be as powerful as anything else we have considered. The results of Section 8.34 (see in particular Figure 8:10, p. 171)

TABLE 10:1

The key of Fig. 10:3 gives us five classes with the following features and members ("/" means "not applied"):

CLASS	FEATURE P A Q	NO. OF MEMBERS	MEMBERS			ADDITIONAL OTUS
			TYPICAL SETS (and number of members)	TYPICAL GROUPS (outside sets)	EXCEPTIONS (OTUs in the typical sets, but not in the corresponding classes)	
CLASS 1	+ / /	41	I (34) II (2)		146 (in Set I)	36 (from Set VII) 35 (Set IV) 38 (12 G) 90 (Residue) 101 (Residue) 11 (Residue)
CLASS 2	− − +	24	III (15)	3B (3) 12H (2)	105 (in Set III) 77 (in Set III)	146 (from Set I) 57 (from Set V) 44 (Set IV) 34 (12G) 49 (10 D) 43 (Residue)

				5? (in Set V)	
		10	VI ? (9)		77 (from Set III)
					65 (from Set VII)
					58 (10 D)
					79 (Residue)
					54 (Residue)
					114 (Residue)
					64 (Residue)
CLASS 4	– + –	50	VII (27)	65 (in Set VII)	116 (Set XI)
			VIII (5)	136 (in Set VII)	122 (Residue)
			IX (9)	134 (in Set VII)	131 (Residue)
			X (4)	36 (in Set VII)	110 (Residue)
			XII (4)	117 (in Set XII)	130 (Residue)
					124 (Residue)
CLASS 5	– – –	13			105 (from Set III)
					136 (from Set VII)
					134 (from Set VII)
					117 (from Set XII)
					145 (Set IV)
					132 (Set XI)
					100 (12 G)
					96 (12 G)
					78 (Residue)
					108 (Residue)
					135 (Residue)
					133 (Residue)
					113 (Residue)

In the final column, "36 (from Set VII)" means that OTU 36 is in Set VII, which has been associated with a class (Class 4); "35 (Set IV)" means that OTU 35 is in Set IV, which has not been associated with any class; and similarly for the other examples.

suggest that N_1gender and N_2gender might in practice often be valuable, but they could not be entirely satisfactory.

The double use of C could be obviated by using C after — P as well as after $?P$, to make the first criterion "P and/or C", but this would mean unnecessary use of C on OTUs which have $-P$, $-C$, $+A$; and since almost all $-P$ OTUs have $-C$, and the majority have $+A$, this is not negligible[1]. Table 10:1 gives the five classes with the features and members.

Excluding Class 5, it appears that there is what can be called, very roughly, a scale of cohesion in strings consisting of verb plus one prepositional phrase, with Class 1 representing the closest cohesion between the structural elements and Class 4 the least. In support of this appraisal see Table 10:2, which shows the number of OTUs in each class possessing the various "degrees of cohesion" (see Appendix 3).

TABLE 10:2

DEGREE

	5	4	3	2	1	
CLASS 1	31	7	2^1	1^1		41
CLASS 2	1	7	12	1^2	3^3	24
CLASS 3			4	3	11	18
CLASS 4			4	12	34	50
CLASS 5	1	1	3	3	5	13
	33	15	25	20	53	146

[1] OTUs 35, 90 and 36. All these have -C.
[2] OTU 48.
[3] OTUs 71, 76 and 63. See Appendix 3, p. 249.
At this point the original classification is less misleading than this key.

[1] In our data we had:

+P	$?P+C$	$?P-C$	$-P+C$	$-P?C$	$-P-C+A$	$-P-C?A$	$-P-C-A$
38	2	1	4	2	58	3	38

It is noteworthy that the large sets I and VII are to be found in the classes at the poles, whereas the numerically small sets and, more especially, the single, marginal OTUs (which have resisted grouping on the basis of the *total* number of features) are largely placed in the intermediate classes.[2] This fact suggests that the selected key criteria are most adequate for the extreme classes and least adequate in the intermediate region.

Class 1, which is the second largest class, shows the greatest degree of cohesion, all strings admitting $+P$. This property predicts $-A$ and $-M$ and, almost always, $+Q$, and hence these criteria need not be applied for a simple, economical classification (see Section 3.4 on predictability and Section 8.34, pp. 155 ff.). For illustration, see Sets I, etc. (pp. 197 f.).

Class 2 also exhibits considerable cohesion ($+Q$, but not $+P$). There are no $+M$ and hardly any $+A$ in this class. For illustration, see Sets III, etc. (p. 199).

Class 3, the smallest class (excluding Class 5), accepts $+A$ and $+Q$ but not $+P$. For illustration, see Set VI, etc. (p. 200).

[2]   This is well shown in the two tables below: the first compares the proportion of members in each class that come from one of the twelve sets; and the second the number that are correctly assigned by use of the typical sets.

	CLASS 1	CLASS 2	CLASS 3	CLASS 4	CLASS 5	TOTAL
In a Set	38	18	13	45	6	120
Not in a Set	3	6	5	5	7	26
Total	41	24	18	50	13	146

	CLASS 1	CLASS 2	CLASS 3	CLASS 4	CLASS 5	TOTAL
Correctly predicted by Set	35	15	11	44	0	105
Remainder	6	9	7	6	13	41
Total	41	24	18	50	13	146

Class 4, the largest class, is characterized by $+A$ and $-P$, $-Q$. It is characteristic of this class that it has a wide range of different p exponents. The 50 OTUs of Class 4 have 26 different prepositions as compared with the 41 OTUs of Class 1, which have only 10 different prepositions (and, indeed, only 21 different exponents of $V + p$). For illustration, see Sets VII, etc. (pp. 200 f.). There are a number of additional questions that arise in connexion with our final key, and it seems simplest to deal with them piecemeal.

First of all, does the key give a reasonably adequate representation of the results in Chapters 8 and 9? Considering fn. 2 or the results of Chapter 8, it appears that it does, within the limitations of its simplicity. There are, indeed, both improvements and deteriorations with respect to, for example, the computer output. The deteriorations are not all of the same type; they include the transference of OTU 36 from Set VII to Class 1 (through what may be an anomalous P response — an inevitable hazard in using a key, unless the key criteria are of the constituent type) and the absorption of a group (12H) containing OTUs 76 and 71 (see p. 203). On the other hand, many of the OTUs in the Residue are, intuitively, reasonably placed. In any case, it seems likely from Chapter 8 that a completely adequate representation can only be obtained by considerable over-refinement. Whether this would remain true if we extended the experiment, or rather, whether only a key that was extremely complex would be sufficient to represent the linguistic situation, we cannot decide merely on the basis of this experiment.

Another problem is the mutual relationship of the classes, or at least of Classes 1-4. Part of the answer to this has already been posited: that the classes form a cline, but with the largest classes at the extremities. The results of Appendix 5, and the analysis of Section 8.3, suggest that this is not the complete picture, however. Similarly, the final results of Section 8.34 suggest that the situation is basically a cross-classification (see Section 7.24). Very tentatively, we may say that the situation seems to be one of "serial relationship", that is, one in which there are various grammatical categories of common occurrence, with a number of less

common intermediate or marginal categories, which might be diagrammatically represented as in Figure 10:4.

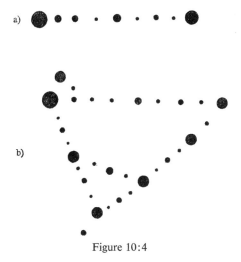

Figure 10:4

To this argument it could be objected that the intermediate
classes that we have found have been admitted to be ill-founded,
and also that Class 4 should be redivided; but it seems likely that
the general picture is of this type nevertheless.

The key has been defined as incomplete, since Class 5 has been
selected for re-analysis. Apart from this, we may consider the
adequacy of the classification; this is rather difficult to consider,
and perhaps all that can be said is that it seems on the whole
reasonable, but is far from adequate (see Appendix 3, pp. 247 ff.).

This key is considerably coarser than the "taxonomic" key.
The main reason is that this was designed as a pilot experiment
in numerical taxonomy applied to linguistics, and in view of the
insufficient size of the material and number of criteria, we cannot
hope to produce now a both reliable and refined classification
which should be applicable to new instances outside the material.
It is perhaps worth emphasizing that, although the OTU classification and the diagnostic keys derived from it are based on the
corpus used for the experiment, our ultimate aim is not to obtain

the best classification of this closed corpus but rather to gain insight into the particular problem in order to obtain a classification which can then usefully and economically be applied to an infinite corpus.

A general assessment of the success of the experiment will be made in the next chapter.

11

CONCLUSION

In this study we have discussed some general problems of classification in linguistics and described an experiment in numerical taxonomy applied to a segment of English syntax (N_1 V p N_2-strings). In this connexion, our principal aim has been to provide material for an evaluation of our methods rather than to gain insight into the specific illustrative problem.

The question, therefore, that remains to be answered here is the suitability of this technique for linguistic research. The program we have used was, after all, primarily intended for the classification of bacteria, and one may expect such work to present rather different problems from the classification of prepositional strings. Certainly, the originator of the program has never claimed that it is appropriate for all kinds of data. The program imposes only one restriction on the type of data on which it is to be used, viz. that the material should *segment into natural classes in a single way*. Even with data that segment in more than one way, it may still be valuable to find out *one* of the ways in which it does so. The origin of the program is relevant only insofar as it was designed to obtain a unique set of exclusive classes (and thence a nested hierarchy); it was not designed to look for a partitioning (see Appendix 1). We have found, in this and a subsequent experiment, that the aims of the program were achieved quite successfully. In addition to using the basic facilities of WHI (see Section 7.11, pp. 67 ff.), we have used other techniques, such as inter-group analysis (Section 8.3, pp. 141 ff.), which enabled us to refine the output further, to define certain overlapping groups and to relate to the classification OTUs not placed in these groups.

It may be asked how far mutually exclusive classes are suitable for descriptive statements in English syntax. We have attempted to begin an answer to such a question by conducting the present experiment. Our work has not presupposed any particular linguistic theory, and indeed we assume that increased knowledge of linguistic structure, as in our illustrative example, would be valuable for any approach.

In evaluating the suitability of the method for our particular problem, it is to be noted that the results give us a few fairly distinct classes with some partially overlapping classes. There is a certain amount of subsidiary or minor cross-classification, but the program is quite capable of dealing with this, provided that the cluster-analysis is supplemented by visual inspection of the similarity matrix or by inter-group analysis.

We must distinguish between major and minor cross-classification. A simple example of major cross-classification represented on a shaded matrix could resemble the following figure:

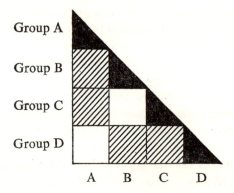

Here, the OTUs of Group A are as much like those of Group C as those of Group B, and there is a similar situation in the other cases of intermediate shading. Consequently, it would be equally valid to divide the OTUs in either of two ways: A + B, C + D, corresponding to the matrix we have shown, and also A + C, B + D, corresponding to a precisely similar matrix.

An example of minor cross-classification could resemble:

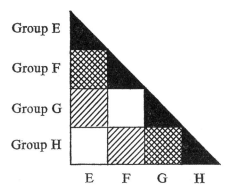

Here it is likely that there is a set of features which distinguish Group E from Group F, and Group G from Group H, but the set is small in number, so that for example the OTUs of Group E and Group F resemble each other more than those of Group E and Group G. In any case, the division E + F, G + H is satisfactory but the division E + G, F + H is not.

It is likely that various monothetic methods (see Ch. 6, pp. 60f.) would be efficient in giving good diagnostic keys, although they would probably be on the whole less illuminating. (For an account of some of these methods, see Lance & Williams 1965; and, also, Appendix 1.8, p. 230).

The suitability of program is a less serious problem in our case than that of setting up a feature matrix to represent the material adequately. Some aspects of this difficulty have been discussed in Sections 7.12-3, pp. 72ff. Here, we may further mention the lack of information due to insufficient number of criteria as suggested in Appendix 3. This insufficiency may be attributed to the fact that we need many criteria which will be relevant at only a small number of points in the classification. It may be difficult for the linguist to find sufficient criteria and, even if this were possible, there are the problems of obtaining responses and encoding them.

We should also consider whether the sample is reasonably adequate to represent occurrences of the structure we have chosen to classify. The large number of virtually unclassified OTUs (29 out of 146, i.e. almost 20%) suggests that 146 OTUs are insufficient to provide a comprehensive classification.

Another cause for concern is the rather narrow genre of English that constitutes our present corpus (see Section 4.2, p. 41) — especially in view of the fact that the OTUs are taken from only two stretches of 5000 words each and can hardly be representative of the language as a whole. We may add that there is an additional skewing factor: strings are frequently repeated almost word for word, so that a particular class might consist of several instances of a single phrase, such as *look at*. This is not to say that repetitious usage is necessarily unrepresentative; it may be in fact that repetition or more abstract recurrence of structurally similar items may be a characteristic of language as such.[1]

---

[1] In comparing the texts with the final classification of the OTUs in Chapter 9, we formed the impression that OTUs close together in the classification were relatively frequently close together in a text. We have not investigated this fully; it might be profitable to do so with a larger corpus. One factor that would contribute towards such a phenomenon is any stylistic bias towards particular categories. We had:

SETS

		I, II	III-V	VI-VIII	IX-XII	REMAIN-DER	TOTAL
TEXT	a	12	10	31	11	13	77
	b	24	11	10	8	16	69

(The Sets have been grouped together in this way to avoid very low values in the cells.) This table considered as a 2×5 contingency table is significant at the 99% Level. (We used the χ^2-test; see Kenney & Keeping 1951, p. 232.) The effect of mere lexical repetition on this table was not considered, however.
Another factor that could result in the same phenomenon is a variation from place to place in a particular text, in the relative frequencies with which items are chosen from particular categories. This factor may well occur in both texts, but we have not verified this. The evidence for such a variation seems stronger in Text a; for example, if we consider the five cases where there are two Text a OTUs with different exponents of V in the same sentence,

We may now briefly recall the specific aims stated in Section 3.4. (pp. 33 ff.) and question the extent to which the experiment has been successful.

(*a*) SIMPLE. If we think of the results presented in Chapter 10, the answer must be "yes".

(*b*) COMPREHENSIVE. As can only be expected in a pilot experiment, this aim has not been attained.

(*c*) GENERAL. On the whole, the answer is "yes".

(*d*) PREDICTIVE. Our impression is that this requirement has been met, which is borne out by the results in Appendix 3.

(*e*) OBJECTIVE. We are confident that this requirement has been met.

(*f*) CONSISTENT WITH INTUITION. On the whole, "yes". It might be objected that, if a classification gives exactly the results the linguist hoped for, there is no need for experiments. However, our use of "consistency" here does not mean that the results can be forecast but rather that, confronted with the results, the native speaker should find them sensible and, preferably, also suggestive.

(*g*) EXTENDABLE. Since this is the first experiment of its kind, this question must be left open, but we are inclined to believe that the answer is "yes".

(*h*) STIMULATING. Despite the obvious defects of our provisional classification, it seems fair to say that it does give some insight into the nature of the specific problem and, which is perhaps more interesting, into the more general nature of linguistic structure.

---

we find that on three of the five occasions they come from the same subdivision of the classification. The chance that this would happen if there were no association is less than 1/300. The smallness of the numbers 3 and 5 does not reduce the force of this result, but the fact that we have only found such a result for one part of one novel certainly prevents us from generalising from it. No similar result can be established with regard to the sentences of Text b. A full investigation of this problem would require considerable linguistic and statistical care. (The five pairs of Text a OTUs cited above were:

OTUs 112 & 113 in Set X and the Residue respectively
OTUs 74 & 102 in Set V (13F) and Set VII (13A) respectively
OTUs 55 & 41 in Set VII (13A)
OTUs 60 & 61 in Set VI (10C)
OTUs 142 & 127 in Set VII (13A).)

To the question, therefore, "Does the procedure yield worthwhile results for the type of problem considered here, bearing in mind the labour it involves?", we can give a provisional affirmative answer, subject to the requirement that there is available a program with the facilities of CLASP and preferably also the capacity to produce a diagnostic key. (Some diagnostic facilities are proposed in Appendix 4.)

There are also numerous other problems which remain to be solved before the merits of the method can be finally assessed. We have already mentioned some of the difficulties involved in finding criteria, in the satisfactory assessment of their inter-relationships, and in their encoding. To this may be added the importance of improving methods for eliciting informant reactions, and the whole question of the nature of criteria, including a refinement of the present rather crude division of criteria into overt and covert. These difficulties might be overcome by "experiment-chains", that is, by performing a series of computational experiments, the output of one experiment being used to help in the selection and encoding of criteria and string types in subsequent experiments. This procedure is potentially cyclic and cumulative.

APPENDIX 1

PREDICTIVE POWER

We begin by stating the underlying ideas of this appendix, and then apply them to a number of situations. We consider a set of OTUs together with its feature matrix. (See Section 7.11, pp. 66 ff.) Unless otherwise stated, we suppose that we are interested only in these OTUs (and not in some larger population from which they have been drawn), and that all that is known about them is coded within the feature matrix.

We suppose now that we do not have direct access to the feature matrix, but that instead we know certain facts about it. These facts might, in a simple case, consist of the feature inventories, and, perhaps, certain logical relations between the criteria. (See, for example, Section 7.12, pp. 72 ff.) More generally, we might suppose that the OTUs had been divided into groups, and that we know the feature inventories for each group. Plainly such knowledge places restrictions on the possible feature matrices consistent with it; the more extensive the knowledge is, the smaller the number of permissible feature matrices.

A possible measure of our lack of knowledge is the total number N of distinct feature matrices for these OTUs which are consistent with the knowledge we have. In conformity with information theory, we take logarithms (the results are not affected by the choice of base), and define IGNORANCE as $\log N$. If the OTUs are partitioned into a number of groups, the ignorance for the whole is the sum of the ignorance of each group.

Since only one of the N possibilities is correct, $1/N$ could be construed as the probability of selecting the right feature matrix provided we considered all the possible feature matrices as equally likely. This, however, is not very illuminating; N is usually very large, and the various incorrect possibilities are not all equally poor.

A more realistic probability measure of the value of the knowledge can be obtained by considering the totality of possible entries instead of the totality of possible matrices. We may consider, under the same conditions of equal likelihood as those mentioned in the preceding paragraph, the probability of selecting a correct entry in a given column when an entry position is chosen at random. We call this the ENTRY-PROBABILITY.

Another useful measure is one which compares the ignorance under two different conditions, an initial condition and a derived condition in which additional knowledge has been supplied. If the initial ignorance is $\log M$ ($\log M \neq 0$; if $\log M = 0$ we already have complete knowledge) and the lessened ignorance after supplying the additional information is $\log N$, we define

$$ gain = \frac{\log M - \log N}{\log M} = 1 - \frac{\log N}{\log M} $$

gain is a number between 0 and 1 which commonly has values that are convenient to work with, inasmuch as, in practice, it takes values distributed fairly uniformly between 0 (in which case the additional knowledge is worthless) and 1 (in which case we have acquired complete knowledge).

APPENDIX 1.1

If any group of these OTUs is given, we may make various assumptions concerning what is known about it. Our normal assumption will be that we possess its feature inventories, that we know for example that there are 12 cases of P, 1 of $?P$ and 19 of $\sim P$; 15 cases of $N_1 pron$ and 17 of $N_1 noun$; and so on. This could also be expressed by saying that we know both the proportion of members possessing each feature and the total number of members in the group. The ignorance in the group is then the logarithm of the number of ways in which the features could be distributed among the OTUs while still preserving the inventories. This seems reasonable: if every feature is either universal in the group or never occurs at all, then there will be only one way in which features can be assigned to the OTUs, and we shall have no doubt at all about the nature of OTUs in the group. If, however, there is feature irregularity in the group, we shall have doubt because there will be many ways of making the assignment. Ignorance is a more delicate measure than calculating the chance of assigning the right features to a random OTU, and is easily calculated with the aid of a table of logarithms of factorials, as, for example, Dwight 1961. It can of course be calculated for the group consisting of all the OTUs.

The a priori knowledge we assume concerning the group can be made more complex. For example, we can suppose that we are given some relationships between criteria, in particular that one is subordinate to another (e.g. Ap to A), or that features are conditional on each other (e.g. N_2an and $\rightarrow N_2an$). The knowledge required to cover these cases is simply knowledge of which entries in each test are incompatible with certain entries for the other tests. More generally, we could assume that there was knowledge of the actual co-occurrence of features, if it was felt that such knowledge was trivial; for example, we could supply the information that in 94 cases of N_1pron, 4 are indefinite and 90 definite, whereas in 29 cases of N_1noun, 12 are indefinite and 17 definite. Similarly, we could assume knowledge of the *likelihood* of co-occurrence of features, although this would complicate the calculations. The simplest assumption to make would of course be that we knew nothing, but this seems futile: if we are going to use groups, we presumably wish to associate some knowledge with them.

In Appendix 1.2-7 we suppose that some partitioning of some or all of the OTUs into groups is given. How it has arisen is immaterial; it could be the output of a program, an intuitive clustering, a partitioning by texts, a partition made according to a selected criterion, or merely a random division. As usual, we assume that the feature inventories are given with the partitioning.

APPENDIX 1.2

We can consider the diagnostic value of each criterion with respect to a partitioning. In assigning such a value to a criterion, we consider the result of applying it to the OTUs, i.e. we suppose that we know which OTUs have each of the features appertaining to the criterion. We then consider in how many ways we can place the OTUs in the groups, subject to this knowledge; let this number be n. (Suppose, for example, that there are two groups, one with 10 members, 9 of which accept P and 1 of which does not, and another with 5 members, none of which accept P. This gives 15 OTUs in all, 9 of which accept P and 6 of which do not. In placing them in groups, our only uncertainty will be which of the 6 not taking P should be placed in the first group — there are 6 ways of making this decision, and so n is 6.) Then, as before, we take logarithms, so that the DIAGNOSTIC UNCERTAINTY is $\log n$. This number (or n itself) is adequate to order the criteria as we did in Section 8.2, but it is more convenient to consider a new parameter, the diagnostic value, obtained from the diagnostic uncertainty by a "normalising" process: if the overall uncertainty as defined in Appendix 1.1 is p and the diagnostic uncertainty is q, the DIAGNOSTIC VALUE of a criterion is defined as $(p - q)/p$. This is a number which varies from 0 to 1; it is 0 if the criterion is of no help at all, which can only happen if it is always answered in the same way, and it is 1 if the groups are completely determined by it. (If we are dealing with a large population beyond the OTUs in the data, the definition should be framed so as to give the value 0 if the answers appear to be randomly distributed with respect to the groups, but *not* here, since it is helpful to know the exact distribution even if it *is* random.)

The CRUDE PREDICTIVITY of a feature, as used once in Section 8.2, is the probability of choosing the right group if, each time, the group with the greatest number of occurrences of the feature is chosen; for a criterion, the crude predictivity is the sum of the crude predictivity of the corresponding features each multiplied by its own frequency of occurrence. Its only advantage is its extreme simplicity.

APPENDIX 1.3

We can also define the PREDICTIVE VALUE of a criterion in any group G (which could, in particular, consist of all the OTUs). To do this we partition the OTUs of G according to the features corresponding to the criterion, and calculate the OVERALL UNCERTAINTY (see Appendix 1.1) of the partitioning. This quantity can be "normalised" with respect to the uncertainty of G itself to give the predictive value (as in the definition of diagnostic value in Appendix 1.2, where q was normalised with respect to p). We consider the criterion with the highest predictive value (or lowest overall uncertainty) as the most predictive in G.

APPENDIX 1.4

Both Appendices 1.2 and 1.3 can be generalised to include considering a number of criteria simultaneously, but this would normally be too unwieldy to be worthwhile, because of the large number of possible sets of criteria and the labour of finding the co-occurrences of the various features. A reasonable application would be in the case of related criteria; this idea was used in Section 8.34.

APPENDIX 1.5

With regard to a single group, the reasonable way to define the deducibility of a binary criterion is "the probability of giving the correct answer". If, for example, a group has P 9 times and $\sim P$ once, it would be sensible to guess P, and this would be right in 9/10 cases. However, this is inadequate if there are more than two features. In our experiment, $N_2 form\text{-}class$ had three features, and we would say that it was better known in a group with $N_2 pron$ 16 times, $N_2 name$ 5 times, $N_2 noun$ once than in one with $N_2 pron$ 16 times, $N_2 name$ 3 times, $N_2 noun$ 3 times.

We therefore define AMBIGUITY for a criterion with respect to a partitioning as "the logarithm of the number of ways of assigning the criterion's features to the OTUs, given the feature inventories of the OTUs in the groups".

An example of the way the definitions work when there is only one group may make the situation clearer. Suppose there is a criterion with two features, each of which occurs twice in the group, so that the group has 4 members; the possible assignments are as follows:

	Correct	Other possibilities consistent with inventory					
OTU 1	+	+	+	−	−	−	24 assignments of entries: 6 cases, applying to 4 OTUs
OTU 2	+	−	−	+	+	−	
OTU 3	−	+	−	+	−	+	
OTU 4	−	−	+	−	+	+	
correctly marked +	2	1	1	1	1	0	
correctly marked −	2	1	1	1	1	0	
Total correct	4	2	2	2	2	0	12 correct assignments

The probability of guessing the entry correctly for any particular OTU is 12/24 or 1/2, and if, for example, we consider only OTU 1 above, this could be construed as meaning that the first 3 possibilities give the correct answer, and the same number give the wrong answer. The ambiguity is $\log 6$, 6 being the number of columns; so that in considering ambiguity we are considering the chance of every OTU being simultaneously given the correct feature rather than the chance of an arbitrary OTU being given the correct feature, and we are ignoring the fact that some incorrect combinations are worse than others. The advantage of this system is that it generalises easily.

We could alternatively define DEDUCIBILITY as the entry-probability defined in the introduction to this appendix, that is, the probability, given an arbitrary assignment consistent with the feature inventory in the group of the particular criterion, that any particular OTU will be assigned the correct feature. This definition is better than the original, being more sensitive, equally general, but more complex. We give a three feature example, in which features are coded as 1, 2, 3:

	correct	
OTU 1	1	1 1 1 1 1 1 1 1 1 1 1 2 3 2 3 2 3 2 3
OTU 2	1	1 1 1 1 1 2 3 2 3 2 3 3 2 1 1 1 1 1 1
OTU 3	1	1 2 3 2 3 3 2 1 1 1 1 1 1 3 2 1 1 1 1
OTU 4	2	3 1 1 3 2 1 1 3 2 1 1 1 1 1 1 3 2 1 1
OTU 5	3	2 3 2 1 1 1 1 1 1 3 2 1 1 1 1 1 1 3 2

$$\text{probability} = \frac{44}{20 \times 5} = \frac{11}{25}$$

This definition gives a lower probability than the former definition. Thus, taking this particular case, the probability according to the original definition is 3/5, because we should always guess feature 1, which would be right in 3 cases out of 5, whereas the probability just calculated is $\frac{11}{25} < \frac{15}{25} = \frac{3}{5}$. (This is quite general: if the proportions of features 1, 2, ... r are $p_1, p_2, \ldots p_r$ respectively, where $p_1 \geqslant p_2 \geqslant \ldots \geqslant p_r$, it can be shown that the first definition gives p_1, while the second gives $p_1^2 + \ldots + p_r^2$.

Furthermore $p_1 = p_1[p_1 + \ldots + p_r]$ (because $p_1 + \ldots + p_r = 1$)

$$= p_1^2 + p_1 p_2 + \ldots + p_1 p_r$$
$$> p_1^2 + p_2 p_2 + \ldots + p_r p_r$$
$$= p_1^2 + p_2^2 + \ldots + p_r^2$$

The first definition does not in any way represent our *total* knowledge, however.

In generalising to many groups, the complexity grows because the total number of guesses and the number of correct guesses have to be calculated separately.

Once again, the criterion-ambiguity can be normalised as for diagnostic value in Appendix 1.2, to give DEDUCTIVE VALUE, which represents the improvement in performance of the classification with respect to the criterion concerned after making the partition. (This is of more interest for some purposes, as indicating at what point it is sensible to predict a feature, i.e. it helps to indicate that a feature should be predicted when we are satisfied that an OTU is in one subgroup, but not before.)

APPENDIX 1.6

If we considered all possible divisions of the OTUs into two groups, we could rank these divisions by comparing their uncertainties; we should in general discover that one partitioning was the best. However, unless the number of OTUs was very small, the process as described would not be feasible: if we make the assumption that a computer could deal with each partition in 10^{-6} seconds, which is certainly untrue at present, the process applied to our data (146 OTUs) would take perhaps 10,000000,000000,000000 times a very recent estimate of the age of the universe. However, a process such as this but with various different evaluations has been used by Dr. R. Needham, and the method is, roughly, to try one partition and then vary it until every variation gives poorer results. There is no reason to suppose that the resulting partition is the best; but it is at least the best among its neighbours. The process is repeated until new partitions fail to appear, and will normally have yielded a number (possibly only one) of partitions all of which we may call *maximal*.

This leads to a simple definition of CROSS-CLASSIFICATION: the data form a natural cross-classification if and only if there is more than one maximal partition. It would even be possible to measure the extent of cross-classification by the difference between the various maximal partitions. Thus, if there were just two, and these differed only in their placing of 2 OTUs, we should say that the degree of cross-classification was negligible, and normally ignore it.

We may extend these ideas in two ways. In the first place, we could consider arbitrary partitions into any number of groups; this is hardly feasible as a practical measure, except by selecting the partitions initially on some other grounds. Alternatively, we could divide the groups formed earlier by applying the process described above.

This leads to the search for a best partitioning in complete generality. The more groups we have, the less the uncertainty can become, until, with as many groups as OTUs, it is bound to be 0. However, it seems sensible to use a variety of intermediate stages, and we normally think of one stage as optimal; this can be made precise *if* we can "count the cost" of having a certain number of groups.

Another aspect that may be considered is that of a "NATURAL" GROUP. We can approach a definition in some such way as this: there is a graph that can be drawn of the average ignorance for a group of given size, extending from its maximum, when the group is all the OTUs, and descending to 0, when every group has only one member; if a group is "significantly" better than the average group of its size, it is a natural group. It would perhaps be better to restrict the definition rather more; we need an evaluation of the value of a group for its size, which, if a group is to be natural, should be significantly high (so that there is now the possibility of having no natural groups of some sizes), and we should add the restriction for a natural group that this evaluation should not increase if an OTU is added or removed, nor perhaps if one is exchanged with one in its complement. These considerations lead us to modify the earlier definition of "local" (see Section 7.12, p. 83): a "local" group is one whose members satisfy some condition amongst themselves without reference to the members of the complement, *even if* the condition is defined with reference to the *whole data*. We have made these definitions because we found them helpful in thinking about the nature of clustering techniques, and have only used them illustratively. Such groups will normally be expected to be maximal in some way, but when they have been established, their members must satisfy the internal condition. We may notice that McQuitty's methods (see fn. 1, p. 66) can produce natural and overlapping groups; linkage methods can also do this, although single linkage will not produce overlapping groups. Natural groups are local. The union of all natural groups might leave a "rubbish dump" or residue (the complement of the union).

APPENDIX 1.7

Given any partition, we can calculate its uncertainty as in Appendix 1.1. We can therefore use Appendix 1.1 to evaluate the merits of various partitions, whether produced by programs or not. We have not attempted to do this here, except in Section 8.34, and since many of our partitions are into different numbers of groups, it is not easy to compare them with confidence.

APPENDIX 1.8

The idea of Appendix 1.7 immediately supplies a reasonable method of ranking criteria directly from the feature matrix, without reference to any given partition. The criteria are ranked by the partitions they induce, that is, by how successful they are in forecasting the features of the remaining criteria. The process could be extended to give a hierarchical classification; thus, one criterion could be obtained, with its induced partitioning, and then the whole process could be repeated on the two or more induced groups separately, leading to two or more new rankings of the remaining criteria. (In practice these rankings are often appreciably different from each other.) Successive repetitions generate more refined subdivisions of the various branches. The process could in theory be refined by considering complexes of criteria, and by following up more than one line if, at some point in the process, there was little to choose between a number of criteria. If one criterion was applied on all those branches immediately depending on another criterion, this could be considered as minor cross-classification; and if the two criteria were virtually equally powerful, it could be considered as major cross-classification. (See Chapter 11, pp. 216f).

APPENDIX 1.9

We began by making certain restrictions. One was that the population was finite and that every member was accounted for in the data, and in our case this is very inappropriate. The situation could very easily be remedied if we assumed that the proportions of features in groups would remain constant; in fact the formulae become somewhat simpler. However, this assumption is unrealistic. We assumed in a separate experiment that the groups would persist, however many OTUs were added, and we attempted to base the calculations on a reasonable notion of how much variation in the proportions of features there might be. Again, we know that the feature matrix does not contain all the information about the OTUs that exists, but this seems a difficult point to discuss. There are situations in which new information is added continually, e.g. that of a program trying to form concepts in a game such as chess and learning to improve them and its use of them by play; it has no method of gaining information without playing, and so its situation is essentially one in which it must start from nothing and build up to success. We do not put our program in this situation, but if we consider *ourselves* as inside the process, we can consider the *whole* process as being of this type.

Furthermore, it seems theoretically possible to have programs which are used on various sets of data and which apply what they have learned from one set to another, although this is perhaps more than we can reasonably demand in practice.

APPENDIX 2

SOME STATISTICAL CONSIDERATIONS

The principal problems have already been mentioned in Sections 8.1 and 7.13: they are the viability of the groups when considered in relation to the whole population, the significance of any association between these groups and the features, and the extent to which the classification would persist if different criteria were used. There are perhaps two approaches to assessing the significance of the results; one is to apply numerical tests to the output, and the other is to repeat all or part of the experiment on new data, or to use a different classification method.

APPENDIX 2.1 — NUMERICAL TEST ON THE OUTPUT

There are two related questions that need to be answered for the type of data under consideration in this study: whether or not there is any appearance of structure in the output beyond what might reasonably be expected if the features were assigned to the OTUs at random (or, more precisely, if they were assigned at random in such a way as to preserve the feature inventories, and so that any logical constraints between the criteria were observed); and whether or not there is sufficient evidence to show that such structure would extend to the whole population of OTUs. A perfect answer to the second question would include a consideration of the effect of using different criteria, but it is obviously not possible to do this in the absence of appropriate data. Since we do not possess such data, either for this or for any similar experiment, we shall not consider this aspect further. It is not easy to predict what form of output should be expected with a random assignment of features, especially since the criteria are not logically independent, and hence it might be useful to have a taxonomic analysis of a data matrix that had such a random assignment. We shall discuss the treatment of the output under a number of headings.

APPENDIX 2.11 — THE UNORDERED SIMILARITY MATRIX

This is simply the collection of all the similarity coefficients, and the problem is to compare the actual distribution of this set with the distribution that could be expected with a random assignment of features. It does seem fairly evident from the similarity matrix itself and from using the groups of the output, that there is a natural clustering, and in particular that the collection of similarity coefficients is not a random collection. It is still desirable to have some numerical evidence for this, and, furthermore, it seems useful to know what type of distribution of similarity coefficients is likely to be associated with a particular type of clustering.

The most obvious and simple comparison between the observed and expected distributions would be through various elementary statistics, such as the mean and variance, although in practice even this would require a computer. However, these two quantities cannot be expected to be very valuable. If, for example, WHI is used in either of its versions (see Section 7.11, pp. 68 ff.), and if NC is not used, the mean is completely determined by the feature inventories, and is therefore wholly uninformative. The most natural comparison is then between the two distributions as a whole, and the most obvious figure to give is a grouped frequency curve for the similarity coefficients. Such a graph is however liable to be misleading. This is because the collection of similarity coefficients consists of sets of similar coefficients (such as 20/22, 19/21, 18/20; or 10/22, 9/20, 8/18; or 5/22, 5/21, 5/20); this is clearest for the coefficients nearest to 0 and 1. The grouped frequency curve is sensitive to the relationship between these sets and the points of division that have been chosen for setting up the groups; and since the sets do not occur at regular intervals, it is extremely difficult to give a fair representation of the situation. (This would not be so if there was a very large variation in the number of points of comparison.) We therefore present the information in a different form. We consider the similarity coefficients in terms of their defining numerators and denominators, that is, as $\dfrac{\text{number of agreements}}{\text{number of comparisons}}$ (see Section 7.11, p. 68). The data are given in Figure A:1, which shows the number of occurrences of each such fraction, together with summations to show the frequencies of the various numbers of agreements, comparisons, and disagreements. Thus, the "550", which is in a cell near the centre of the tableau, means that the situation of 15 agreements, 8 disagreements, and 23 comparisons (giving a similarity coefficient of 15/23) occurs 550 times. Again, the "34" at the left hand end of the row "TOTALS" at the bottom of the figure means that there were 34 pairs of OTUs with no disagreements, that is, 34 similarity coefficients equal to 1; the 34 is made up of the numbers of the tableau that are in the slanting column through the 34, viz. 1, 1, 5, 13, 7, 4, 3, which means that there was one similarity coefficient with 27 agreements and comparisons, no disagreements; one with 26 agreements and comparisons, no disagreements; and so on. Similarly the "3847" in the centre of the inner left hand vertical column means that there were 3,847 similarity coefficients arising from 23 comparisons, that is, with denominators of 23. "Mean = 22.7" at the foot of the extreme left hand vertical column means that the average number of comparisons was 22.7. In certain cases there are a number of cells corresponding to one similarity coefficient; for example, there are three cells corresponding to the similarity coefficient 2/3 or .67. One is associated with 14 agreements, 7 disagreements, and 21 comparisons, and contains the number 113; one is associated with 16 agreements, 8 disagreements, and 24 comparisons, and contains the number 192; the third is associated with 18 agreements, 9 disagreements, and 27 comparisons, and is empty. In two cases of this type there is a possibility of a very small error in some cells; however, such error could never make any significant difference. Lines joining the centres of cells corresponding to a single similarity coefficient are *not* parallel, but meet at the centre of the cell associat-

Figure A:1

ed with no agreements, no comparisons, and no disagreements, which would appear in an extension of the tableau below the page.

There are a few points which are immediately noticeable. As was to be expected, the amount of variation in the number of agreements and disagreements is much greater than that in the number of comparisons. There is a gap in the top right hand portion of the tableau, reflecting the fact that there are *relatively* more agreements, that is, higher similarity coefficients, when there is a high number of comparisons. This is more interesting, but is principally explicable by our use of "positives" (see Section 7.11, p. 70). In addition, it is probably true that OTUs which are alike in possessing optional overt features about which further questions were asked, are, in general, more similar than average. On the other hand, the number of comparisons is relatively low for OTUs with *P*, and this set of OTUs furnishes most of the pairs with high similarity coefficients. The situation is summarised in Table A:1.

TABLE A:1

	Number of comparisons	Mean number of agreements	Average similarity coefficient for the number of comparisons (per cent)
	27	23.7	88
	26	21.2	82
	25	19.7	79
	24	17.9	74
	23	15.8	69
	22	14.0	64
	21	12.9	61
	20	12.1	61
	19	13.2	69
Overall average	22.7	15.5	68

The apparent anomaly of the case of 19 comparisons is based on only 6 similarity coefficients, and so is of no interest. The situation can also be expressed by the following facts: for similarity coefficients greater than 70%, the most common numbers of points of comparison are 23 and 24; for coefficients between 70% and 50%, the most common numbers are 22 and 23; and for the small number below 50%, the most common numbers are 21, 22 and 23.

In Figure A:2 we give four curves showing the number of times various numbers of agreements occurred for the four most frequent numbers of comparisons. These curves therefore show the distributions of similarity coefficients of constant denominator for the denominators 21, 22, 23 and 24; this includes over 94% of the coefficients. The extreme right hand points all represent similarity coefficients of magnitude 1. One curve has been drawn dotted for visual clarity.

It is noticeable that the larger the number of comparisons, the steeper the corresponding curve is.

In Table A:2 we give the distribution of the number of coded features excluding NC: the mean number of features is 26.0.

TABLE A:2

Number of features	Number of OTUs with corresponding number of features
29	8
28	11
27	22
26	46
25	48
24	10
23	1

It is considerably more interesting to compare some of these figures with the values that would be expected if there were no "structure" in the data, that is, broadly speaking, if the features were distributed at random. In order to make this comparison the expected values under three variants of this hypothesis were computed for the comparison, agreement and disagreement frequencies. The three variants were used to test the effect of the logical constraints between the criteria (see Section 7.12, pp. 72 ff.),

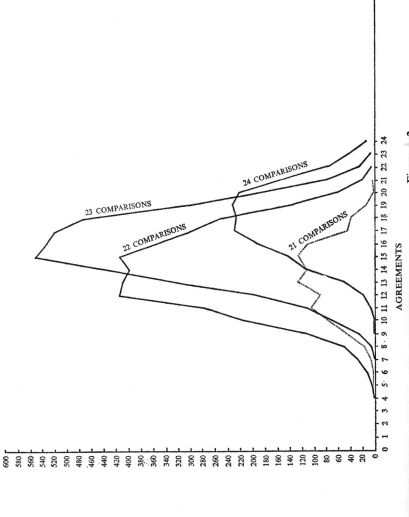

Figure A.2

and the three assumptions were (progressing from the weakest, which would imply the least apparent structure in the similarity matrix, to the strongest, implying the most):

(i) INDEPENDENCE ("IND"): that all the criteria were completely independent.

(ii) LOGICAL DEPENDENCE ("LOG"): that all the criteria were independent subject to the strictly necessary logical constraints, such as "at least one of $\rightarrow N_1 an$ and $\rightarrow N_1 in$ must be true"; "$N_1 pron$ and $N_1 name$ are incompatible".

(iii) MAXIMUM DEPENDENCE ("MAX"): as (ii), but assuming in addition that such pairs of responses as "$N_2 an$" and "$\nrightarrow N_2 an$" — that is, "N_2 is observed animate" and "N_2 cannot be animate" — are impossible.

It might appear that (iii) was a logically necessary constraint, but in the form in which the informant understood such criteria (which was rather, for example, "would it be natural and normal for N_2 to be animate here?"), there was possibility for inconsistency, which did indeed occur on a number of occasions. An example, for N_1, is OTU 60:

A sigh came **out of** the poplars *and a few bright discs spun down and settled round their feet.* (a26)

which was coded as $N_1 in$, $\nrightarrow N_1 in$. The constraints of (iii) are therefore too strong, although it is closest to the truth. The results are summarised in Table A:3, in which " $\times$ " means "impossible"; "0" means "predicted nearer 0 than 1"; and dots imply continuation, indefinitely, or until a new symbol occurs, possibly beyond the limits of the table.

If there is structure in the data it should transpire that some pairs of OTUs are more alike than would be expected at random, whilst other pairs are less alike. The effect of adding logical constraints between the criteria will be the same. Hence in both cases we should expect that there were more cases of high and low similarity coefficients, and fewer of the central similarity coefficients, than the assumption of independence of the criteria would predict.

TABLE A:3

AGREEMENT FREQUENCIES

	0	1	2	3	4	5	6	7	8	9	10	11	12	13	14	15	16	17	18	19	20	21	22	23	24	25	26	27	28	29	30	31	32	33	34	35	36	… = number of agreements
FREQUENCIES OBSERVED					3	11	22	38	77	205	375	518	733	923	1076	1263	1210	1148	1049	749	527	339	184	86	39	8	1	1										
PREDICTED MAX	×	×	0	0	0	0	2	7	27	77	183	369	641	972	1294	1514	1556	1400	1094	734	417	196	74	22	5	1	0	0	0	0	×	×	×					· · ·
PREDICTED LOG	×	×	0	0	0	0	1	6	23	70	175	367	656	1011	1351	1571	1590	1396	1057	685	374	169	61	17	4	1	0	0	0	0	×	×	×					· · ·
PREDICTED IND	0	0	0	0	0	0	2	11	38	114	280	577	997	1445	1755	1782	1506	1052	603	280	104	31	7	1	0	0	0	0	0	0	0	0	0	0	0	0	0	0 ×

COMPARISON FREQUENCIES

	12	13	14	15	16	17	18	19	20	21	22	23	24	25	26	27	28	29	30	31	32	33	34	35	36	37	38	39	40	41	42	43	44	45	46	47	48	49	= number of comparisons
FREQUENCIES OBSERVED							6	107	939	3467	3847	1713	429	68	9																								
PREDICTED MAX	×	0	0	0	0	0	9	121	892	3107	4065	1960	383	44	3	0	0	0	0	0	×	×	×																· · ·
PREDICTED LOG	×	0	0	0	0	0	1	14	154	986	3139	3974	1901	370	43	3	0	0	0	0	0	×	×	×															· · ·
PREDICTED IND	×	0	0	0	0	0	1	14	158	1016	3192	3860	1825	446	66	6	0	0	0	0	0	0	0	0	0														0 ×

DISAGREEMENT FREQUENCIES

	0	1	2	3	4	5	6	7	8	9	10	11	12	13	14	15	16	17	18	19	20	21	22	23	= number of disagreements
FREQUENCIES OBSERVED	34	116	264	579	915	1199	1306	1367	1328	1104	983	619	399	213	88	41	20	9	1						
PREDICTED MAX	4	33	137	375	764	1231	1621	1781	1651	1297	863	483	226	86	26	6	1	0	0	0	×	×	×		· · ·
PREDICTED LOG	3	27	120	347	733	1212	1627	1811	1689	1326	876	483	220	81	24	5	1	0	0	0	×	×	×		· · ·
PREDICTED IND	1	14	78	270	664	1218	1735	1966	1799	1344	825	417	174	60	17	4	1	0	0	0	0	0	0	×	

Thus the frequency curve will be more flattened and the variance greater than we should have supposed.

Speaking in terms of the number of agreements, etc., there should be more cases of "many agreements, few disagreements", and "few agreements, many disagreements" than we should have expected. Obviously, if there are constraints *and* structure, we should expect this effect to increase beyond what we should expect with the constraints but no structure, that is, complete independence otherwise. (What to expect in the case of the number of comparisons is not obvious!) Table A:3 does in fact show precisely the effects described. If we pool the values at each end so that all the tabulated numbers are greater than 25, and use the χ^2 test (see

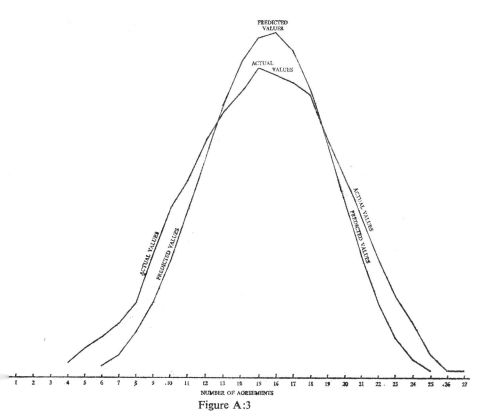

Figure A:3

Kenney & Keeping 1951, §5.13), we obtain an overwhelmingly low p-value, suggesting extremely strongly that the constraints between the criteria are not sufficient to account for the observed concentration of high and low coefficients.

Figures A:3 and A:4 show graphs of the square roots of actual number of agreements and disagreements, and also the expected values using assumption MAX. Square roots were taken in order to display the differences for both high and low numbers clearly; notice that the number of similarity coefficients between n OTUs is roughly of the order of n^2.

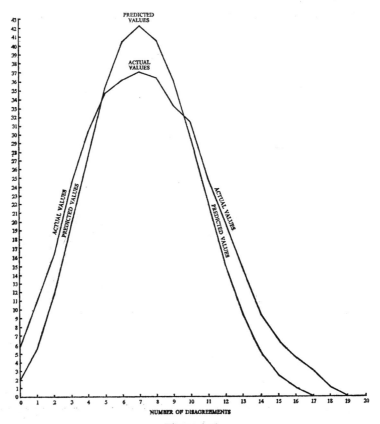

Figure A:4

APPENDIX 2.12 — THE ORDERED SIMILARITY MATRIX

We may either attempt to measure the structure of the ordered matrix without reference to its unordered form, in which case the ordered matrix is being taken as the norm, or we may attempt to measure the improvement that is obtained by passing from the unordered form. In addition we might consider the statistical significance of either measure. It is obvious in our case that ordering the matrix has improved it considerably, but it would be reassuring to have a numerical confirmation that the ordered matrix was significantly better than an ordered matrix based on random data. A possible method would be to compute measures such as those proposed in Section 7.31, fn. 5, p. 95. For example, we could consider the average of the products of neighbouring similarity coefficients as a measure of the extent to which the ordered OTUs could be considered as partitioned. This measure would have to be related to the mean of the similarity coefficients, and would increase as the ordering became more conformable to a partitioning. It would not be very sensitive. In a similar way we could attempt to measure the extent to which the ordered matrix represented a cline by calculating the average of the products of similarity coefficients with some measure of their distance from the diagonal. These methods do not seem very satisfactory; better measures of the worth of clusterings are suggested in Appendix 1. See also Appendix 5.

APPENDIX 2.13 — THE RELATIONSHIP BETWEEN
THE FEATURES AND THE GROUPS

This approach has been discussed already in Section 8.21 and applied in Sections 8.23, 8.34.

APPENDIX 2.14 — RELATIONSHIPS BETWEEN THE CRITERIA

To discuss these in any sense comprehensively would be to provide an independent and perhaps very lengthy analysis, but it is reasonable to examine the "key criteria" only. Most of the criteria, and all those that appeared to be important, were in one of three sets: the N_1 constituent criteria, the N_2 constituent criteria, and those transformational criteria which involved structural change, e.g. P as opposed to $\rightarrow N_1 an$. (Criteria such as the last were not considered in Section 8 because of their close relationship with the corresponding constituent criteria. When we have analysed them, the only one that has appeared useful has been $\rightarrow N_2 an$, both when taken independently and when it was taken as subordinate to $N_2 an$). It seems certain on the basis of the results we have so far considered that the criteria in each of these sets are highly associated with each other, and, in particular, that P, C, A, Q, and M are highly associated. Since we have at various points stressed the near-equivalence of P and C, we give the contingency table for these two criteria, but it seems unnecessary to give the remaining nine tables for the other pairs of criteria in this list:

	P	$?P$	$\sim P$	
C	35	2	5	42
$?C$			1	1
$\sim C$	3	1	99	103
	38	3	105	146

It would be pedantic to give a significance level for this table. The OTUs that do not show agreement for P and C are given by the following table, which suggests that they are of a number of different types:

OTU number	P	C	Set (if any)
35	+	−	IV
36	+	−	VII
90	+	−	
13	?	+	II
27	?	+	I
34	?	−	12G
96	−	+	12G
146	−	+	I
125	−	+	VII
101	−	+	
49	−	+	10D
86	−	?	IX

We also give the contingency tables between one criterion from each of the three sets, choosing N_1*form-class*, N_2*form-class*, and *P*.

		N_2 *pron*	N_2 *name*	N_2 *noun*		
N_1	*pron*	23	6	65	94	(a)
	name		1	12	13	
	noun	4	1	24	29	
	ØS	2		8	10	
		29	8	109	146	

		P	*?P*	*~P*		
N_1	*pron*	27	3	64	94	(b)
	name	4		9	13	
	noun	3		26	29	
	ØS	4		6	10	
		38	3	105	146	

		P	*?P*	*~P*		
N_2	*pron*	12		17	29	(c)
	name	2	1	5	8	
	noun	24	2	83	109	
		38	3	105	146	

Table (a) does not appear to be significant, but Tables (b) and (c) look closer to significance. They are perhaps easier to comprehend in a slightly simpler form.

		P	*~P*			
N_1	*~noun*	31	73	104		(d)
	noun	3	26	29		
		34	99	133	$\chi^2 = 3.55$	

		P	*~P*			
N_2	*pron*	12	17	29		(e)
	~pron	26	88	114		
		38	105	143	$\chi^2 = 3.03$	

Neither of these tables is significant at the 95% level, although the reductions to the 2×2 forms have been made in such a way as to maximise the apparent significance. They would become significant if treated as "single-tail" tests, which we might find acceptable in the case of Table (c). (See Kenney & Keeping 1954).

The overall impression we have formed is that the associations among the criteria of any one set are quite high, while the remaining associations are low, and are principally between the TR criteria and the remainder.

APPENDIX 2.2 — THE SAME PROCEDURE APPLIED
TO DIFFERENT SAMPLES

We applied the classification method manually to a sample of sixteen OTUs from the corpus, firstly using all the criteria, then the TR criteria only, and finally using the CON criteria only. Furthermore each analysis was repeated with the feature inventories unaltered but with the entries placed at random. The general impressions we formed were that the classification of the small sample was on the whole consistent with that for the entire corpus; that the CON and TR analyses were appreciably different from each other, although they were related (this relationship was verified numerically); and that the "randomised" results were clearly poorer than the original ones.

Other analyses that might prove of value are an analysis using new, or perhaps independently chosen, criteria; and a complete analysis of a new corpus, including the finding of a diagnostic key.

APPENDIX 3

OBJECTIFYING INTUITION: A NEW APPROACH

A line of approach which we believe would be very rewarding is to relate a *given* partition (or other classification) of OTUs to their features and, if possible, to find a diagnostic key. The given classification will normally be an intuitive clustering, and frequently a judgment of the degree to which some factor obtains. There is a variety of approaches that might be made, and a successful result could be regarded as the objectifying of an intuition. We could consider the problem as one of pattern-recognition.

We made a preliminary venture into this field using the concept of "degree of cohesion". The illustrative problem used in this study may be described for instance in terms of collocation, expectancy, or cohesion: the degree of cohesion between V and p is felt to be greater in the string

(OTU 9)   *Emma* looked **at** his face *and said* ...   (b96)

than in

(OTU 112) ... *her face had* hollowed **underneath** the cheek-
            bones, ...   (a17)

In the latter example, there is greater cohesion between p and N_2 than between V and p. Although strings of the structure $N_1 \, V \, p \, N_2$ are usually divided into two groups (see Section 2.1, pp. 15 ff.), we have good reason to believe that there are intermediate degrees of cohesion between these two extremes. Consider, for example, the variety shown by the OTUs above, and the following:

OTU 122 *She handed the lead to Madeleine and* strode
        towards the church.   (a26)

OTU 132 *"With Mr Eborebelosa it's his colour, and with this*

OTU 134 *The swans* slid **out of** sight, *making for some known evening haunt in the creek's upper reaches.*

OTU 137 *He* pulled **into** the kerb *and* ...

For the experiment outlined in this appendix, a linguistically trained speaker of English was asked to estimate the degree of cohesion between V and p in a number of OTUs. The responses were to be given immediately after each OTU was read out to him, and no attempt to objectify his intuitive judgments was called for. The degree of cohesion was estimated for each OTU on a five-point scale, 1-5, in which "Degree 1" indicated very low cohesion, and "Degree 5" very high. The only methods of prediction we had envisaged were, firstly, to find the "character" (as defined in Section 8.42) of each group of OTUs with the same degree of cohesion and to use this in the obvious way, by matching the features of a new OTU against the characters of each of the groups, and, secondly, to weight the features so that the sum of the weights of the features possessed by an OTU should give a value corresponding to one of the degrees. Thus, we might have $P = 5$, $A = -2$, $\sim A = 1$, and so on, and an OTU accepting P and $\sim A$ would have weight $5 + 1 + \dots$ The key might then place totals of at least 15 as Degree 5, of between 12 and 14 inclusive as Degree 4, and so on. Both these methods are so simple as to seem trivial, but they were not pursued, one reason being that there are OTUs which have virtually identical features but which were assigned Degrees 1 and 4, for example, OTUs 63 and 45, and OTUs 145 and 44; and while an error of one degree seems reasonable, it is plain that pairs of OTUs such as these are considered, intuitively, to be very different. This situation suggested that the position was rather subtle, and that our features were not fully successful in giving an adequate description of the OTUs: more "information" was needed.

An example of a pattern of features which is associated with a wide variety of degrees of cohesion is provided by the TR features $\sim P$, $\sim C$, $\sim A$, Q, $\sim M$. In the corpus we have:

Degree of cohesion

P	C	A	Qa & Qb	M	D	1	2	3	4	5	Total
—	—	—	+	—	+	2	1	6	4	—	13
—	—	—	+	—	?	1	—	1	—	—	2
—	—	—	+	—	—	—	—	4	1	—	5
					Total	3	1	11	5	—	20

We quote the four OTUs indicated in the Table with Degrees 1 or 2, and, for comparison, two OTUs with Degree 4:

OTU	Degree of Cohession	Group	OTU
69	4	12D	"*I thought you were* agreeing **with** us *?*"
45	4	13E	"*You should stop* worrying **about** your conscience *so much.*"
48	2	13E	*They* went **out of** the gate *and* ...
71	1	12H	*The dog* bounded back **with** a stick, ...
76	1	12H	*A waitress* came **with** a cloth.
63	1	13E	*She walked away* ... *and presently* returned **with** a large garden spade.

It is noteworthy that OTUs 63, 71, and 76 are three of the four OTUs in the corpus where $p \ N_2$ may be paraphrased as *Ving* (*bringing*) N_2. The other OTU is 118; compare also OTU 102. OTUs 71 and 76 form a computer group (12 H); OTU 63 is closer to both OTU 71 and OTU 76 than any other OTU. See also the last table in this Appendix.

The results we give below seem to show conclusively that there is very considerable association between the degrees of cohesion on the one hand, and both individual features and the classification on the other. We begin by showing the truncated tree (TREE I) with the number of members in each class possessing each degree; in 11A, for example, there are 18 OTUs of Degree 1, 10 of Degree 2, and so on. It will be seen by considering 1A that Degrees 2 and 4 are relatively infrequent.

The patterning in this tree seems convincingly clear. This is reassuring because it suggests that both objective and subjective classifications, however differently based, are in some sense valid.

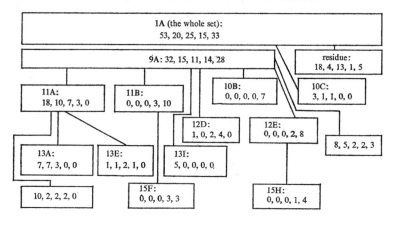

9A: 21, 5, 14, 1, 5

The following groups show high cohesion: 10B, 12E/15H, 11B/15F. 13I has low cohesion. 11A/13A and 10C have a core of low cohesion with a steady trail of higher cohesion.

It is interesting that one group, 12D, is strikingly anomalous here, outside the mammoth group 9A, and that this group was the only one marked as counter-intuitive on the original inspection, the posited reason being overstressed N_2pron. 13E also seems unusual. Note the strikingly high proportions of Degree 3 in the residue from 1A.

We give below the OTUs in 13E and 12D in the order in which they came from the computer, showing the degree of cohesion:

13E	OTU 45	4	"*You should stop* worrying **about** your conscience *so much*". (b106)
	OTU 63	1	*She walked away ... and presently* returned **with** a large garden spade. (a 27)
	OTU 48	2	*They* went **out of** the gate *and ...* (a 17)
	OTU 81	3	*She* fished **for** her handkerchief *and ...* (a 28)
	OTU 84	3	*Carfax sat down and began* to puff *militarily* **at** his pipe; ... (b103)
12D	OTU 77	1	*He* kneeled down **in front of** her *and ...* (b 96)

OTU 69   4   *I thought you were* agreeing **with** us?"

(b104)

OTU 56   4   "*It* went **for** him *again and again* —
screeching. /it = the rat/   (a25)

OTU 46   4   "*It doesn't* worry **about** you, *you know*".
/it = your conscience/   (b106)

OTU 105 4   "*I don't* know **about** you, *but I've enjoyed
this*".   (b95)

OTU 83   3   *They also looked benevolently on a morose,
barrel-chested artist named Herman, and the
woman he was* living **with**.   (b99)

OTU 62   3   "*Should we* run **for** him?"   (a26)

We may also compare the degrees with the output of the other keys. First of all the inter-group analysis:

Level 13 groups	Degree of Cohesion 1 2 3 4 5
A	7 7 3 — —
B	3 — — — —
C	3 — — — —
D	1 1 2 — —
E	1 1 2 1 —
F	1 — — 1 —
G	1 — — 1 —
H	— — — 3 7
I	5 — — — —
J	— — 2 1 —
K	— — — 1 6
L	— — — — 2
M	1 1 — — —
N	— — — — 5
O	— — — 2 —
P	1 — 1 — —
Q	1 1 — — —
R	2 — — — —
S	— — — — 2
T	— — 2 — —
U	2 — — — —
V	— — 2 — —

A	7 7 3 — —
B_1	4 2 4 3 —
B_2	— — 4 7 22
B_3	13 1 1 — —
B_4	5 1 — — —
V	— — 2 — —
Total	29 11 14 10 22

C_1	24 10 8 3 —
C_2	4 2 8 10 22
C_3	5 1 2 — —
C_4	20 8 4 — —
D_1	24 10 12 10 22
D_2	11 9 11 10 22
$\overline{C_1}$	5 1 6 7 22
$\overline{C_2}$	25 9 6 — —
$\overline{C_3}$	24 10 12 — —
$\overline{C}^c$	9 3 10 10 22
$\overline{D_2}$	18 1 3 — —

and finally with the output of the concept-formation key:

Ai	— — — 3 10
Aii	3 1 5 3 1
Aiii	3 — 2 — —
Aiv	— — 1 5 19
Av	12 4 10 3 2
Avi	7 4 3 — 1
Avii	15 8 1 — —
Aviii	11 3 — — —

Among these there are:

Bi	3 — — — —
Ci	1 5 2 — —
Cii	— 1 1 — —
Ciii	— — — — 1

We conclude by giving bar charts of the number of occasions each feature co-occurred with a given degree of cohesion (Figure A:5), and a graph comparing the percentage of times that a few selected

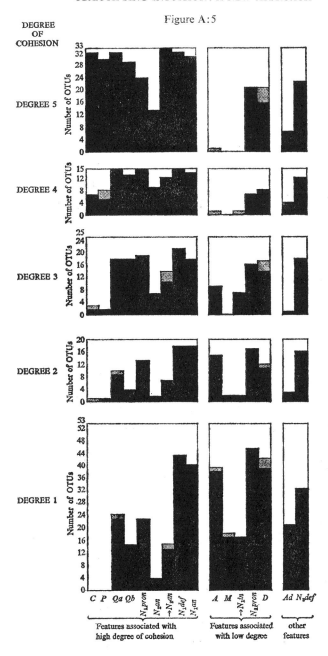

DEGREE
OF
COHESION

Figure A:5

Five bar charts (one for each degree of cohesion) showing the number of OTUs possessing certain features. Stippling indicates query responses. The thin line above each chart shows the total number of OTUs of the corresponding degree of cohesion.

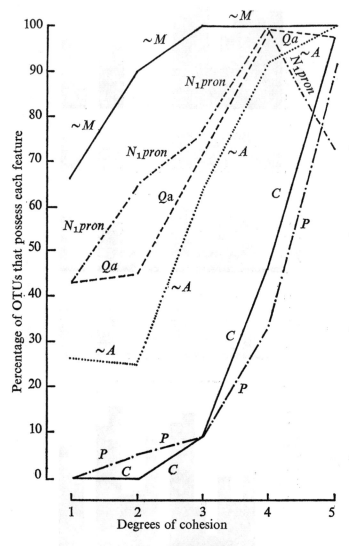

Figure A:6

features co-occurred with each degree of cohesion (Figure A:6). In order to facilitate comparison, features have been negated if they were more frequently associated with low degrees of cohesion.

If we consider the four criteria P, A, Q, and M of Chapter 9, it seems that the best way to order the OTUs so as to correspond to the degrees of cohesion is first by P, then by M, then by A, and then by Q. Thus, we first place all OTUs with P above those with $-P$. Then we take each of these groups and place those with $-M$ above those with M (in practice there were no OTUs with P and M, and so the roles of P and M are interchangeable). The process is repeated with these groups, placing OTUs with $-A$ above those with $+A$, and finally placing OTUs with Q above those with $-Q$. We give two tables, the first ranking by A and Q only, the second using all four criteria:

A Q	Degree of Cohesion 1 2 3 4 5
$-$ $+$	3 1 12 12 29
$-$ $-$	8 4 3 1
$+$ $+$	11 3 1
$+$ $-$	19 5 1

P M A Q	Degree of Cohesion 1 2 3 4 5
$+$ $-$ $-$ $+$	4 28
$+$ $-$ $-$ $-$	1
$-$ $-$ $-$ $+$	3 1 11 5
$-$ $-$ $-$ $-$	2 3 2
$-$ $-$ $+$ $+$	9 2 1
$-$ $-$ $+$ $-$	13 5 4
$-$ $+$ $-$ $-$	5
$-$ $+$ $+$ $+$	2
$-$ $+$ $+$ $-$	6

In this table the first column stands for P and C; cases of disagreement are omitted. Using this table only, the diagnostic values (expressed per cent) of these four criteria for predicting the five degrees of cohesion are:

$$P \quad 63$$
$$A \quad 52$$
$$Q \quad 49$$
$$M \quad 44$$

(See Appendix 1.2, p. 224.).

The whole corpus is included in the final table, in which Q is entered as "?" if Qa and Qb conflict or if either is "?":

P C A Q M	Degree of Cohesion				
	1	2	3	4	5
+ + − + −				4	28
+ + − ? −				1	1
− − − + −	3	1	11	5	
− − − ? −	3		1		
− − ? + −			1		
− − + + −	9	3	1		
− − + ? −	5	3	2		
− − + ? +	2	2			
− − + − −	13	6	4		
− − + − +	6				
− − − − −	2	3	2		
− − − − +	5				
− − + + +	2				
− − − − ?	1				
− − ? − +	1				
− − − ? +	1				
+ − − − −		1	1		
− ? + ? −		1			
− + − + −			1		1
− ? + − −			1		
+ − + ? −			1		
− + − ? −			1		1
? + − + −				2	
? − − + −				1	
+ + − − −					1
− − ? ? −					1

The diagnostic values (expressed per cent) for the whole corpus for these and some other criteria are:

C	32	Qa	14
P	30	M	9
A	22	$\rightarrow N_1 in$	9
$\rightarrow N_2 an$	20	D	7
Qb	15	Ad	6

A criterion answered with 73 $+$'s and 73 $-$'s distributed independently of the degrees of cohesion would probably have a diagnostic value near 3 (see Appendix 1,2, p. 224).

APPENDIX 4

A PARTIALLY SUBJECTIVE CLASSIFICATION METHOD

We outline in this appendix a process which could be programmed and which might be useful for the kind of data treated in these experiments. It has the disadvantage of being partially subjective, but has a number of advantages; it is capable of being very flexible, and is likely to be comprehensive (that is, able to account for the unclear, ambiguous, and marginal cases) without the necessity of eliciting and coding the responses of a very large number of OTUs to a very large number of criteria. The process is reminiscent of the recommendations in Wexler 1966 (see Section 8.43, p. 190). It consists of a "conversation" between the computer and the linguist, but on-line communication would not be necessary. We shall describe the process in two somewhat different forms.

In the first, the program is provided with a feature-matrix, as in the case described in this study. On the basis of this matrix, the computer produces a classification and a diagnostic key, and applies the latter to the OTUs, printing out the results. If the linguist is not entirely satisfied because the output conflicts at some point with his intuition (*not* because the output fails to make some criterion as important as he believes it should be) he tells the computer which OTUs seem to be misplaced. The machine attempts to rectify this by taking other features into consideration; if this fails, the computer requests supplementary information about those OTUs which it finds no reason to distinguish from each other but which the linguist believes to be essentially different. The additional information will take the form of the responses of these OTUs only to new criteria. If this process eventually gives a satisfactory result, the original key criteria may be applied to a much larger set of OTUs, and the program will suggest to which OTUs the additional criteria should be applied; alternatively, this operation could be executed manually. The output is then inspected by the linguist, and the whole operation is continued until the classification appears to be satisfactory. If it appears to be impossible to achieve this happy outcome, the presumption is that the intuition itself is faulty.

In the second form of the program, the data consist, in addition, of some form of "linguist's intuition". In the initial stage of the process this would perhaps be best applied to cases which seemed clear, and the additional data would then consist of a simple dichotomy. Thus, in the case of the problem discussed in this study, we should probably have used only the OTUs which were assigned Degrees 1 and 5. In some unrelated experiments, the intuition consisted in dividing the data into groups that were not ordered on any scale, but for which it was still possible to conflate them into two major groups. The process does not necessitate this conflation. The program attempts to predict the degrees or groups from the features it is given, and, when successful, it is applied to more difficult cases, for example the Degree 3 cases. There are obviously some difficulties in this type of analysis. There is, incidentally, no reason why the program should not be more ambitious than the original intuition; thus, if we propose a three-point scale, the computer might suggest an eight-point scale.

As before, if success cannot be achieved, even with new criteria, we may suspect that the original intuition was faulty. In one of the unrelated experiments referred to above, something like a breakthrough was achieved with the 27th criterion that was proposed; before it had been considered, the analysis had been fairly complex. It should be added that, even if success is achieved, there is no guarantee that perfect comprehension has been obtained; there may be other aspects to the problem. In this connexion compare the tables of diagnostic values in Section 8.34 with the table in Appendix 3, p. 257.

APPENDIX 5

A TWO-DIMENSIONAL MODEL FOR A SUBSET OF THE OTUs

We have already referred, in fn. 1 (pp. 59f.) and fn. 13 (pp. 151f.)' to two methods of representing OTUs in a space of any number of dimensions, given a similarity matrix. Through the kindness of J. Doran, of the Experimental Programming Unit of the University of Edinburgh, we were able to use his program (The Analysis of Similarities Program, Sept. 1965) on a subset of our OTUs. We shall first describe briefly how this program functions; further details may be found in its accompanying manual, and in Kruskal 1964, Shepard 1962.

APPENDIX 5.1

The program is supplied with the similarity matrix for the OTUs, and, implicitly, the maximum and minimum number of dimensions in which configurations are required. It supplies the user with configurations in these and all intermediate dimensions; broadly speaking, the farther apart the points representing two OTUs are, the lower their similarity coefficient. The representations will, except in artificial cases, be better when the number of dimensions is large, sometimes much better, but, of course, only low dimensional representations can be used as visual aids.

The method employed is roughly as follows. The program begins with an initial configuration, either one supplied by the user or a random one generated by the program itself. This configuration is in the highest number of dimensions required. The program then generates a succession of configurations, each one depending solely on its immediate predecessor.

The *pairs* of OTUs can be arranged in two orders: one the

numerical order of the corresponding similarity coefficients, the other the numerical order of the corresponding distances in the current configuration. In passing from one configuration to the next, the program simply attempts to equate these orders. There is no metric, that is, no pre-assigned relation between the similarity coefficients and the distances. The basic tool of the program is a measure, calculated for *each* pair of OTUs, which increases as the correspondence between the two orders diminishes. It does not take account of the magnitudes of the distances, only their ordering, but it does take into account the magnitudes of the similarity coefficients, so that if several similarity coefficients are close together, confusion in the order of distance of the corresponding pairs of OTUs is not so important as if the similarity coefficients were far apart. This measure is used in two ways: to determine the movement of points in passing from one configuration to the next, and to assign to the configuration a value (δ) which measures how successfully it has achieved its object. The iteration process continues until either the amount of change becomes less than the user has prescribed, or until the number of iterations reaches a value he has assigned. If configurations are required in a lower dimension, the final configuration is projected into the next lower dimension, and the whole cycle is repeated.

At each iteration both δ and a measure of the amount of change are printed out, and the configuration itself is also printed out as often as the user desires.

There is no guarantee of perfect convergence; indeed, it is virtually certain that after a certain point the process will cease to bring the configurations closer to an optimum. In our case we used 20 iterations; in three dimensions the 5th was the best, in two dimensions the 10th. It is quite possible that different initial configurations will lead to substantially different results. The program does not purport to give a perfect representation of the data, but it is almost certain to be a useful visual aid in interpretation.

APPENDIX 5.2

In order to be reasonably economical of computer time, we used the program on 30 OTUs only. They were chosen to represent what our classifications suggested were the principle groups of OTUs. In addition we included OTU 68, which had shown little affinity with any of the major groups, although closely related to OTU 52, and slightly to OTU 67; and two OTUs, 124 and 133, which showed little relationship to each other or to any other OTU or group. These principles of selection would lead us to expect that there were fewer high similarity coefficients than there would normally be in a random sample, since these would be fewer pairs very close together and a slightly high proportion of unusual OTUs. On the other hand, however, the OTUs from the groups were chosen as fairly typical members, and sometimes more than one was chosen; and in addition the intermediate regions were underrepresented. In fact the average similarity coefficient for this sample is 73%, as opposed to 68% for the whole sample.

In Figure A:7 we compare the distribution of the similarity coefficients for the sample and the whole corpus; there appears to be no very significant difference between them. (The difference between them is in fact statistically significant, but not very strikingly, and provided the relation of the chosen OTUs to the whole corpus is understood, there seems no reason, on this account, to suppose that the sample is misleading.)

We begin by listing the OTUs, together with their relation to the various classifications we have discussed, some of their features, and the degrees of cohesion. Q has been marked "?" if either of Qa, Qb was "?", or if Qa and Qb conflicted. Class 5 was the class selected for re-examination; 1A was the final WHI group consisting of all the OTUs, and so OTUs marked as 1A were the last to be absorbed by any group. The order of the OTUs is that derived from a single linkage classification for this set of OTUs considered in isolation; and in order to show as much as possible of the relationship between these OTUs, we give the tree for this classification beside the table. Frequently, groups are united by links formed by

Figure A:7. Grouped frequency distributions for the similarity coefficients in the corpus and the sample.

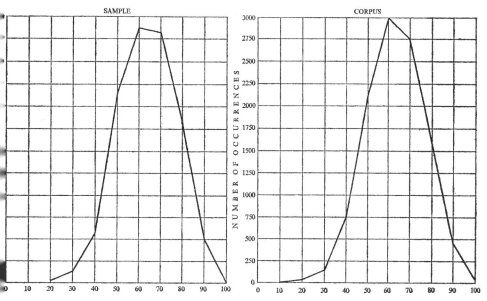

The numbers on the horizontal axis represent (per cent) the lowest value similarity coefficients in the corresponding totals; thus '50' stands for '50% or more, but not less than 60%'. The scales for the two graphs are almost, but not quite, equivalent.

Lower limit for similarity cofficient value (per cent)	0	10	20	30	40	50	60	70	80	90	100
Sample			1	5	22	86	115	113	73	20	
Corpus		3	31	144	684	2025	2991	2730	1563	380	34

adjacent OTUs, one from each group; the ordering has been arranged to cause this wherever possible; more generally, to cause similar OTUs to be near similar OTUs, though this was not always possible. The links *not* by adjacent OTUs are shown by dotted lines; the only case where the link is not obvious from these considerations is OTU 100, which in fact is linked to OTU 77 at the 87% level. It is *not* similar to its other neighbour, OTU 10; the similarity coefficient is 681 per mil., virtually the average for the whole corpus. See Table A:4.

As a further comparison between the sample and the corpus, we considered the "profiles" of some of the OTUs in the sample with respect to the sample itself and with respect to the whole corpus. (By "profile" we mean the set of similarity coefficients between the OTU concerned and all other OTUs, arranged in numerical order. Profiles can be represented graphically as bar charts or grouped frequency distributions.) There appeared to be reasonable agreement between the two sets of profiles. The profiles turned out to be intrinsically very interesting, often differing substantially from the overall distribution of similarity coefficients, and differing even more between themselves. The most obvious differences are exemplified by the following three cases:

(i) The profiles for OTUs 61 and 55 are very similar, but that for OTU 55 is farther to the right, that is, it corresponds to higher similarity coefficients than that of OTU 61. Speaking geometrically, this indicates that OTU 55 is more central than OTU 61.

(ii) The profiles for OTUs 61 and 68 are almost identical in shape and position, but that for OTU 61 has a long low extension to the right, extending into the high numbers. This indicates that OTU 68 is almost isolated.

(iii) The sets of similarity coefficients for OTUs 112 and 133 have similar, low means ($57^0/_0$ and $53^0/_0$ respectively), but the profiles are completely different in shape; that for OTU 112 is long and low, while that for OTU 133 is narrow and steep, with fewer low and fewer high similarity coefficients. This might be explained in two dimensions by thinking of OTU 112 as at the end of a "cigar", and OTU 133 as at the side of the cigar, and a little distance from it. OTU 124 has profile similar to that of OTU 133, but starts farther to the right, i.e. it corresponds to higher similarity coefficients.

We have not reproduced either set of profiles because some of the curves are easily confused when they cross one another.

Order as given in App. 5.2	WHI GROUPS, given up to absorption by 12A or a group containing 12A	Inter-group analysis group	Concept	Set	Class	P	C	Q	A	M
124	1A	—	v	Residue	4	—	—	?	—	+
68	15O, 3B, 2A	V	v	—	2	—	—	+	—	—
133	1A	—	vi	Residue	5	—	—	—	—	—
112	13R, 5B, 4A	B_4	vii	X	4	—	—	—	+	+
61	15N, 11C, 10C, 5A	B_4	v	VI	3	—	—	+	+	
75	13Q, 10C, 5A	B_4	v	VI	3	—	—	+	+	
86	8A	—	iii	IX	4	—	?	—	+	—
94	13M, 10A	B_3	vii	IX	4	—	—	—	+	—
87	13I, 10A	B_3	viii	VIII	4	—	—	—	+	?
95	12C, 10A	—	vii	VII	4	—	—	—	+	—
117	11A	—	vi	XII	5	—	—	—	—	—
55	13A, 12A	A	vii	VII	4	—	—	—	+	—
41	14B, 13A, 12A	A	v	VII	4	—	—	?	+	—
85	13D, 12A	B_1	v	VI	3	—	—	+	+	—
127	13A, 12A	A	vii	VII	4	—	—	?	+	—
145	13G, 12A	B_1	viii	IV	5	—	—	?	—	—
65	10A	—	v	VII	3	—	—	+	+	—
48	13E, 12A	B_1	v	III	2	—	—	+	—	—
84	13E, 12A	B_1	v	III	2	—	—	+	—	—
57	13F, 12A	B_1	v	V	2	—	—	+	?	—
2	15I, 11B, 10A	B_2	iv	I	1	+	+	+	—	—
30	10A	—	iv	I	1	+	+	+	—	—
7	15F, 13H, 12B, 11B, 10A	B_2	i	I	1	+	+	+	—	—
40	15F, 13H, 12B, 11B, 10A	B_2	i	I	1	+	+	+	—	—
62	13J, 12D, 10A	B_2	ii	III	2	—	—	+	—	—
77	12D, 10A	—	ii	III	4	—	—	+	+	—
100	12G, 8A	—	v	—	5	—	—	?	?	—
10	15K, 13K, 12E, 10A	B_2	iv	I	1	+	+	+	—	—
12	13K, 12E, 10A	B_2	iv	I	1	+	+	+	—	—
8	15L, 13N, 12F, 10B, 9A	B_2	iv	I	1	+	+	+	—	—

We now present, in Figures A:8 and A:9, the best two-dimensional configuration obtained by the program. This was obtained at the 10th iteration. The 20th iteration was almost identical save for two minor exceptions: the points corresponding to OTUs 117 and 124. In the 20th iteration OTU 117 is level with OTU 145, and is in consequence much nearer OTU 48; and OTU 124 is farther to the right and slightly higher, so that it is almost over OTU 95. The symbol "⊗" is at the centre of the configuration (mathematically, the centroid). In Fig. A:8 the dots are labelled with the OTU numbers (small figures) and also the class numbers (see Chapter 10), the inter-group analysis group if any (see Section 8.31, pp. 141 ff.), the concept groups (see Section 8.4, pp. 174 ff.), and the set numbers (see Chapter 9). In addition, lines analogous to isoglosses have been drawn dividing the "map" into regions by the responses to the criteria P, Q, A, M, N_1 *form-class*, and N_2 *pers*; the lines for constituent criteria cut right across the figure from left to right, while those for transformational criteria are closed curves. Where there are queries in Table A:4, these curves go *through* the dots. It should be remembered that Class 5 is the class of unclassified OTUs.

Except for OTU 133, the OTUs are distributed inside a slightly elongated oval area. The central region is the most densely populated, and the left-hand region is more diffuse than the right. The configuration is not that of a perfect cline, but nevertheless is closely related to a cline.

From Fig. A:8 we may consider the degree to which the existing classifications conform to the appearance of the map. The classes conform moderately well, but only Class 1 corresponds completely satisfactorily. The sets fit better, except for the two OTUs of Set VI and, perhaps, the OTU of Set XII. The concept groups conform fairly well. The most satisfactory association is found with the inter-group analysis groups, which might perhaps have been expected; the only anomaly is the two OTUs of B_3. However, as stated in Section 8.32 (p. 149), B_3 was not defined as a natural group. There is no exact correspondence between any of these

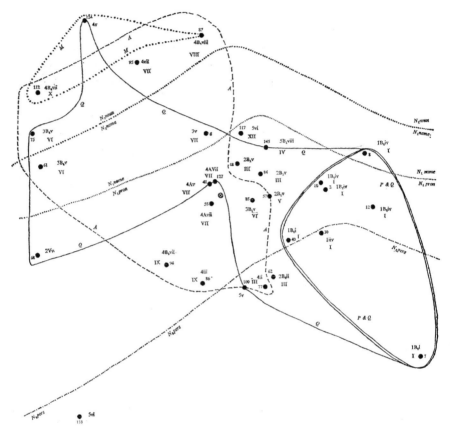

Figure A:8

classifications and the groups one would draw by eye on the map; but since the map is not a perfect representation, and since the sample is not an adequate set either, this is probably not important.

The feature curves have some interest. Since the CON features divide the top from the bottom, roughly, whereas the TR features are more associated with the axis of the cline, we may suspect that the TR criteria alone would have led to a more perfect cline; but this is uncertain. Other noteworthy aspects of the feature divisions are:

(i) The unity of the P and M regions, and their opposition at the extreme ends of the configuration.

(ii) The apparent existence of two Q regions, one often associated with P, and the other with A. These meet at the centre of the configuration, with a large number of query respones associated, and two Class 5 OTUs. The A dividing line also passes through the region. See Sections 8.233 (p. 137); 8.234 (pp. 137 ff.); 8.32 (pp. 148 ff.).

In view of the close agreement with the inter-group analysis groups, in Fig. A:9 we mark off the regions containing OTUs in Groups C_1, C_2, and C_3; and mark the OTUs as in B_1, B_2, C_3, or

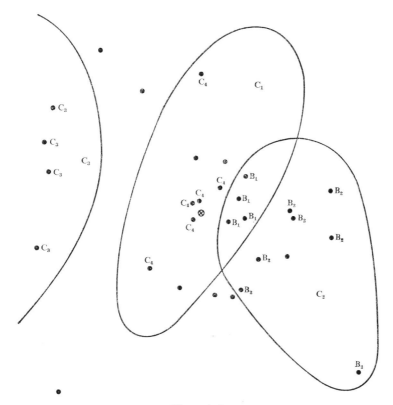

Figure A:9

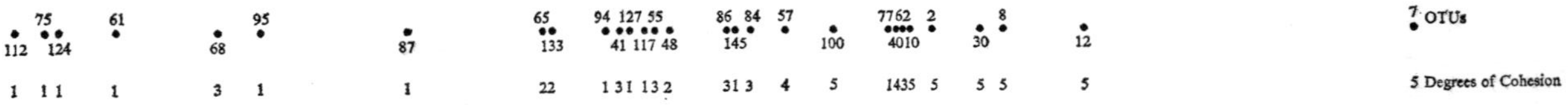

Figure A:10

A representation of the OTUs as a cline. The degrees of cohesion (see Appendix 3) are shown below the corresponding points.

C_4. (C_1 was defined as the union of B_1 and C_4, C_2 as the union of B_1 and B_2.) OTUs that were not among the 86 OTUs used in the inter-group analysis experiment have been ignored. The consistency of these groups with the configuration, and, indeed, with the axis of the cline, is very striking.

In conclusion we present in Fig. A:10 a representation as a cline; it is more or less implicit in Fig. A:9, and requires no further comment. It is of interest that according to the measure δ mentioned in Appendix 5.1, which is small for good representations, the three-dimensional representation is scarcely better than the two-dimensional one (δ for the three-dimensional case is approximately 0.0142, and for the two-dimensional case 0.0144; for the initial random configuration, $\delta = 0.0674$). On the other hand, the one-dimensional representation is a good deal poorer: $\delta = 0.0190$. We may infer tentatively that the situation is in some sense close to being a two-dimensional one.

BIBLIOGRAPHY

a. See R. Lehmann, below.

b. See M. Bradbury, below.

Bonner, R. E., "On Some Clustering Techniques", *IBM Journal of Research and Development*, vol. 8, no. 1 (Jan. 1964), pp. 22-32.

Bradbury, M., *Eating People is Wrong* (Penguin Book 1670, 1959), pp. 90-107.

Chomsky, N., *Aspects of the Theory of Syntax* (Cambridge, Mass., 1965).

Crystal, D. and R. Quirk, *Systems of Prosodic and Paralinguistic Features in English* (The Hague, 1964).

Dale, A. G., N. Dale and Pendergraft (eds), *A Programming System for Automatic Classification with Applications in Linguistic and Information Retrieval Research* (Linguistics Research Center working Paper LRC 64 WTM-4, Texas, 1964).

Dwight, H. B., *Mathematical Tables* (New York, 1961).

Ellegård, A., "Statistical Measurement of Linguistic Relationship", *Language*, 35, pp. 131-156 (1959).

Gaddum, J. H., "Lognormal Distributions", *Nature*, Oct. 20 (1945), pp. 463-6.

Good, I. J., "Categorization of Classification", *Mathematics and Computer Science in Biology and Medicine* (London, 1965), pp. 115 ff.

Gower, J. C., "Some Distance Properties of Latent Root and Vector Methods Used in Multivariate Analysis", *Biometrika*, 53 (London, 1966), pp. 325-38.

Halliday, M. A. K., "Categories of the Theory of Grammar", *Word*, 17 (1961), pp. 241-92.

Herdan, G., *Quantitative Linguistics* (London, 1964).

Hudson, L., "Intelligence; Convergent and Divergent", *Penguin Science Survey*, 1965B (Penguin Book 2226, 1965), pp. 9-22.

Hunt, E. B. and C. I. Hovland, "Programming a Model of Human Concept Formulation", *Computers and Thought*, ed. E. Feigenbaum (New York and London, 1964).

Jespersen, O., *A Modern English Grammar* (Heidelberg and Copenhagen, 1907-49).

Kenney, J. F. and E. S. Keeping, *Mathematics of Statistics*, Part I (Princeton, 1954).

——, *Mathematics of Statistics*, Part II (Princeton, 1951).

Kruisinga, E., *A Handbook of Present-Day English* (Groningen, 1931-32).

Kruskal, J. B., "Multidimensional Scaling by Optimising Goodness of Fit to a Nonmetric Hypothesis", *Psychometrika*, 29 (1964), pp. 1-27.

Lance, G. N. and W. T. Williams, "Computer Programs for Monothetic Classification (Association Analysis)", *Computer Journal*, 8:3 (1965), pp. 246 ff.

Lees, R. B., *The Grammar of English Nominalizations* (Bloomington, 1963).

Lehmann, R., *The Echoing Grove* (Penguin Book 1262, 1958), pp. 16-30.

MacNaughton-Smith, P., W. T. Williams, and M. B. Dale, "An Objective Method of Weighting in Similarity Analysis", *Nature*, vol. 201, Jan. 25 (1964).

Michie, D., "Machine Intelligence", *Penguin Science Survey 1965B* (Penguin Book 2226, 1965), pp. 55-78.

Möller, F., "Quantitative Methods in the Systematics of Actinomycetates", *Giornale di microbiologia*, vol. 10 (1962), pp. 29-47.

Moroney, M. J., *Facts from Figures* (Pelican Book A 236, 1956).

Needham, R. M., *Classification and Grouping*, unpublished Ph. D. thesis, Univ. of Cambridge (1961).

Olsson, Y., *On the Syntax of the English Verb* (Göteborg, 1961).

Poutsma, H., *A Grammar of Late Modern English* (Groningen, 1904-26).

Quirk, R., "Descriptive Statement and Serial Relationship", *Language*, 41 (1965), pp. 205-217.

Quirk, R. and J. Svartvik, *Investigating Linguistic Acceptability* (The Hague, 1966).

Rose, M. J., "Classification of a Set of Elements", *The Computer Journal*, 7:3 (1964), pp. 208-11.

Shepard, R. N., "The Analysis of Proximities: Multidimensional Scaling with an Unknown Distance Function", *Psychometrika*, 27 (1962), pp. 125-140, 219-246.

Sneath, P. H. A., "Some Thoughts on Bacterial Classification", *Journal of General Microbiology*, 17 (1957a), pp. 184-200.

——, "The Application of Computers to Taxonomy", *Journal of General Microbiology*, 17 (1957b), pp. 201-266.

——, "A Comparison of Different Clustering Methods as Applied to Randomly-spaced Points", *The Classification Society Bulletin*, 1:2 (1966), pp. 2-7.

Sokal, R. R. and P. H. A. Sneath, *Principles of Numerical Taxonomy* (San Francisco and London, 1963).

Svartvik, J., *On Voice in the English Verb* (The Hague, 1966).

Sweet, H., *A New English Grammar* (Oxford, 1891).

Wexler, P. J., "Distich and Sentence in Corneille and Racine, *Essays on Style and Language*, ed. R. G. Fowler (London, 1966), pp. 100-17.

Williams, W. T. and J. M. Lambert, "Multivariate Methods in Plant Ecology I. Association-analysis in Plant Communities", *J. Ecol.*, 47 (1959), pp. 83-101.

Zandvoort, R. W., *A Handbook of English Grammar* (London, 1963).